Immokalee's Fields of Hope

Carlene A. Thissen

iUniverse Star
New York Lincoln Shanghai

Immokalee's Fields of Hope

iUniverse Star
an iUniverse, Inc. imprint

For information address:
iUniverse, Inc.
2021 Pine Lake Road, Suite 100
Lincoln, NE 68512
www.iuniverse.com

ISBN: 0-595-31654-9 (pbk)
ISBN: 0-595-66357-5 (cloth)

Printed in the United States of America

In memory of Kathleen Elizabeth Thissen

"It is important that you write this history so that our children and grandchildren know what we went through to get here and how we fought for our rights. This book will tell them our stories—the stories of immigrants. Once the book is written, we will look forward to having it to show to our children."

—Pedro Lopez and Andres Mateo

Contents

Preface

If you don't live in Southwest Florida but know about Immokalee, you may be familiar with National Football League running back Edgerrin James who was raised there. It's primarily an agriculture town, so you may have read press coverage of the Coalition of Immokalee Workers and their protests for better farmworker wages. Or you may have seen the famous documentary "Harvest of Shame" that included information about Immokalee's farmworkers in the 1960s. Other than that, very few people have ever heard of this place.

I live in Naples, about forty minutes southeast of Immokalee. I'm a U.S.-born white woman, just over fifty years old. My husband Barry Kotek and I run a supermarket technology consulting business. We have a fairly large home on five acres, where we have planted a tropical garden.

Most people would call me "eclectic." Barry and I are members of a nearby country club called "The Vineyards," where we play golf and tennis. We also ride motorcycles. I go to school, and have gone to school most of my life, part time. I just like it. On Wednesdays I volunteer at the Guadalupe Family Center in Immokalee, teaching music to pre-school children, and I am part of the English choir at the Catholic Church in Immokalee. That's how I got to know some of the people I want to tell you about.

I wrote this book because I learned what the immigrants who live in Immokalee experienced in their home countries. I wrote it because I see how hard they work, how much they love their children, and how devout they are when they pray. I wrote it because they are fine people, and their stories deserve to be heard. It's also my way of saying "thank you" to them for adding so much to my life.

I also wrote this book because many people from nearby coastal communities like Naples and Fort Myers won't even go to Immokalee because they are afraid. I'd like to help change that impression. Immokalee is a fascinating community with many different cultures, like being in several Latin American/Caribbean countries and the United States all at the same time. The Immokalee people I know are good people. They have welcomed me into their community with kindness, and I am a better person because I know them. The more I learn about them, the more impressed I am with their drive and determination and the simplicity of their dreams. They are like my grandparents and great-grandparents. They just want to work and make a better life.

Another reason I wrote this book is that some people are prejudiced against these immigrants. Based on the dictionary definition, prejudice can be good or bad. I have struggled with this, but in the end I decided that I'm personally very prejudiced because I have many preconceived notions about groups of people. But the ones I have tend to be good notions. Or, if they're bad, I try to accept them and understand them. I know that by making positive generalizations, I'm really doing the same thing as the people who make negative generalizations. How can I be upset when someone claims a particular group is lazy, or mean, or stupid, when I will just as easily say a group is hard-working, or devout, or dedicated to their families? Am I not doing exactly the same thing? I am. The difference comes down to how you focus—on good things or bad things.

The last reason I wrote the book is to let other people know how volunteering has helped me. My life has changed unbelievably and I have never been happier. I'm even starting to see how I can use my business skills and knowledge to help some of the people in Immokalee.

I've been told that books should take their readers on a journey. When I started writing this, I meant to take you on the journeys of the immigrants from their home countries to Immokalee, Florida. But as it turned out, I'm also going to take you with me on part of my journey. It started when I made a telephone call and became a volunteer at Guadalupe Family Center. Then, after a year of singing with children, I almost lost my voice. I found a voice teacher who taught "centering" that fixed my voice and fixed my life. It's a longer story that I will tell you more about later, but he got me back to graduate school, where I ended up studying Latin American history. My thesis was based on Immokalee's immigrants. After I received my Master's degree, I wrote this book.

Between 2000 and 2002 I interviewed thirty-five of the immigrants who live in Immokalee. I chose the more typical stories to share with you in this book. I focused on the three largest population groups: the Mexicans, the Haitians, and the Guatemalans. I asked them questions like these: Where did you come from? What was it like there? Why did you leave? How did you get here? What do you do now? What are your dreams for the future? Their stories, by the way, are not unique to Immokalee. Other immigrants in nearby towns have similar experiences. Actually, immigrants all over the United States have similar stories. I put their stories together with what I learned while getting my Master's Degree at Florida International University.

Most of Immokalee's immigrants are rural poor people who were hungry, persecuted, and frightened. They came looking for the America that opens her doors so that people can realize their dreams. Immokalee has opened its doors to thousands of immigrants who live there today. They just want to work, make a better life, and live in peace.

Acknowledgements

First and foremost, I want to thank the people of Immokalee for helping me write my Master's Thesis and then this book. Lucy Ortiz and Desilus Nicolas told me their own stories, arranged interviews with new immigrants, and sometimes helped me translate. For their knowledge and insight, I also thank Sister Judy Dohner, HM; Brother Jim Harlow, Irish Christian Brothers; Joe and Charo Brueggen; Paul Midney; Lesvia Martinez; Patty and Frank Ligas; Anne Goodnight; Mildred Sherrod; Gloria and Andy Contreras; Albert Lee; Greg Asbed; Father Vilmar Orsolin, CS; Esther Montero; Maria Rodriguez; Ed Laudise; Father Ettore Rubin, CS; and Father Jean Woady Louis.

Those who previously worked in Immokalee and helped from a distance include Sister Eileen Eppig, SSND; Sister Barbara Pfarr, SSND; Sister Marie McFadden, SSND; Father Isaia Birollo, CS; John Witchger; Rob Williams; and Greg Schell.

The professors at Florida International University supported me in my focus on Immokalee's immigrants. I most of all want to thank Victor Uribe who encouraged, guided and inspired me through almost all of this research. Other professors who were particularly helpful include Sherry Johnson, N. Noble Cook, Brian Peterson, James Sweet, and Terry Rey.

People who provided important resources include Marlene Foord; Sister Alice Zachman from the Guatemalan Human Rights Commission/USA; H. Rhea Gray; Gail McGrath; Becky Kokkinos; and Helene Caseltine.

For agricultural information, I want to thank Jamie Williams, Paul Everett, Joe Procacci, and Mike Procacci.

I want to thank my mother, Mary Elizabeth Thissen, for her memories, her insight and her love; and my nephews Karl, Eugene, Keith, and niece Valerie Pickett, just for being wonderful.

For their careful editing, I thank my friends Sister Maureen Kelleher, RSHM, Beth Callender, and Peggy Diaz. Sister Maureen also deserves a very special thank you for her help with research, her memories, and a lawyer's attention to detail. And I thank my husband, Barry Kotek, for his direction, editing, patience, support, and love, throughout the writing of this book.

Last and most importantly, I thank the immigrants of Immokalee for their courage and their perseverance in coming to this country and for what they have added to my life. Their stories are told in the following pages.

Acknowledgements for the Second Edition—The second edition had many additional helpers. For guidance and inspiration I thank Maria Stone, author of many faithful histories of Collier County. Business friends, journalists, and editors Michael Garry and John Karolefski helped with copy-editing, as did Becky Farrar-Koch, editor and publisher of *Neopolitan 50 Plus*, and my cousin Diane Hayward. And for information about organizations that has been added to this edition, I thank Rev. Lisa Lefkow, J. Douglas Burke, Flo and Ted Huey, Barbara Mainster, Bonnie Rosenmeier, Yolanda Wohl, Jim Sanders, Pete Gallagher, Laura Stacell, Virginia Quillinan, Nancy Powers, and Benny Starling.

Introduction to the Second Edition

It may seem unusual to publish a second edition of a book within a year of the first edition. I chose to do it because I received valuable feedback from people who read the first version. I wanted to incorporate it, and I also wanted to clear up a few things.

First, some people who read the first version felt compelled to argue with me about the problems, dangers, and costs of a large population of new, poor immigrants in the U.S. My response is that it was never my intention to argue those issues, and I am still not interested in doing that. I only want to show the human side of the immigrants—the farmworkers in particular. I want you to have compassion for what these people lived through and what they risked to come here. I want you to understand that they have the same feelings that we all do, and I want you to appreciate their hopes for the future. Their dreams are simple: they want to work and make a better life, and they want their children to go to school. They want the same things that most of our grandparents and great-grandparents wanted when they came to this country.

Second, I wanted to make it clear that the stories of Immokalee's immigrants are likely same as the stories of poor Mexican, Haitian, and Guatemalan immigrants all over the United States. There are similar towns all over our country. Immokalee just happens to be located near my home. Regardless of where you live, the Mexican man who bags your groceries, the Haitian woman who buses tables at your favorite restaurant, and the Guatemalan man who works at your golf course probably all have stories very similar to the ones you are about to read.

I am saddened and confused by the anger toward new immigrants that I hear from many people. I wonder how they can forget what their ancestors went through to come to this country and how they worked to establish themselves here. I offer the following in the hope that memories of my ancestors will help readers remember their own.

My father's mother, Anna Katherine Scharfhausen, and her husband, Peter Matthias Thissen, were German immigrants. Their families were poor and they came to the United States to work and make a better life, just like the people I know in Immokalee. My great-grandmother, called "Oma," told her grandchildren that in Germany, they did not have "a pot to pee in or a window to throw it out of." They knew how to weave velvet, however, and they heard that there was work in velvet-weaving in Connecticut, in the United States, so they came. They wanted to work, just like the people who came to Immokalee.

My German grandmother never learned English because she did not need to. I mention this because the new Latin American and Caribbean immigrants are often criticized for not learning English, but there is little free time in the day for poor people. They do not need English in order to work; English is a difficult language, and they have little opportunity to study or to practice, the same as my grandmother. At home, my grandparents spoke two languages, as do most of the people in Immokalee today. The German grandmother spoke only German, and my father's father spoke English. The children were therefore bilingual, a great gift to have from childhood.

There are other prejudices against the new immigrants. Prejudice is not a primary focus of this book, because the people I spoke with did not mention it, although I am certain they have felt it. I had a friend in Chicago whose parents came originally from Mexico. Paul went on vacation to Mexico once, and when he came back, he told me it was the first time in his life he wasn't ashamed to be Mexican. He had never mentioned it before.

My father knew something about this. His name was really Karl, but he changed the "K" to a "C" during World War I so it would not be so obvious he was German. His sister Isabelle did not even go to high school because she was taunted about being German. My father went, but the other children would hit him and kick him on his way home from school, calling him "Kaiser! Kaiser!" He never forgot what it felt like. Hatred of groups of people is a terrible thing, especially when you see it in children.

My mother's Irish grandparents, Charles O'Hanley and Elizabeth Murphy, dropped the "O" from O'Hanley when they got to Ellis Island. Once they got established in Jersey City, Charles built houses and Elizabeth would go out in the freezing cold to collect the rent. She walked, to save bus fare. Often when she got there the people couldn't pay, but instead of pressuring them for money they did not have, she would go out and buy groceries for them. She helped people when they were sick or needed money and she delivered their babies. At the end of her last walk, she collapsed on the street and later died of pneumonia. They called her "The Saint of Manning Avenue."

Charles and Elizabeth Hanley were very much like the immigrants in Immokalee today, except that they lived in the city, and Immokalee is in the country. I even talked to a Mexican woman, Juanita, whose mother was like the Saint of Manning Avenue. She made a meager living giving injections to sick people in their homes in Mexico. When her patients ran out of money, she gave the shots for free and also brought them food.

My Irish and German ancestors supported themselves, sent money back home to their families, and paid to bring other relatives here. When they came, the relatives lived with them until they could get a place of their own. Mexicans, Haitians, and Guatemalans do exactly the same thing today. They send money home, and they help their relatives.

Most of the people I talked to have decided to remain in the United States. The conditions in their home countries are dismal, and while they love their countries, they say there is nothing to go home to.

Most of my relatives stayed in the United States, but they never forgot Germany and Ireland. Life here was better than it was in their countries, so they stayed, and they brought their heritage with them. The Mexicans, Haitians, and Guatemalans are adding much to our culture now and will continue to add more in the future.

My mother said there was hatred and discrimination against Irish, German, and Italian immigrants when she was growing up in Jersey City. She remembers signs that read, "No Irish Need Apply."

"I think most of it was a matter of economics," she explained. "They all came here with a common purpose—they wanted to make a better life. And when they did finally earn a place in this world, a new group came in, threatening their jobs."

The new immigrants are just like my ancestors. Nothing has changed.

Volunteering started me on the path to being able to feel compassion for these new immigrants. A few years before I turned fifty, I looked back at a very successful business career and felt as if I had wasted my life. Then I got involved as a volunteer in Immokalee, teaching music to preschool children, and my life has changed completely. I am a much better person today.

It may seem like a simple thing—teaching music to little children—but it is very important. I teach them skills that will give them confidence as they get into elementary school, and concepts that will help them learn. It is my way to contribute, to change the world just a little. A woman who builds houses with Habitat for Humanity feels the same way. Her name is Erikka Thalheimer, and she summed up the feeling in one of the Habitat newsletters:

"I so enjoy the time I spend at the building site," she wrote. "My family now knows not to ask anything of me on Saturday mornings because that *is my time. My time* to do *my* part to change the world."

We both volunteer because we care about the new immigrants. We want to help them make their way in our country, the way our ancestors made theirs. But in order to care about the new immigrants, I think it is important to understand something about them, and that leads me to the key purpose of this book. It came to me when I re-read a quote from Sister Eileen Eppig, whom you will meet in Chapter Six.

"Caring for the whole person doesn't just mean caring for the person who is in need now," she told me. "It means connecting with the reality that the person left part of their life behind, in another country."

My goal is to help my readers connect with that reality. The first edition of this book had that effect on some people.

"For some reason," one wrote, "I have always held the Central Americans in contempt. Now that I understand what they went through, I see them so differently."

"With this book," said another, "you're shaking us into the reality of how good we have it in the United States, and that it's essential to be willing to share what we are blessed with here."

"I like the way you call them the 'last heres,'" said a third. "It's a good reminder that we were all 'last heres' at one time, all looking for a better life for our families. I came away from this book understanding that these people need and deserve our help and support."

The most touching response was from an old friend who called to ask, "How can I help Rosalinda bring her children here from Guatemala?"

Carlene Thissen
March, 2004

P.S. I also learned that the name of this place is hard to pronounce, so I offer this tip: Immokalee rhymes with broccoli.

Introduction to the First Edition

Before we talk about the immigrants and what they have meant in my life, I need to tell you about Immokalee. To get there, I drive northeast from Naples and watch the scenery change from golf courses to gated communities to swampy areas of the Everglades and then to citrus groves. After forty minutes, I'm in Immokalee. I read somewhere a perfect description of Immokalee's Main Street:

"It looks like a movie set with a lot of extras milling around, waiting for the filming to start."

Immokalee is the center of Southwest Florida's multimillion-dollar agricultural business. It is located in the northeast corner of Collier County, about five miles from the Hendry County and Lee County borders, making it an agricultural hub for the three counties. The main crops in the area are tomatoes, watermelons, peppers, cucumbers, potatoes, and citrus.

It is one of Florida's largest farmworker communities. Large-scale production of winter vegetables in the area expanded between 1960 and 1990 and the big growers needed labor to work their fields. At the same time, immigrants from Latin American and Caribbean countries were escaping poverty, corruption, and oppression. The word spread, from northern Florida to Louisiana to Texas to Mexico to Haiti and to Guatemala: "There is work in Immokalee." So people came.

The coming of new groups to Immokalee wasn't anything new. The community has changed before, and it will probably change again. In the middle 1800s, it was a Seminole Indian camp called "Gopher Ridge." Later, in the 1870s, white settlers started coming. One of the first was Charles W. Hendry, a cattleman, but after two years he moved north.

His homestead was taken over by William Allen who, after the hurricane of 1873, moved inland from Ft. Myers, and for a short time they called the small community "Allen's Place." Later, Bishop Grey of the Episcopal mission in Allen's Place changed the name to Immokalee. According to the Collier County Museum, in 1893 the Bishop asked eleven-year old Rose Brown the Indian word for "My Home" and she replied "*I-mok'-a-li.*" He used the spelling "Immokalee" on the application for the first post office, and it became the name of the community.

Immokalee grew and changed in the twentieth century. White ranchers came, then poor Whites and poor Blacks, then *Tejanos* (pronounced *teh-HA-nos*, meaning Mexicans from Texas), then Mexicans, Haitians, and Guatemalans. Other immigrants came, too, from other places in Latin America and the Caribbean. Today, over nineteen thousand people claim Immokalee as their permanent home. This number grows to more than thirty thousand people when migrant workers move in to work the fields during the winter months.

Immokalee is about forty-five miles northeast of downtown Naples. That's where I live, but I'm on the outskirts on the northeast side, so Immokalee is only thirty-four miles away. Naples is a vacation and retirement town for wealthy people, one of the richest communities in the United States. Other nearby wealthy communities include Marco Island, Bonita Springs, Fort Myers, and Sanibel.

In spite of the agribusiness in the surrounding areas, Immokalee is still very poor, especially compared to affluent Naples. Federal funding for social programs is sometimes hard for Immokalee to get, because the people of Naples make Collier one of the wealthiest counties in the United States. At the time I wrote this book, Immokalee was still unincorporated. That means it is not really a town, although I will use that term in this book. It has no mayor, no city council, and no hospital, but it is growing and has the promise of becoming a fascinating multi-cultural community. For me, it already is.

Immokalee and the other coastal communities have very similar growth and migration trends, but for completely different reasons. Many Naples winter residents (we call them "snowbirds") are retired wealthy people from the U.S. Midwest and East Coast. They live in Florida just over six months of the year, claiming the state as their primary residence for tax reasons. Many immigrant farmworkers also consider Immokalee their permanent home, but their reason is that it is a hub of activity related to the migrant worker stream. Wealthy Naples residents go north in April to escape Florida's summer heat and humidity. The migrant field workers go north in April too, as South Florida's growing season winds down. They go to the Northeast and the Midwest not to cool off, but to pick summer crops. Both groups return in the fall every year.

The immigrants who came to Immokalee in the second half of the twentieth century were different from the workers who came earlier. The new ones spoke different languages and had different cultures. They have changed Immokalee more than any group before them.

Many of these new immigrants came here legally, but some of them didn't. They risked their lives, crossing deserts on foot, swimming across a river, or sailing across the ocean. Some even floated across the Rio Grande in inner tubes! Many of those who came illegally at first "got their papers" after they worked in the U.S. for a while. Sister Maureen Kelleher, an Immokalee immigration attorney, said it is not possible for most of these people to come here legally. If they can, it takes up to twelve years. Some of them would have starved or been killed while they waited.

That's because life is hard in the places they came from, and that's what I want to tell you about. It explains why, in the individual chapters about the Mexicans, Haitians, and Guatemalans, you will find some of the history of their countries. The history helps us understand the immigrants, and that is really the reason I wrote this book, after all: to help people understand the immigrants.

The Mexicans I talked to spoke mostly about poverty. Economic conditions in Mexico have always been difficult, especially for poor people. The gap between rich and poor in their country is huge. The poor people's plight got worse and worse from 1950 to the 1990s, the same time Florida's winter vegetable and citrus production really took off. Before coming to the U.S., many of Mexico's poor tried moving to Mexico's large cities. Mexico City has become the largest city in the world because of the number of poor people who moved there and built makeshift shacks on the outskirts of the city. We called them "shantytowns" in the Great Depression. Eventually, many of them decided to risk their lives to cross the border to the United States, and some of them came to Immokalee.

The Haitians lived under the oppression of two dictators named Duvalier, known as "Papa Doc," and his son, "Baby Doc." Even after they were gone, the corruption in the government and the military remained. In Haiti, the land doesn't have enough nutrients to support even small crops because the trees were logged out and erosion took away the topsoil. It's so bad that if you look at some satellite weather maps, Haiti is brown. Like the Mexicans, rural Haitians moved to their capital city. A whole community of people in Port-au-Prince today live in shacks they built on top of a garbage dump. The place is called *Cite Soleil*—"City of the Sun." Haiti is the poorest country in our hemisphere. Many of the Haitians made their way across the waters of the Caribbean to U.S. shores to find jobs and safety. Some of them came to Immokalee because there was work here, and peace.

Most of the Guatemalans in Immokalee are Mayan Indians who have been persecuted for centuries. The Guatemalans lived in the same kind of poverty as the Mexicans and the Haitians, but some of them also went through the persecution of Guatemala's "Dirty War," an extended civil war between the government and the indigenous people that lasted thirty-six years—from 1960 to 1996. Thousands of Mayan Indians were killed, tortured, or driven out of their homes by their own government. Many of them left Guatemala because they were afraid for their lives. After a while, the violence eased up, but the poverty was still there, and the Mayas moved to their capital, Guatemala City. They faced the same conditions there that the Mexicans and the Haitians faced in their big cities: "shantytowns," no work, no food, and no hope. The first Guatemalans who came to Immokalee found it because a man came to their town and told them there was a place in the United States where the indigenous Indians were free; that there was even a town in the Indians' language that meant "my home."

The need for labor that drew these immigrants to Immokalee started with Castro's takeover of Cuba in 1959 that left a void in the U.S. supply of winter vegetables. In the 1960s, big growers in Southwest Florida set out to replace that supply, and as a result, agriculture in the area around Immokalee turned into big business: "agribusiness." Thousands of acres were dedicated to winter vegetable crops, and thousands of workers were needed to plant and harvest those fields. People started coming in from Latin America who would work for lower wages, and when they started coming, the U.S.-born White, Black, and *Tejano* field workers were offered even less money than before. Naturally, the workers already here resented the ones who came after them. It was true when my mother was growing up, and it's true today.

I asked Albert Lee about this. Albert is a paralegal who works at Florida Rural Legal Services in Immokalee. Here's how he explained it.

"It's my experience that 'last here,' whoever that is, normally gets the most work," he explained. "Because they're the most vulnerable, they are more apt to do anything and everything that needs to be done for less money than the ones who have been here."

This book is really a chronological history of the "last heres." The prologue explains how I got to know Immokalee and how volunteering has helped me. Chapter One is the early history of Immokalee, and how the people there changed with changing uses of land. Chapter Two tells the story of the most significant change, the one that brought the new immigrants: small-scale vegetable farming that turned into "agribusiness."

In Chapters Three, Four, and Five, we meet the people this book is really about: the new immigrants. The Mexicans—the dominant ethnic group in Immokalee today—came in the 1970s and kept coming. The Haitians came in the early 1980s and the Guatemalans in the mid-1980s. Both those groups kept coming, too. I framed the stories they told me about their lives with the histories of their countries. If you are a history buff, I hope you will particularly enjoy these chapters, but if you are not that interested in history, don't worry. I did my best to have the immigrants' personal stories narrate the story to keep it interesting.

Chapter Six describes what Immokalee was like when many of the immigrants first arrived and describes how social and legal services developed to help them. Chapter Seven shows how things changed in the 1990s, when the new residents started to become one people. It also describes Immokalee today and where it seems to be headed in the future.

Immokalee is a fascinating community that has been enriched by people of many different cultures. Most of them came to Immokalee because there were jobs available, planting, harvesting, and packing crops. They just wanted to make a better life and live in peace. They just wanted to work.

Prologue—About Me and How I got to Know Immokalee

"The best way to find yourself is to lose yourself in service to others."

—Mahatma Gandhi

A few years before I turned fifty, I looked back at a successful business career and decided I had wasted my life. For more than twenty-five years I had been a career-driven businesswoman who worked, made money, and spent money. Looking back, I can't even believe that person was me. It was almost as if I had lost my soul. My earliest dream—to be a doctor working with the poor—had stayed with me through my mid-twenties, but then something changed and I followed a different path. Not long ago something stirred in me, I made some changes, and now my life has meaning again. Immokalee's immigrants did that for me.

I believe there is a plan. People are put into your life (and you are put into theirs) for reasons, and the reasons are part of the plan. A very wise woman I once knew explained that we don't always get to know what the plan is.

"God doesn't have to tell us," Ginny would say. If things get blocked, she explained, particularly if they get blocked strongly, then it just means you're not following the plan. "He'll break your leg if he has to," she would say. I learned from her that there are two tricks to following the plan. The first is to watch for signs. The second is to do things that come easy; they are usually the right things.

I didn't set out to get to know Immokalee. I didn't even set out to live in Florida. Everything changed in 1993 when I was happily living in Chicago. I owned a successful business: consulting in supermarket technology and marketing. I had my own Harley Davidson motorcycle that I had wanted all my life, and through that I met my friend Joyce, who is a "biker chick," too. I had season tickets to the Lyric Opera, Chicago Symphony, and the Goodman Theatre. I had one charity—the battered women's organization in my neighborhood—and I had wonderful friends, especially Carolyn and Joyce. I spent about a third of each year in Costa Rica, two, three, or four weeks at a time. I had even gotten a consulting partner there and an apartment. I was studying Spanish and hoped one day to move to Costa Rica permanently.

On one flight from Costa Rica to Chicago, I remember being particularly conscious of how perfect my life really was. The only thing that could mess this up, I thought to myself, would be a man. Then I heard a voice.

"Hey, what are you reading?" And so entered Barry Kotek.

Eight months later, my new husband and I moved to Naples, Florida.

I believe Barry Kotek was put in my life to be my husband and he is a wonderful husband. He led me to Naples and to his mother, Theresa. She was in her third battle with cancer, and this time she had said "no" to chemotherapy and radiation. She lived her life to its natural end and enjoyed it as much as she could. She was grateful to have three grown children and their families in Naples with her. In a way, you could say that Theresa was the one who got me to Naples and to Immokalee. I got to spend a whole year with her before she died. I loved her. I also got to know Barry's wonderful sister, Julie, who introduced me to her friend Rolf, and Rolf introduced me to Ursula, who became another very good friend. Ursula introduced me to Yolanda, who taught me about Raja Yoga meditation, and indirectly, Yolanda led me to Immokalee. Here's how it happened.

After one meditation session, the Raja Yoga group discussed life in general. For the first time, I expressed the disappointment I felt about how I had lived my life. I was still a successful businesswoman, author of several business publications, and had an incredible lifestyle. But all I had ever done with my efforts was make money, and I had done very little for anyone else. I once read a quote that went something like this: "If just one person slept easier because you existed, your life was worthwhile." I couldn't think of very many people who slept easier because of me, and it was beginning to bother me.

Someone at the meditation group observed that I love to sing and I like children, so why not find a place where I could sing to children? I play the guitar and the piano and I knew some children's songs because my mother taught kindergarten and first grade for many years. Of course I could sing music with children. *Do what comes easy.*

The very next morning I was reading the Naples Daily News and saw an article about the Guadalupe Family Center. Every year, back then, Snyderman's Shoe Store provided discounted shoes to Immokalee's poorer school-aged children through the Guadalupe Family Center. *Watch for signs.* I called the Family Center and offered my services as a volunteer. "I can sing and play music," I said. Marianne Morrisey was the director of the Family Center then. Here's what she told me.

"We have a full-time staff. We have someone who comes and teaches computers. Another lady teaches art. The only thing we don't have here is music," she said. "When can you start?" *Watch for signs* and *Do what comes easy.*

The Guadalupe Family Center is a very nice facility. It used to be a nursing home, but then James Near organized funding so the Guadalupe Center could buy it and turn it into a Family Center, daycare, and after-school care center. It is not for the extremely poor, nor is it for migrants. (The migrants have other daycare services through Redland Christian Migrant Association and Immokalee Child Care Center.) Guadalupe Family Center provides preschool and after-school care for the children of people who have gotten off the migrant circuit and settled down into stable lives, but life is still sometimes a struggle for them. Parents pay for childcare at the Family Center, but the cost is subsidized by donations. They pay varying amounts, depending on their income.

The children at the Guadalupe Family Center are mostly Mexican or of Mexican ancestry. There are a few Haitians, an occasional Guatemalan child, and some U.S.-born Whites and Blacks. The teachers are not certified teachers, but they are trained in early child-care, and they are very good with the children. Some of them worked in the fields for at least part of their lives.

Although almost all of the staff is bilingual, they speak only English to the children, because the goal of the Family Center is to prepare them for school here in the United States. I was, however, encouraged to sing in Spanish and Haitian Creole if I liked. I did like that idea, mainly because I like languages so much. Also, it's important that the children know songs from their own culture and that they learn each other's languages, since Immokalee is such a multi-cultural town.

I went once a week on Wednesdays. At Thanksgiving, Marianne, the director, asked me to play my guitar on the Guadalupe Family Center float in Immokalee's parade. I looked forward to this experience and I met the Family Center staff across the street from *La Favorita* Bakery just off Main Street. Sister Judy Dohner, then the director of the overall organization of Guadalupe Center, was there, too. I had seen her a few times before, and she became my first "nun-friend." I have several of them now. My nun-friends are dedicated, they are smart, and they are strong. They figure out what God wants them to do, get themselves ready, and then they do it.

That Thanksgiving, Sister Judy brought her guitar to the parade and we played together easily because we both had played in church. The floats in the Immokalee Thanksgiving Day parade were mostly flatbed trucks, otherwise used in the fields. A few, like the one from Immokalee High School, were quite sophisticated, decorated with colors and lights. Ours, like many of the others, had only a few makeshift seats and a poor amplifier and microphone that didn't really work. It was decorated with crepe paper. A few of the pre-school children sat on the truck with us. One of them, a white boy named Scottie, wore an elaborate Mexican sombrero that nearly covered his whole head.

We sang, but were hardly heard because of the poor quality of our amplification system. Marianne kept repeating, with a determined smile, "Next year I want a generator!" We sang and threw pieces of candy to the people of the town who were watching the parade, standing or sitting along the sidewalk of Main Street that is also Highway 29. This was before they installed streetlights, and Main Street was dark and seemed very lonely, but the people in Immokalee were happy with this parade. You could tell that from the looks on their faces.

Afterwards, I drove home and experienced culture shock for the first time, going from Immokalee to Naples. It was still early in the evening, about 8:30, and I was to meet some friends in downtown Naples at an expensive restaurant on Fifth Avenue South. I stared at my closet and could not decide what to wear, because nothing seemed normal. When I arrived at the restaurant, my friends were dressed as usual, with beautiful clothes, perfect hair, and perfect make-up. I always enjoy their company and always like the lights, the crowds, and the activity downtown, but somehow this night I was not able to make the transition. I could not stop thinking about Immokalee.

That's how it went. I kept singing with the children at the Family Center on Wednesdays and grew to love it more and more. I remember the Busy Bees—the oldest group of children—from that first year. They were three years old when I first met them, and I knew them for a year. The teachers were Ms. Delma, a U.S.-born woman of Mexican ancestry, and Ms. Queenie, a U.S.-born Black. The Busy Bees I remember most are Candace, Joe, Sonny, Scottie, Brandon, and Fabian. They were good singers, these children, and I loved them. When I arrived each week, they would run up to me and hug me, shouting, "Ms. Carlene, Ms. Carlene!" They loved to sing. One of their favorites was a song by John Anderson about the destruction of the Everglades: "Blow, blow, Seminole Wind. Blow like you're never gonna blow again…"

The children sang and they danced. Sometimes I let them play my guitar. I do this today, too, when I have time. They stand in front of me with the guitar pick and strum the strings while I play the chords. I sing along with their strumming, at the speed and beat they play. It teaches them quickly how to keep pace and rhythm. Some are very natural at it. A Busy Bee named Carlos, who had big ears (like mine), and a wonderful smile, was very good on the guitar. One day we were all playing some kind of instrument, using blocks, jingle bells, and triangles. Carlos had drumsticks and played them on the table. He played them very well, too.

I said, "You have drums at home, don't you?"

He smiled shyly, came over, touched my guitar, and said, "We got one of these at home, too."

The first year I taught at the Family Center, the children had a kind of spiritual connection to me. I almost got to thinking that my father was somehow reincarnated into one of them, or all of them. Here's why; I would bring my father's guitar to the Family Center sometimes, to show them the differences in guitars. My father gave me my guitar as a present for my grammar school graduation, and I acquired his when he died. I point out to the children that the guitars are both made of wood, but one is bigger (his) and one is smaller (mine.) One has "f-holes" (his) and the other has an "o-hole." But the Busy Bees were always more interested in my father than the construction of his guitar.

"Whose guitar is this?" I would ask them.

"Your dad's," they would reply in unison.

Then they would ask, "Where's your dad?"

"He died," I would say. "He's in Heaven, with God."

The next time I brought his guitar, they would all ask the same questions again.

"Where's your dad?"

And I would reply, always patiently, "He died. He's in Heaven, with God."

This happened repeatedly, same children, same questions, and same answer. One day I brought them a photograph of my father playing his guitar. It was an 8 X 10 enlargement, so it was easy to see him and the guitar. The Busy Bees stood on line to look at it, without saying a word. Each child stared at the picture for over a minute, and the other children made no sounds as they waited for their turn to see the picture. Each child stared silently, almost reverently, at this picture of my father playing his guitar. They were only three years old, and of course they had never met him, but it seemed they loved my father as much as I did. This still amazes me, especially since they were so young.

One day I arrived at the Family Center and the Busy Bees told me about their field trip on a train in Fort Myers. I had my father's guitar with me that day.

"Where's your dad?" they asked as usual, staring reverently at his guitar.

"He died," I answered, patiently, as usual. "He's in heaven, with God."

"No he's not," they all insisted. "We saw him. We saw him on the train."

I stared at them. They nodded their heads. Absolutely, they said, they saw him.

Of course, it was probably just an older man who looked like the picture they had seen of my father. But they were sure it was him. I got such a strong sense of connection, as if my father were sending me a message. A message like this:

"What you're doing here is good, my little Carlene; very, very, good. And I'm so happy to see you playing my guitar."

I continued my volunteer work at the Family Center once a week, then Marianne moved up north and Marie Morales took over as director.

That was fun, because Marie played the guitar and sang with the children and me, and I gradually got to know Sister Judy better. We started having lunch on Wednesdays after I was done singing with the children.

Several years later, Judy moved away to Lake Providence, Louisiana, and then moved on to Haiti where she works as a nurse in a hospital and street clinics. We keep in touch by email, and she visits sometimes, but I miss her very much. I miss her spirituality, and I miss her laughter. I especially miss playing our guitars together.

Judy always made me feel appreciated. Once she said the most beautiful thing to me:

"I don't know how long God is going to let us keep you, but I am so grateful you are here."

I tried to explain that really, it was the reverse. I was grateful to be in Immokalee. I finally had meaning in my life, because I was doing something that meant something for other people. She understood, because she lived it.

In December of that year, Sister Judy invited me to join her and the small choir at the tri-lingual Christmas Eve Mass. Three priests took part, because some of it was said in English, some in Spanish, and some in Haitian Creole. For the "Our Father," the priests asked all of us to say it together, but each in our own language. It was a very interesting and very moving thing to hear. The choirs alternated the songs—one in each language. The Guatemalans played guitars and sang, too, in Kanjobal, their native Indian language. That experience was all I needed to know that I loved this place. I went once or twice more to St. Williams church in Naples, and then switched over to Immokalee completely. The "whiteness" of many of the churches in Naples bothers me now. I've gotten used to different colored skin, different accents, and customs from other countries. White churches are nice, but I prefer Immokalee and Our Lady of Guadalupe.

I became a regular member of the choir at Our Lady of Guadalupe's English Mass, and I still am. Back then I played the guitar with Sister Judy, but since she left, I play the guitar alone. Joe Brueggen sings and introduces each part of the Mass. Tara Norman from Naples became our organist, and her husband, John Norman, takes care of our sound system and helps get the Masses on a local radio station. Joe's daughter, Michelle, plays the flute. The Brueggen's older daughter, Cece, used to play maracas and tambourine, but she went away to college, so their younger brother Joey has taken over the rhythm section of the choir. Paul Midney and his daughter Elizabeth also sing with us now, and Sister Kelly Carpenter plays the cello.

I have gotten to know quite a few people, like the Brueggens, who moved to Immokalee in the 1980s. Like the immigrants in this book, they also came because there was work. Not farm work, but work that helped make Immokalee a home for the immigrants. Quite a few of these people who came to help had worked before in different countries in Latin America and they have interesting stories of their own. Some of them brought spouses from these countries, like Joe Brueggen's wife Charo, who came from Peru, or Paul Midney's wife Reina, from Paraguay. These spouses were also new to the U.S. and are part of Immokalee's small melting pot.

Little by little I got more involved in the Immokalee community. I continued to teach music at the Guadalupe Family Center because I loved the children and the teachers. Many of them are former fieldworkers.

The third year I was involved with Immokalee, I almost lost my voice. The hoarseness started in the fall and kept getting worse. Singing with little children and singing at church shouldn't hurt your voice, but it turned out that I was using my voice incorrectly.

As an alternative to vocal chord surgery, I went to see a retired opera teacher named Michael Trimble. Michael helped me fix my voice by teaching me how to use it properly, and he helped me fix my soul by teaching me how to be "centered."

Once I learned how to stay centered, I started doing more of the things I loved, like going to school, and I decided to finish the Master's degree in Medieval History that I had started when I lived in Chicago.

Why? Just because I liked it. I contacted my professor from the University of Illinois for recommendations, and he suggested Florida International University, FIU. It is the closest major university to Naples where I could take graduate courses in Medieval History. The main campus is located precisely one hundred miles from my home, right at the end of 41, on the outskirts of Miami. *Do what comes easy.*

One of the first courses I signed up for was a research seminar that was a required part of the coursework for all history majors. When I arrived, Professor Sherry Johnson told us that the focus of the course had been changed and it had become a research course specifically in Latin American History. *Watch for signs.* I had the option of changing to a different class if I wanted, but I was curious. Because of Immokalee, I had some interest in Latin America, and I really did think this might be a sign, so I stayed in the class. I asked if I could do my research on Our Lady of Guadalupe Church in Immokalee. She not only agreed, but also encouraged it, so I wrote a history of the church and the social services that developed because of it.

After that course and that paper, I changed my major from Medieval to Latin American History, and I began to think about writing this book. Every professor I had at FIU encouraged me to research Immokalee as part of my coursework. I was working on a degree in Latin American History, with a focus on recent history. What better way could there be to learn than to hear it from the people who had lived it?

The story I would write would be a different kind of history, as most history is written from the perspective of the educated, ruling classes. I learned something about the history of the lower classes once when I took a course in American History at San Francisco State University. I took it because there were no courses in Medieval History—at that time my primary interest—but also because I was interested in learning about the founders of our country, especially about Thomas Jefferson and Benjamin Franklin. Our professor stopped those expectations with her opening words.

"We are not going to study about the 'Great White Men' who dominated early history," she said, sternly. "We are going to learn about the everyday, ordinary people and their role in the history of this country."

I was disappointed at first, because I really wanted to learn about Jefferson and Franklin, but the course turned out to be very enlightening. Instead of the usual history about governments and great white men, we studied the people whose voices were hardly ever heard—voices of black slaves and poor white women, poor white men and American Indians.

And I learned a historical concept about the value of the history of ordinary people. That's one of the reasons this book is both different and important; it is the stories of ordinary people, and ordinary people matter.

To do oral research in Immokalee, I needed to improve my language skills. I had studied German in high school, but that was no help, although I remember my father telling us that when he sailed to South America he only spoke German.

"They hate Americans down there," he said "so I always tell them I'm a 'Heinie.'" (A slang word for German.) It was not until I studied Latin American History that I understood what he was talking about.

My Spanish was passable, but not good. I started listening to advanced Berlitz tapes in the car on my way to and from school in Miami, and my Spanish improved. That left Haitian Creole.

Because languages have always come easy to me and I enjoy them, learning another one did not frighten me. I had worked in Belgium and Paris a few times, so I knew a little French, and the accent is similar. Accents come easy, too, I think because of the music: the skills for listening and reproducing sounds are similar. But where and how could I learn Haitian Creole? I bought a set of tapes that taught basic words and phrases, but I needed to go beyond that.

I found my first Haitian Creole teacher on Good Friday at the tri-lingual Stations of the Cross, where we have a procession through local streets in Immokalee. I saw a young Haitian man and woman with song sheets for the Haitian music, so I walked near and motioned that I would like to read along with them. They both smiled and shared their paper. Afterwards, in the church parking lot, they came over to me. She spoke first.

"You want to learn Haitian Creole?"

"Yes. Yes, I do," I replied.

He spoke next. "I need to learn English."

We made a deal. We would teach each other. I asked their names. His name is Socrate, and hers is Carline. It is pronounced just like my name. *Watch for signs.*

My new teachers had come from Haiti only a few months before, but Carline had studied English there, while Socrate had not. We met each week on Sunday. I would sing at the 9:00 English Mass, finish at 10:00, and then go to breakfast. At 11:30 I would go back and meet Carline and Socrate at the end of the Haitian Mass. I bought a book for English-speaking people learning Haitian Creole that we used for our lessons. It worked well for learning Creole and English.

Carline was quite elegant, about my height but very thin. She became the teacher as we sat in chairs around the teacher's table in a classroom next to the church. When I had a question about something, she would stand up and say, "All right. Let me explain you." Then I would say "…to…you" and she would smile, slightly embarrassed, and say it correctly, "Let me explain it *to* you." Then she would write on the blackboard, explaining the subtleties of their language.

There are a few more things I want to mention before we start into the history of Immokalee. The first is about the number of people you will meet in these pages. I recommend that you don't try to remember them all; there are too many. I want to take you on a journey you will enjoy, not frustrate you. If I mention people more than once or in different places, I will add a little information to remind you of who they are. You can also find most of them in the index.

The second thing I want to say is that one of the words you will not find in this book except in quotations is the word "illegals." It is commonly used, but I try not to use it. For example, when I started this research I asked several people when the first immigrants started coming from other countries. This was a typical answer, "There were *Tejanos*, and a lot of Blacks in the fields, and some Whites, but there weren't many illegals here then."

A young woman named Damara Luce who works in Immokalee sensitized me to the use of the term "illegal." Damara came to Immokalee in 1997 from Vermont. She was a volunteer at the Guadalupe Family Center when I first met her and later she went to work at Guadalupe Social Services. Today Damara works with an inter-faith group that supports the Coalition of Immokalee Workers.

"People can't be illegal," she explained. "They came to this country illegally, but they themselves are not illegal, so we shouldn't call them illegals."

I agree with Damara. These people are not illegal. They crossed our border illegally, and I have no problem saying that, but they are not themselves "illegal." I've also heard the term "aliens." Although the term is technically correct, I am not comfortable calling human beings "aliens." "Illegal aliens" sounds even worse.

Is there a better word to describe people who crossed our borders without legal authorization? Damara and most of the social and legal-services people in Immokalee use "documented" and "undocumented." But I don't use those words because I always seem to want to translate them for people. I like to say something simpler, like "with papers," and "without papers."

So in this book you will find "They were here without papers," or "He got his papers in 1986." It's very clear, and very simple.

The third thing I want to mention is that most of the people who come to this country illegally would rather come legally, but they are not allowed to because they are poor. The rules are complicated. Sister Maureen Kelleher helped me understand them and we will go over them later, but here's what we in business call the bottom line: poor people who do not have a close relative in the U.S. with enough money to support them cannot come to this country legally. If they could, most of them would.

Because of the people of Immokalee, many things in my life have changed. Now, instead of just working to make money, I do other things with my life. I have a Master's degree in Latin American History, and I have written this book. My life is unbelievably better because I have gotten to know people in a place that is like being in the United States plus several foreign countries at the same time, and I only have to drive forty minutes to get there. It all happened because I offered to do one thing for other people: sing with little children.

I now understand what Gandhi meant when he said, "The best way to find yourself is to lose yourself in service to others."

I seem to have found myself, and I am very happy today. And that's all I'm going to say about myself for the moment, because this is not my story.

It is the story of the immigrants and a multi-cultural community they are creating. They fled from poverty, repression, and violence, risking their money, homes, families, and sometimes their lives to get here. They came to find a better life. They just wanted to work, and there was work in Immokalee.

1

Immokalee's Early History and the Changing Uses of its Land

"It was just a little community, and everybody helped each other."
—Mildred (Roberts) Sherrod

Today, Immokalee is filled with many types of people who are becoming one people. I originally meant to focus only on the waves of new immigrants—those who came from other countries, but then I took a look at the community's early history. Not only is it fascinating, but it would be difficult to understand the impact of the immigrants if you did not know about the early days.

Somewhere between 1500 and 1800, some Calusa Indians probably hunted in the Immokalee area. The Calusa were actually a coastal tribe, but they did come inland. They are sometimes called "The Shell People" because they built their homes on shells and they left shell mounds as evidence of their existence. The Caloosahatchee River that connects the Gulf of Mexico to Lake Okeechobee, about twenty miles north of Immokalee, was named for them. (Caloosahatchee means "River of the Calusa.") The Calusa was one of the most powerful tribes in Florida. The Tequesta Indians who lived in the Miami area were subject to them, in a loose kind of a way. It was like old Ireland when they had "High Kings," where all the tribes were independent, but one was respected more than the rest. In Florida, the Calusa were the High Kings. It is commonly believed that they gradually disappeared after the Spanish discovered Florida, and that by the early 1800s there were no Calusa Indians left. However, Pete Gallagher, one-time historian for the Seminole Tribe, says some of the Calusa lived on in Florida, and that today's Seminole Tribe of Florida claims direct ancestry to the Calusa and other aboriginal peoples of Florida.

"They began to merge with other tribes—Maskoki speakers from across the Southeast—and fleeing black slaves," Gallagher explained. "This amalgamation of peoples who settled in the Florida outback became known as the Seminole Indians."

Gallagher also mentioned something that would be of great importance to vegetable growers and explains why, although much later, agribusiness started in Immokalee. "Immokalee...was high ground, between the Okoaloochee Slough and Fakahatchee Strand."

In the mid-1800s, the Seminoles used the Immokalee area as a base camp. Other Indians who shared the Maskoki language came to join them after the Creek War of 1813–14 when Andrew Jackson forced them out of Alabama. Together with the Indians already in Florida, they developed maroon or runaway communities in the Everglades. Some say the name Seminole is taken from the Spanish word for maroon, which is *cimarone*. "Seminole" is also similar to the Maskoki word for "free people"—*yat'siminoli*.

Many African slaves escaped from the Southern states and ran south to the Florida Everglades where they lived with the Seminoles. The ex-slaves could not survive in the Florida wilderness alone, so the Seminoles helped them. In return, the ex-slaves brought farming skills and the language of the white people.

Later, as white settlers came across Florida's borders, the Indians fought against them. Then General Jackson marched across the Florida border and started what became known as the First Seminole War. His troops burned Indian towns and hanged one of the most powerful medicine men. More wars took place when the U.S. forced more than 3,000 Maskoki Indians to move from Florida to Oklahoma. This tragic event was called the Second Seminole War. For twenty years the Seminole people were hunted, rounded up like cattle, and forced onto ships that took them to New Orleans, and then farther up the Mississippi.

Osceola was one of the most famous Indians who fought in the Seminole Indian Wars. They say he was as passionate as he was intelligent, and he masterminded successful battles against five U.S. generals. He was eventually captured and died in 1838 in a prison in Charleston, South Carolina. At that time, according to Seminole history, he was the most famous American Indian. They say newspapers all over the world covered the story of his death, and Osceola became the symbol of non-surrender for the Indians in Florida.

In the end, the Seminoles won—the only native-American Indian tribe to withstand the efforts of the U.S. government to control them. In 1858 the government gave up and signed a peace treaty with the Indians, but it was 1957 before a constitution was forged and the U.S. Congress officially recognized "The Unconquered Seminole Tribe of Florida." It was then that one group of Seminoles asked for separate recognition. This was granted to them, and in 1962 they were officially recognized as the Miccosukee Tribe of Indians of Florida.

White families from Georgia and Northern Florida started coming to Immokalee in the late 1800s. At that time, the community was called Gopher Ridge, a name that came from the large numbers of gopher turtles there. Those settlers were very much like the pioneers that settled the American west, and were also like everyone else who came to Immokalee. They just wanted to work, make a better life, and live in peace.

William Allen was one of the early residents, and for a short time Immokalee was called "Allen's Place." Later, in 1893, as I mentioned in the Introduction, Bishop Grey of the Episcopal mission in Allen's Place asked a young girl the Seminole word for "my home" and she said, "*I-mok-a-li.*" The Bishop used the spelling Immokalee on the application for the first post office, and it became the name.

Soon more white pioneer families came, bringing their cattle to graze in Immokalee. Robert and Sarah Roberts and their children were one of the first cattle families.

Mildred (Roberts) Sherrod, Bob Roberts' daughter, still lives in Immokalee. She said there were nine children. Seven came with the family when they moved from Desoto County, and Mildred and her brother Bob were born in Immokalee.

"The oldest was a boy," she told me. "He had to be a man by the time he was twelve. And there were six girls. I'm the seventh daughter of a seventh son. They always told me there was something special about that."

I met Mildred at her home in March of 2001. She still lives next door to the house she was raised in. When her family first came in 1914, it was a log cabin. Later her father added a chimney and fireplace to that cabin, and later still, he built a real house there. The Collier County Museum had just finished restoring it as a museum, and interestingly, it opened to the public the day after I met Mildred.

John Lawson, the director of outreach for the Guadalupe Center where I sing with the little children, arranged my meeting with Mildred. I would have been uncomfortable calling her directly, because I had never met her. I was actually a little intimidated because the Roberts family is well known in the area and I felt as though I were meeting pioneer royalty. But Mildred put me at ease immediately because she is very kind, warm, and gracious. She has a pleasant, educated, southern accent.

Her ranch-style living room reminded me of a western home, filled with paintings and pictures of cowboys and some things from the Seminole Indians. She likes the Seminoles very much, and was wearing Indian earrings when I met her. Mildred said her father first came to Immokalee on a trip from their home in Desoto County to bring some cattle here.

"He saw this place down here and he liked what he saw," she told me, "so he gave this fellow fifty dollars and said he'd be back to buy the place.

The fella decided that he wanted to go back where he came from, so he and Papa traded places. No money, just the sixty acres with an old log cabin. He brought about three hundred head of cattle."

This was in 1914. Northern Desoto County is about a hundred miles north of Immokalee, and it didn't seem like much of a trip until I remembered that there were no roads back then. Mildred said it took them three days to cover the hundred miles in wagons. The land was Florida wilderness, filled with thick pines, swamps, alligators, snakes, and mosquitoes. In addition, Mildred said hostile locals stopped the family at the Caloosahatchee River.

"One story was that he had to pay to come in, and the other was that they didn't want any family people here. Well, my father pulled his rifle across his saddle and said, 'Come on, boys, we're goin' across.' He was little, but he was strong. My father was really something. My mother was, too."

Mildred became very sad when she talked about her father, although he died a long time ago, in 1963. At one point when she was talking about him, she started to cry. I understood. Some kinds of sadness never go away.

"He just worked so hard—mentally and physically—that by the time he was sixty, his heart was so enlarged that the doctor took him off the horse. Told him he couldn't ride anymore. He rode old Tony out to pasture, and that was his last ride."

Mildred said there were very few people in Immokalee when her family first came, maybe a dozen families. I think that meant a dozen white families. She said they had a few Blacks come through. The Seminoles were here, too, of course. They had been here all along. Later, more white families arrived and Immokalee became a small cattle town that sounds very much like the old west.

"It was just a little community, and everybody helped each other," she explained. "That was back in the 1920s. My mother and Dad made coffins, washed bodies, and laid them out because there was no undertaker. That's the way they got along, by helping each other. If one butchered a cow, they'd send for the neighbors. If somebody had a horse and wagon, they would go to Ft. Myers, which was a three-day trip, to buy their supplies for a month. There were no roads."

Mildred said the new white settlers got along well with the Seminoles.

"The Seminoles were always here—before anybody," she remembered. "They've always been our friends. Indians used to bring in their hides, like alligator hides, and they'd meet a buyer at the Collier's First Mercantile Store to sell them." Later, her brother Dyas bought the store and called it Roberts' Store.

Mildred loves to tell stories about the Indians. "If they find they can't trust you, you're off their list, but if you're trustworthy, you're their friend. An Indian named Paul Buster told me a joke."

Here it is. A white man picked up an Indian in town and took him down to the church on the reservation. When they got there, they got out of the car, and the white man said, "Well, should I lock my car?" The Indian said, "No, you don't need to. There's not another white man within twenty miles of us."

Today the Seminoles receive a substantial income from casinos owned by the tribe. Mildred said some people resent them for having what they have from those casinos, but she disagrees. "I say they've been through the worst times, and if people are foolish enough to give them their money, well…anyway, it does me good to see them doing well."

She said some of the Indians worked in the cattle business, at least for a while, but I got the impression it was only when special jobs had to be done. For example, the Seminoles helped with the tick eradication when, in the 1930s, tick fever wiped out two thirds of the cattle in the area. Mildred remembers it like this:

"That was a terrible ordeal. The groups of Indians and Whites would get together to dip the cattle. They built dipping vats with some kind of poison. It was a big vat, dug, with cement walls. They'd run the cattle into it and the cows had to swim across and go out the other side.

The cattle had to be dipped every two weeks, I think. That was the hardest time. There was no money, no transportation, no anything."

The ticks were eventually eradicated and cattle remained big business in Immokalee. It still is today. There are no dairy cows here, though. Immokalee's cows are all range cattle, grown for beef.

The next big change in Immokalee was the railroad. Before 1921, the Atlantic Coast Line Railway Company came south as far as Palmdale and Labelle, a town about twenty-five miles north of Immokalee, in Hendry County. Mildred mentioned, incidentally, that Labelle was named after two daughters of Captain Hendry, whose names were Laura and Belle.

Barron G. Collier, who gave Collier County its name, extended the rail line south to Everglades City, and Immokalee was one of its stops. He was born in Memphis and had made a fortune selling streetcar advertising. In the early 1920s he purchased 1.3 million acres of land in the area, and in 1923 the part of that land that included Immokalee was separated from Lee County and became Collier County. Mildred joked about this. "I was born in Lee County, but I was here." The Colliers are still one of the most powerful families in Florida.

U.S.-born Blacks came to Immokalee because labor was needed to build the railroad. The stories of these early black people in Collier County have only been told once, when a woman who taught school in Immokalee, Maria Stone, wrote a book of their oral histories. She called it *We Also Came*. The title of that book reflects the reality that Blacks were left out of the other histories that were written. The few histories that were written about Collier County before the 1950s are interesting, but they ignore the black people.

The black people interviewed in *We Also Came* talked about the railroad. I borrowed a few of the voices Maria Stone recorded to help with this history. Orlo Carson was one of them (page 187 in *We Also Came*). He was born in Immokalee in 1912. He remembered a small black settlement when he was a boy, but later, "two or three dozen American Blacks came to put down the rails for a railroad."

Most people living in Immokalee in the 1930s and 1940s had farms where they grew enough to feed their families, and they had livestock. They only sold what they grew if they had more than they could use. It was a while before vegetable production became a business, and it was even longer before it became big business.

Since Mildred grew up in the 1930s and 1940s, I asked her what it was like to live in Immokalee then.

"Uptown, down on those four corners where you come in from Naples," she remembered, "there were three corners with two-story buildings with porches all around, on both floors. There were rooms upstairs, and there was a business downstairs. They had dances, but I wasn't allowed to go. They were pretty rough dances when they had them."

During the 1930s, lumber developed as a new use of the land around Immokalee. Northern Florida's trees were logged out right around 1900 and the sawmills started looking south. Collier County had one of the largest remaining stands of virgin cypress and pine timber in Florida, so it was a natural place for them to come. Mildred remembers the sawmills starting in 1935.

"Mr. Collier had bought all of this land, and he sold the timber to Mr. T.T. Scott from Live Oak. Mr. Scott brought in about five big mills. Down there on one side of the highway was the Sherrod's Mill and the other side was the Wingate Mill. They were two big families that came in here. The third was the Frizzells." The pine they logged was called "slash pine" or Dade County pine or southern yellow pine.

Now, more Blacks came. They had been sawmill workers in Northern Florida and Georgia until the trees were logged out, and they came to Immokalee because there was timber and that meant work. The sawmill owners built living quarters for the workers, and provided a company store for food and supplies. Arizona Daniels was another Black who was interviewed by Maria Stone in her book (on page 209 of *We Also Came*). Arizona explained how things worked at the Babbit Mill. "Back then, the blacks worked for nine or ten hours for five dollars a day. They paid us in babbit. That's a little piece of metal we could trade for what we needed at their commissary."

There are logging trails that you can still see today on maps of this area. They look like a jagged white line, like a crease through the trees. Those were logging tram roads. Workers would start down a section line and "sheet-cut" pines and load them on trams, then the pine logs were shipped out on the railroad.

Eventually, the cypress and pine were logged out, and the sawmills closed down. There is pine in this area now, but it is all new trees called "second growth." The cypress here are second growth, too, but they grow much more slowly than pine, so most of them are quite small. They are called "bald cypress" because they turn brown in the fall and lose their needles in the winter—the closest thing we have to fall colors here in south Florida. I love the cypress trees. In the summer they are brilliant green, soft and graceful. John Anderson's song "Seminole Wind" that I sing to the children at the Family Center mentions the cypress.

> The last time I walked in the swamp
> I sat upon a cypress stump.
> I listened close and I heard the ghost
> Of Osceola cry.

The Everglades were once filled with cypress, but they will not grow back to their full size for at least a thousand years. I will never see them.

Frank Ligas saw the end of the timber business in Immokalee. I know Frank and his wife Patty, because they go to our church. Frank came to Florida in 1952 to work for the Federal Fish and Wildlife Service, and for a year he lived in a house by the lighthouse in the Ding Darling Refuge on Sanibel Island. Then the Audubon Society was looking for a bachelor who was willing to travel around the country and study eagles, and Frank took the job. He traveled most of the year, marking eagles by putting red dye on their white tail feathers so he could study them. He said they used red dye instead of bands, because with bands you only get data if a bird is caught or if a dead one is found. However, with the red dye the eagles can be spotted in the wild from a distance. Frank traveled to the Midwest and the Northeast, following the eagles.

"We put notices up and posters, saying if you know where there's an eagle's nest, let me know. Then we went out and tramped and walked out to almost every single eagle's nest in Minnesota and Wisconsin. After we located all the nests, others from the Audubon Society would fly over them in the following year in April and see what eagles were sitting on each nest. Then the other Audubon folks would fly over again in June to see how many hatched before the young ones flew off."

Frank met his bride-to-be, Patty, in a Wisconsin camp he was using as a base. Patty was a lifeguard there in the summer. She is twenty-four years younger than Frank, and for a long time they were just good friends. They wrote letters back and forth for four years, and it seems they fell in love through their letters. They married, and when Patty got pregnant with her first child in 1969, the Ligas family settled down in Corkscrew Swamp permanently. They had three children: Julie, Jacqui, and Frankie. When Frankie started kindergarten, Patty became a teacher in Immokalee. She was a great help to me in my research. Following in her mother's footsteps, Jacqui now teaches at Immokalee High School.

Patty told me that Corkscrew Swamp Sanctuary was created when the Audubon Society saved the last stand of uncut cypress as a nesting ground for the endangered wood storks. Many species of animals, fish, and birds were lost when south Florida was developed. My father helped destroy them when he worked dredging the Everglades, but of course no one thought about that back then. Corkscrew Swamp Sanctuary is halfway between Naples and Immokalee. It has a boardwalk that is just over two miles long, and is one of the last few areas where you can see what the old Everglades were really like, where you can still walk in a virgin swamp with its beautiful cypress trees and Spanish moss.

After the big trees were gone, the land, having been cleared by logging, was used for growing vegetables or cattle grazing. I wondered about the stumps. How did they get them out of the fields? Frank Ligas explained.

"The center of the really big pine trees was solid resin, and it never rots," Frank told me. "When they did the logging, they'd cut the tree at about three feet high, and they'd take the tree for timber, but the stump stayed there until all the soft stuff rotted away, and they ended up with resin, really. Companies use it for explosives and medicines. They had things that would lift it right up out of the ground, like a backhoe. The Atlas Company and other explosives companies picked up ours. They took the wood and heated it, and then they got the carbon from it. I think they called it 'destructive distillation.' Then the carbon was turned into explosives."

I learned later that locals refer to the harvesting of this resin as "stumpin'." After the stumps were removed, the fields could be used for planting.

There was even oil found in Immokalee—not in large quantities, and it never became a big business, but it was there.

"There was oil found on our land, thank you, Lord," said Mildred, looking upwards with a smile. "It came at a crucial time, shortly after my daddy passed away in 1963. He knew it was there, but they never had brought it in until he was gone. It was a wonderful help. It was in Hendry County, north of the Collier County line."

She told me that Sun Oil made the discovery in 1964, but it wasn't ever a high production field. Then it gave out, and they finally just gave up.

"There's something about the drilling here that is difficult," she explained. "It's been up and down ever since the first discovery. The geologist from Sun said there's oil down there, it's just a matter of getting it out. They're still pumping pretty strong down in Cypress which is Collier's, and out in Lake Trafford on Pepper land."

Mildred also told me about Lake Trafford, because one of the people she suggested I talk to lives out there. Lake Trafford is a 1,500-acre lake just a few miles west of Immokalee's main street, and it is part of Immokalee. Mildred remembers it from when she was younger. "In the 1950s, they had the nicest fishing camp out there. They had cabins; it was a great place to go. Beautiful place."

Today Lake Trafford is still beautiful, in spite of some problems from fertilizer that was draining into the lake from the surrounding fields. The lake doesn't really have "outflows," or places where the water regularly drains out, so the fertilizer goes into the lake and fertilizes the algae and the Hydrilla water plants. Those plants use up all the oxygen in the water and the fish die. In 1996 fifty thousand fish died out there, all at one time.

There is a Lake Trafford Restoration Effort going on today. Hopefully they will have it restored to its original condition soon. It is still beautiful, however. My husband and I ride out there on our motorcycles sometimes. There is a big wood-covered deck where you can sit and look at the lake, and a bait and tackle shop, and fishing boats, so the fish must be doing all right again. There are also airboat rides. People from Immokalee go there, all different nationalities, to have picnics or to just peacefully look at the lake.

The thing that had an unforeseen effect on Lake Trafford was the same thing that brought the new immigrants: vegetable farming started to expand in south Florida. Farmers were drawn to the land around Immokalee because that land was higher, probably by five or six feet, than the land farther south and toward the coasts, and did not require draining. The land brought agribusiness, and agribusiness brought new and different people. They all came because there was work in Immokalee.

2

The Lure of Vegetable Farming

"I say anyone who wants to call farmworkers lazy, they should be made to do that work for a least a week, and I guarantee you they'd learn to respect it."

—Albert Lee

In the early 1930s, Mr. James T. Gaunt started growing tomatoes and cucumbers in Ochopee, a small community about thirty miles south of Immokalee, near Everglades City. Mildred Sherrod told me about him. She often used his middle initial when she said his name: "Mr. James T. Gaunt." She also did that when she talked about "Mr. T.T. Scott" who built sawmills.

The Post Office in Ochopee was originally Gaunt's tool house. A fire burned everything in town, so they used Gaunt's tool house as the Post Office. It is a tourist attraction today: "The nation's smallest Post Office."

Mr. James T. Gaunt needed a place for his vegetable workers to live, so he built a labor camp called "Bunker Hill." It was about ten acres of land, three miles outside of Immokalee. U.S.-born Blacks and Whites came from nearby southern states to work in his fields. After a while, though, Gaunt moved his farms to Immokalee. Mildred Sherrod remembers when he did it.

"Mr. Gaunt had tried farming on that rocky land in Ochopee until somebody found out they could plant here in Immokalee in this sand. Actually, the first production farmer in Immokalee was Mr. Tooke from Ft. Myers, but Gaunt moved his operations to Immokalee shortly after."

In 1940, Mr. James T. Gaunt and his partner, Mr. C.J. Jones, started Immokalee Growers, Inc., Immokalee's first packinghouse. The packinghouses were key to making Immokalee what it is today. It is one thing to grow vegetables, but quite another to be able to pack the produce and ship it out to market. For packing and shipping, you need packinghouses.

As the farming industry grew in the 1950s, other workers came to Immokalee. Many of them were poor Whites from Appalachia and the Ozarks, described by long-time Immokalee residents as "destitute and alcoholic." People told me these workers were attracted to Immokalee's warm weather, and also by the fact that they could get "day work." I spoke to several people about them, and they all said the same thing.

"They were winos."

Almost everyone I talked to from those early days used that term, "winos," and seemed to share the same opinion of them:

"They were usually single. The majority had been kicked out of their families, hadn't seen their families in years. If you gave them a couple of dollars, they wouldn't show up at work the next day. They slept in the palmettos, and they peed in the streets."

Quite a few of these destitute white people still live in Immokalee. I met some of them once when I went with Sister Judy to sing Christmas carols and hand out Christmas toiletries in Immokalee's flophouses and shelters. Not all of the white workers were winos. Some were just poor, and many of them had children.

In the early 1950s, a group of Mennonites came and provided childcare, food, and clothing to these early migrant farmworkers. A couple named Harold and Ellen Shearer started the Mennonite services in Immokalee. He was known locally as "Preacher Harold." An early member named Ben Hershey told me they provided childcare and a center for help with food or clothing or transportation. Ben said he made many trips to Miami, taking people to clinics, before there was a clinic in Immokalee. They serve the poor of Immokalee still today, under the name Immokalee Neighborhood Services.

There were *Tejanos* in Immokalee in the 1950s and some Puerto Ricans. Of course, both of these groups could travel freely to Florida. Mildred Sherrod remembers, because she taught first and second grade in the early 1950s.

"I had a class full of Mexicans—a lot of Mexicans and Puerto Ricans. I'd studied Spanish, which helped. Some of the first ones came from Texas, and they already had some English."

The black children in Immokalee could not go to the school where Mildred taught. It was for Whites only.

"So how did the Latinos get in?" I asked. I did not think they were usually considered "white."

Albert Lee, a black man who has lived in Immokalee since the 1960s, explained it. "It just depends on what they put down on the application. Spanish can be what they want to be. Puerto Ricans, Cubans, can be what they want to be. Blacks are the only ones who can't be but Black, and that's all there is to it."

In a separate discussion, Mildred Sherrod confirmed that it was the way they filled out the forms.

"They told me that everybody in Puerto Rico has 'white' on their birth certificates," she said. "There were some of them in my class. One boy was black, and his hair was kinky, but he had 'white' on his birth certificate."

Some of the Blacks who had previously cut and processed lumber stayed to work in the vegetable fields. More new black people came in from other places in the United States as the word got out that there was work in Immokalee.

Albert Lee, who worked in Immokalee's vegetable fields in the 1960s, said the Latinos were there, but fieldwork back then was dominated by Blacks and Whites. Albert still works as a paralegal in Immokalee, at Florida Rural Legal Services, although he is seventy-two years old. He said he retired a few years back, but then he just kept coming in on a volunteer basis, so they put him back on salary.

Albert helps new immigrants from Latin America and the Caribbean, particularly when they face discrimination in the fields. He has the perfect background to help him in this job. He was a field worker for the first seven years he lived in Immokalee, and as a black man, he experienced considerable discrimination. Things were different for him than they were for Whites, *Tejanos,* or Latinos from other countries. His story is typical of Blacks during that time.

In 1961, Albert left his wife at home and headed to Florida. They had bills to pay and there was no work for him in Louisiana. He came to Florida to make some money, just like the people from other countries that work in Immokalee today. He went first to the East Coast of Florida to a town called Lantana, but was not happy there. He had never done fieldwork before, and he was not in shape for it.

"I lived at a camp three weeks," he said, "and I couldn't take it no more. I was working day and night. I was pickin' staked tomatoes that came up high."

He motioned up to his neck. Albert is not very tall, maybe 5'8 or 5'9. He said the tomatoes grew so high that you couldn't even see a person his size in a row.

"It was rough, really rough out there," he remembered. "The first week I made eleven dollars, the next week it was sixteen dollars, and I sent that money home to my wife."

Picking tomatoes is piecework, where you make more money the more you pick. It took a little while for Albert to get the hang of it, but he still didn't like it, so he quit.

"The third week I made twenty-five dollars. But I wrote my wife a letter and told her, 'I'm gonna travel with this money. I don't know where I'm going, but you'll hear from me whenever I get there.'"

He and another man headed to a place called Goulds, an agriculture town just south of Miami. The bus, however, stopped somewhere else instead. The bus driver turned off the lights and said he would take them back to Lantana for free the next day, but he wasn't going to Goulds. They got off the bus and tried to figure out what to do next.

"A lady saw us standin' around and said she had a job for us," he continued. "She said she'd pay our rent. The rent was six dollars a week. The next morning she took us out there in the field. The first thing she did was give us a bucket, and we started picking squash. Squash is grown right next to the ground."

Albert found out that picking squash was ten times harder than picking staked tomatoes, because now he was bending down to pick things that grew on vines on the ground. His back was killing him within hours.

He leaned over his desk, looked at me pointedly and said, "I say anyone who wants to call farmworkers lazy, they should be made to do that work for a least a week, and I guarantee you they'd learn to respect it."

I have often thought of going out to work in the fields—just once, just to experience it. Some of my Mexican friends in Immokalee pick on weekends for extra money, and I'm sure they would take me, but I'm also sure that I would end up sitting in the truck having problems with my back, watching everyone else work. That image does not appeal to me, so I've never done it. Albert had problems, too, even though he was quite a bit younger then than I am now.

"I picked squash for about three hours," he told me, "and I told the lady I was knocking off, that I couldn't do it no more. She said, 'But you're a good man.' I said 'I know I am, but I'm in bad shape.' So she said 'I'll tell you what, I'll let you put the lids on; you can cap them.' I didn't have to bend at all. It was physical work, but I didn't mind it."

Albert got used to this kind of work, and he stayed there for a while, then he started picking beans or staking tomatoes. He said that wasn't so hard. Everything was fine while they were picking the crops, but then after some weeks they had to prepare the plants for the next harvest.

"When the work is picking," he explained, "workers usually get paid by the bucket. But when you're tying tomatoes, or sticking stakes in the ground for the beans to run up, they pay so much a foot. It looked like the rows we had was longer than the amount of feet she said."

He meant the rows assigned to the Blacks.

"And then one of us went out and measured it and our rows were longer than the other rows. So we quit."

But he had learned something about fieldwork, now that he had some experience. He learned he could pick up and leave if he wasn't happy, and that some other farmer would be very happy to hire him.

"When you first start, you're in a very 'closed' situation," he explained. "You did what you were told and you didn't ask questions. But I found out that maybe I could survive as a farmworker, because now that I had worked in a couple of different places, I realized it was an open market."

Albert realized what Mexicans, Guatemalans, and Haitians would realize later; he could leave and go somewhere else if he didn't like the situation he was in. Many of the new immigrants do not know that at first. Some of them put up with considerable abuse until they realize their labor will be appreciated elsewhere.

So Albert went south to Homestead and picked potatoes. When the season "started down," they offered him year-round work to stay there, but he had gotten used to moving around.

"Me, havin' a certain amount of migrant in my blood already, I decided no, I got to go. Everybody else was leavin', so I had to go, too."

He went about five hours north, to Labelle, but it wasn't a good place, as far as Albert was concerned, either. At least not back then.

"When I got there, I found a place and asked the lady what was the rent. She said 'Three dollars a week.' That sounded good, but it was just a little shack next to the house. So I said, 'Where's the bathroom?' She said 'There's a tub hanging off the back of the house.' So I said, 'All right, but where do I use the toilet and stuff?' She pointed to the bushes in back of the house. So I said, 'Oh, no, no, no.' So I left.

I asked around about where I could find something different, and people said Immokalee. They said there was work in Immokalee."

Albert came to Immokalee and got a job working for Six L's Farms. He went north with Six L's in the spring, too, from Immokalee to the Carolinas, Virginia, Maryland, and New York. They paid him seventy-five cents an hour.

After a few months, Albert heard from his wife in Louisiana that all their bills were caught up, and she'd saved a little money, and she told him he should "come on home." When Albert's boss at Six L's heard he was thinking of leaving, he offered him $1.25 an hour if he'd stay. So he did.

"Now, where I'd been sending twenty to thirty dollars home a week," said Albert, "I was sending a hundred dollars or more. At that time, Six L's was so poor that they traveled with their equipment. When they finished packing here, they'd load the equipment on a truck and move it to the next place. I moved with them."

When Albert got back to Immokalee, he sent for his wife and she joined him there. They both thought she could work in the packinghouse, but at that time, in 1962, there were no black women working in the packinghouses. There were white women, and Spanish, Albert told me, but they wouldn't allow black women. His wife went on her own to the packinghouse and got a job there.

"Now she's not real dark complexion," Albert said, "but she has curly hair, so we figured it was all OK."

He meant that they figured the packinghouse knew she was Black.

"But then one day I come in off the farm and we had lunch together. We was just like a couple of teenagers back then, I guess, and the two of us were walking around, holding hands. So this guy come up to me and asked me, 'What are you doin' holding that lady's hand?'"

Albert told me he didn't know what the man was talking about. He answered, "Well, I'm supposed to hold that lady's hand. That's my wife."

The man replied, "Well, then she can't work here." It turned out the man thought Albert's wife was Puerto Rican when he hired her.

"We don't work black women in here."

Albert went to the farmer the next day and told them he couldn't stay.

"You've got me doing everything on this farm," he complained, "but my wife can't work in the packing house? I got to leave here."

They wanted to keep Albert, so they let his wife stay on. It seems that Albert and his wife integrated the packinghouse, and it seems Six L's was the first packinghouse to be integrated. I asked Albert how it felt to have to put up with things like that.

"Well, it's something that you grow up with," he explained. "Even now, I hear about things and I don't get as angry as I should."

He said it wasn't as aggravating as some things, like back when he was in the service. He had gone into the Army in 1946 when he was sixteen.

"I recall coming home from Anchorage, Alaska, and got into Great Falls, Montana," he remembered. "We came back on a train, and we came into Kansas City. It turned out we had to change seats on the train because we were goin' across the Mason Dixon line. I was wearing my uniform, we'd all been everywhere together, and now we had to change seats. And later, when we got on a bus, you couldn't sit in the front of the bus, you had to sit in the back."

Albert shook his head. "So there are a lot of things you learn to live with because it's necessary at that time, but it's very annoying and aggravating."

I saw discrimination against Blacks when I was very young. My family used to come to Florida for a few weeks every winter. Our mother would "home-school" us during that time, long before home schooling was called that. Two or three times we stayed longer than a few weeks and went to school in Melbourne.

One of the things I remember about school in Florida was the bus ride. It was the first time I ever saw really bad prejudice. This was back in 1957, when segregation of black people was still the law. They were called "Negroes" or "Colored People" then, at least by polite people. On the drive down to Florida, when we got into Georgia, we saw run-down motels with signs that said "Colored Motel." I remember being confused about why Negroes had separate motels and why those motels were so run down. We didn't have separate motels in New Jersey where I was from. At least I never saw any, but then we didn't have any black people where I was from, either.

The first day I rode the bus to school in Florida we passed some black children standing on the side of the road, waiting for their own, separate, school bus. I had been exposed to the concept of segregation already, because I had seen the Colored Motels, but I had never seen anything like what happened then. Some of the white boys brought rocks with them on the bus, and empty soda bottles. (They called them "pop bottles" in Florida.) The black children were just waiting on the side of the road to go to school. The white boys on my bus yelled at them as they threw the rocks and the bottles.

"Niggers, damn niggers!"

They threw the rocks and the bottles really hard. They meant to hurt those children. I couldn't believe I was seeing this. I was only seven years old, and I had never seen any violence in my life. I especially had never seen kids try to really hurt other kids. I knew our bus driver must have seen it, and I waited for him to do something, but he just kept driving.

The black kids dodged the rocks and the bottles almost casually, and never looked up. I looked back through the bus window to see what they would do next, but they didn't do anything. They didn't even look upset or scared. They just kept on standing there, looking down at the ground.

That was my first exposure to hatred of people as groups, except for the way some of my relatives talked, and I didn't realize then that prejudice and hatred comes toward other groups in addition to Blacks. Some of it, I was to learn later, comes against immigrants just because they're new.

Personally, the ignorance of it baffles me. Sometimes I think it might just be insecurity. The only way some people can feel superior is by the color of their skin.

My mother told me a story that happened in Florida when I was a child. I'm quite sure I must not have been there, because I think I would remember it. It would have hurt me, just like the kids throwing bottles and rocks from the bus hurt me.

My mother and father were in a bar that was owned by their friend, Maggie. I remember Maggie. My sister and I liked her very much. Maggie and her husband, Hershel, were deep-south Whites, originally from Georgia. They called themselves "Crackers," an old Florida term that I heard comes from the cracking of the whips the cowboys used with cattle. I remember Maggie and Hershel's heavy Southern accents. Anyway, my mother said one time a black woman came into the bar. Maggie yelled at her to get out, how dare she come in there. The woman left quickly and everyone at the bar gave a big cheer for Maggie because she'd yelled at that woman and told her to get out. Then they broke into a rousing chorus of "Dixie."

I wonder what that woman felt as she closed the door behind her and heard that cheer and that song. She probably just wanted to buy something to eat or ask directions. Was she hurt? Was she sad? Was she angry? Maybe she just shook her head, thought about the Gospel, shook the dust from her feet, and moved on to somewhere marked "Colored."

As Albert said, "There are a lot of things you learned to live with."

One of the things the Blacks in Immokalee learned to live with was a lack of childcare. Since about 1954, daycare had been provided for white farmworkers, but the Blacks had no daycare for their children. Mr. Eugene Williams, the principal at Bethune, the Black school in Immokalee, was very active in trying to start childcare for "Negroes."

It started in 1962 when Mrs. Fuller and Mrs. Jessup, churchwomen from Naples, took Christmas gifts to the black migrant children in Immokalee. They found abysmal conditions because the parents had only two options: take the children with them to the fields, or leave them home alone. Children were locked inside shacks with no food or left to themselves on the streets without care. Young babies were taken to the fields and placed in cardboard boxes and their mothers pulled them along through the vegetable rows.

The following year the women, now calling their group Church Women United, raised money to start a childcare center for the black children. They found an old open washroom in the county park in the "Negro district" of Immokalee (the south side), leased it from the county for one dollar per year, and opened the Migrant Child Care Center in 1964. The name was later changed to Immokalee Child Care Center, an organization that still serves the people of Immokalee today.

Many black workers stayed in fieldwork until the early 1970s, when civil rights gave them educational opportunities that later helped them get better jobs. Education was key. Albert Lee explained how limited education used to be for Blacks.

"In the community I came from, eighth grade was tops," he explained. "The next school was roughly five or six miles away. Whites rode by on buses furnished by states or counties. There were no buses for Blacks. The only bus I could ride in to school, and I did ride that bus for a while, was the Greyhound bus."

After civil rights, and after many brave black people stood up for those rights, Blacks could finally ride the same buses and go to the same schools.

In Immokalee, the Bethune School educated black children all the way from kindergarten through high school in the same building. It was not until 1967 that Immokalee's schools were integrated.

But education didn't affect the black field workers for some time. In 1970, six years after civil rights legislation was passed, there were still many U.S.-born Blacks and Whites doing fieldwork. It took time before the education of the younger people was reflected in the fields. But there was another thing that caused this change in addition to education, civil rights catching up, and Blacks getting different jobs: new people came in who would do fieldwork for less money.

It is difficult to say exactly when the population started to shift from Blacks and Whites to Latinos; I had to piece it together, using historical clues.

In 1950 three Catholic nuns from the School Sisters of St. Joseph (SSJs) and a priest who lived in Ft. Myers ministered to field workers in the Immokalee area. A brief diocesan history mentions that they taught reading and catechism in both English and Spanish. They taught outside, using boards and vegetable crates for seats. The history says the Sisters drove their station wagon to migrant camps in a fifty-mile radius from Fort Myers to Immokalee, but later I learned that a woman named Rosanne Eldridge from Fort Myers drove them.

The Catholic Church in Immokalee, Our Lady of Guadalupe Mission Church, was dedicated in 1957, a seeming indication that there must have been Mexicans by then. It turned out, however, that the church back then was attended only by *Tejano*s and Whites. The Mexicans from Mexico didn't come into town to go to church. They stayed out in the fields. That's why the "SSJ sisters" taught Catholic catechism in the fields.

Beginning around 1960, there were some Cubans in Immokalee. Castro's revolution took place in 1959 and many people left Cuba immediately. They showed up in Miami, needing money, and some of them came to Immokalee because there was work there. Anne Goodnight remembers them.

I first met Anne at a luncheon at a Collier County School Board meeting at Immokalee High School in the spring of 2000, and I asked if I could visit her. She lives in one of those neighborhoods in Immokalee that people from neighboring communities rarely see—a culturally mixed neighborhood with nice homes. As we sat and talked at her kitchen table, I liked her right away. I liked the way she just says whatever she thinks. She has been in politics in Collier County for years. It is impressive that she's done well in politics, because she does not mince words or tread softly around any issues. Anne said there were Cubans in the 1960s and 1970s, but not many of them ever lived in Immokalee.

"They would send a bus over to Miami and they would work in the packing houses, then the bus would take them back at the end of the day," she told me. "It's 120 miles each way. They didn't want to live in Immokalee. They wanted to live in Little Havana. They got paid at the end of the day, strictly cash."

People came from Puerto Rico in the 1950s, too. A handsome young man named Neftali Ortiz was one of them. He happens to be married to a friend of mine, Lucy Ortiz, and she told me about him.

"Tali" came to Miami from Puerto Rico in 1959 with some friends when he was just eighteen years old. He wanted to be a baseball player, so his goal was to get to New York. He and his friends couldn't afford the airfare to New York, so they went to Miami because the flight was cheaper. When they got into the Miami airport, one of Tali's friends saw a man he knew from Puerto Rico who was waiting for someone from another flight. The man told them he lived in a town called Immokalee, and that there was work there in vegetables.

Tali and his friends needed money to get to New York, so they all got a ride with him to Immokalee. They worked the winter growing season there and then got on the migrant circuit. For a few years Tali worked up and down the migrant "stream," still holding on to his dream of becoming a professional baseball player. At one point, when he was working up north, a scout watched him play and offered him a position in a AAA league, just one level below professional baseball, but Tali's friends told him not to do it.

"You won't be with us," they told him. "You won't have your friends around. And it gets cold up here."

Sometimes that happens with field workers, especially with Mexicans and, it seems, Puerto Ricans. They like working together with their friends. So Tali turned down the offer and went with his friends to the next stop on the migrant stream. He later settled down in Immokalee with his *Tejana* wife, Lucy, where they raised their family. They still live there today.

Tejanos, who usually call themselves "Mexicans from Texas," are one of the dominant groups in Immokalee. During the 1960s and early 1970s, more and more *Tejanos* came from southeast Texas to work in agriculture. Most of them were from the Valley of the Rio Grande, near Raymondville and Brownsville.

Andy and Gloria Contreras were among the early *Tejanos* to live in Immokalee. I met Andy and Gloria one year when I attended "*Posadas*" with other people from our church. *Posadas* are celebrated in every town in Mexico and many other Latin American countries a week or two before Christmas, and they are celebrated in Immokalee. The church bulletin announces them. This one was from 1987:

"Beginning Tuesday 12/16 at 7:30 p.m. we will be walking the streets of Immokalee with Mary and Joseph, looking for a place where Jesus can be born, continuing the tradition of *Las Posadas*."

"*Posada*" means "inn." A similar procession takes place among the Puerto Ricans, but they call it "*Parrandas*." Father Vilmar Orsolin, previous pastor of Our Lady of Guadalupe, explained it to me.

"We go from house to house, knocking, asking if there is room for Mary and Joseph at the Inn. If they say no, we go to the next house. When we find one who says yes, we go in and have some hot chocolate or something and sing Christmas songs."

About fifty people were there the night I went. We carried lit candles as we walked the streets to different houses and sang Christmas carols in Spanish. A very nice woman named Janie shared her paper with me so I could read the words. We went to a few houses where the people came to the door, shook their heads, and closed the door, all set up in advance. The last house, the house that "let us in" that year, was the house of Andy and Gloria. They have a beautiful house, one of the few in Immokalee with a pool. They served hot chocolate and food to all of us.

It was a year or so later that I called Andy and Gloria to ask if I could interview them. Gloria invited me to come to their home after Mass one Sunday. They were curious about what I wanted to know, and interested in talking with me.

They both came originally from the Rio Grande Valley in Texas, but they did not know each other until they met in Immokalee. She came in 1958 and he in 1960. They came from towns on the U.S./ Mexico border. They said these towns have mostly Mexican people.

"Like Immokalee?" I asked. They said no, much more Mexican than Immokalee.

Gloria's mother was born in Mexico and her father was from Texas. She told me how her mother became a U.S. citizen.

"My grandmother came in the early 1940s when they were giving out those cards for a lot of people who wanted to come over," she remembered. "Also, my grandmother's brothers and sisters came over and got U.S. citizenship. They gave them for the whole family. This was in about 1942, when World War II was going on."

Gloria did not know why the U.S. offered citizenship to Mexicans then, but I believe it may have been related to the *Bracero* (laborer) program that brought Mexicans into the Pacific states and Texas as temporary farmworkers. Its formal name was The Labor Importation Program of 1942–1964—an agreement between the U.S. and Mexican governments. Trey Hoover, a University of Texas Spanish student, wrote the following explanation of the program:

"As the United States entered WWII, many farmworkers from all across the country left the fields in order to fight on the battle fields or work in the various war industries. This had a dramatic impact on the American industry. The farmers found that they were lacking sufficient manpower needed to harvest the crops that fed the nation. The United States government realized that this was a major problem that desperately needed to be solved. The solution was what came to be known as the *Bracero* Program. After much negotiation, the governments of the U.S. and Mexico agreed to establish a program for the exportation of workers from Mexico to the United States. The agreement called for basic protections to be guaranteed for the much needed imported workers. The *Bracero* Program went into effect on August 4, 1942. The program lasted from 1942 until 1964."

Under the *Bracero* Program, workers would return home when their contracts expired, but apparently there were circumstances where the Mexicans were offered U.S. citizenship. It seems Gloria's grandmother was one of those.

Gloria worked in the cotton fields when she was growing up, migrating with her family from their hometown of Mercedes, Texas, through other parts of Texas and then to Arkansas. She said there are two different types of cotton-picking: clean and dirty. When she was young, they had to pick the cotton clean. "Picking clean" was really tough on your hands, she told me. Andy brought out some cotton on a branch to show me. They kept it to remind them of the old days. I was surprised to see that cotton that is still on the branch is soft. It looks very much like the processed cotton we buy, but it has a sharp, spiky seed hull at its base. I touched it and immediately stuck my finger. The prick was very much like the kind I get sometimes from fresh artichokes. It must have been horrible work.

They said that when the machines came, the workers could pick the cotton "dirty." Cotton picked dirty is easier to pick because it has the seed hull in it. That meant that the workers could pull the cotton from below the seed hull and strip the cotton off the branch instead of picking at it. The machines separated the hulls from the cotton. Either way, it was tough work. They said it was really hot, and you had to drag your sack to the end of the rows. The sacks weighed up to a hundred pounds. Andy showed me a large painting they had hanging over their fireplace of two men working in cotton fields, dragging a big sack.

Andy's parents were Mexican—probably what they call *Mestizo,* a mixture of Indian and Spanish. His grandparents were Mexican Indians, but he was born in the U.S. Andy did field work in Texas from the time he was eleven years old.

"We followed the crops, the cotton fields," he explained. "Then we switched from cotton to potatoes, migrated to west Texas, then up to Oklahoma. Eventually people started spreading out. I heard about Immokalee from other farmworkers. They said there was work there. We made it to Immokalee with some friends who had already been there. We just came to work for a while and then go back to our home, but when we saw there was a lot of work here, we stayed."

Andy and Gloria met in 1961 at a dance hall on South Third Street in Immokalee. Gloria's friends told her later that Andy liked her, but she was not sure who he was. Then one day, Gloria's crew leader did not have work for her and her family, so they went on a different bus with a different crew leader who happened to be Andy's. Her friends pointed him out and she started paying attention. Soon she got to know him and they began to like each other, but it took two years before they really got together. The crew leaders they worked for went to different places on the migrant stream in the summer, so they only saw each other when they came back to Immokalee in the winter.

After about two years, Andy and Gloria married. When their first daughter, Sylvia, was born, they put her in the Mennonite Daycare on First Street. The daycare took care of her until midnight, while they worked in the packinghouse. Later, Dahlia and Cecelia were born. Although the family was quite well off by the time the girls were teen-agers, Gloria would take them out on weekends to work in the fields.

"They didn't like it," Gloria told me. "People used to ask them did they go to the beach because they had a really good tan? They would say no, we were working in the fields. Their friends used to say to them, 'Your Daddy's got a lot of money, so why are you working?'"

Gloria said she made them work in the fields because it was good experience for them.

"Whenever they would want to quit school, I would say, 'OK, but if you do, you're gonna work in the fields.'"

They never quit school, and all of them went to college. Cecelia earned her degree and teaches in Immokalee today.

I asked Gloria and Andy how many *Tejanos* were in Immokalee when they came in 1958 and 1960. They said, "There were a lot of Puerto Ricans, and a lot of Mexicans from Texas."

It seemed odd to hear them say "Mexicans from Texas." Of course, they are U.S. citizens. But then I realized that most people in the U.S. describe themselves as the nationality of their ancestors. My mother's father was dominant, so she and all of her brothers and sisters said they were Irish. My father and his sisters called themselves German. My sister Kathy always said she was Irish, and I always said I was German.

Andy and Gloria said a lot of white people worked in the fields back then, and Andy used the same term I had heard before. He said, "It was mostly what they called Winos." Gloria said many of them were hillbillies.

"They would work along with us, too," she explained. "There are not many here now. There is one we used to know who is in a nursing home now. He is ninety-seven years old. He used to work at Immokalee Growers. He was a World War II veteran. There used to be some well-educated people, but they were Winos. They were hardworking people, nice people. They didn't harm anybody."

Andy and Gloria also told me something I had not heard before; the Seminoles did field work.

"There were a lot of Indians when we got here," explained Gloria. "They worked in the fields with us. Busloads would come in from the Big Cypress reservation. You would see them in town, too, the older generation, the grandmas, with the big headdresses, all the necklaces, and the long skirts. It was colorful."

Today Andy is retired, but he still does work for the Seminoles, picking up recycled garbage from dumpsters, and he does some land clearing in Immokalee. Andy and Gloria worked hard all their lives.

When they were younger, they both worked in the fields during the day and in the packinghouse at night.

I wondered about the physical aspects of fieldwork. Didn't it hurt their backs? One of the things I've learned from people in Immokalee is that the things we assume about groups of people are not always true. One of the things I assumed about Mexican field workers is that the work doesn't really bother them physically. Maybe, I thought, they just got used to it and it didn't hurt after a while. Andy and Gloria looked at me like I was crazy.

"Are you kidding?" they both exclaimed. "Of course it does! It kills your back! We had aspirins all the time in our lunch pouch. You're bending at the waist the whole time, with your knees just a little bent, all the way to the end of the row."

They both got up to demonstrate. They bent at the waist, moving their hands over imaginary tomatoes on the floor, and quickly moved around the table where we were sitting. I bent over, too, following them around the table. It's a very difficult angle to bend for any length of time. I would have starved if I had to do it for a living. Andy made the corner around the table, still bent over.

"Sometimes you would come down to the end of a row and turn the corner, still bent over like that because you want to move as fast as possible."

Andy and Gloria said that back then, in the 1970s, they used to make $200 to $300 a week, combined. When they asked for more money, they were fired. My first thought was that $200 to $300 a week in the 1970s seemed like good money, but then I realized that they made this by working seven days a week, twelve to fourteen hours a day. And they were hustling.

Another *Tejana* I talked to told me about the wages they paid in the fields when she came in 1968.

"When I got here they were paying up to $12 a day. The piecework was good, and you could make $100 a week."

By piecework, she meant picking. But she said piecework wages haven't increased since then, and that changes have been made to the buckets.

"Back then the buckets for bell peppers were like this short." She motioned about two feet tall. "But now they are three feet tall, and they still pay the same."

There were also problems in the fields with chemicals. Gloria said she had recently been seeing her doctor about problems with her lungs and she thought it was from the pesticides that were used in the 1970s. Not just the pesticides themselves, but also the way they were applied.

"While we were working, they would spray pesticides over us from airplanes," Gloria told me. "We would be tying tomatoes or whatever, and the planes would spray pesticides right on us. And those big tractors, the ones with the sprayers, that look like big spiders? We would be tying tomatoes and the tractor would come and we would have to walk to the ditch to get out of its way. We would all be soaking wet, all our clothing, with pesticides. We didn't want to lose time, so we worked the rest of the day like that."

Today it seems the use of pesticides is much improved. I visited a few of the farms and the proper use of chemicals is a major part of their training. They teach new workers in classrooms and on the job about the handling of pesticides and fertilizers. All new workers who will be handling chemicals are required to go through this training.

After they were married, Gloria kept working in the fields and Andy got a job at a family-owned service station in town, pumping gas and fixing flat tires. Pumping gas paid $47 a week.

"At one time I had three jobs," Andy told me. "I worked pumping gas during the day. During the lunch hour and my supper hour, the railroad hired me to check the boxcars to make sure the diesel was full, because they had small tanks. They were paying me forty-some dollars a week. Then at night I worked in the packinghouse."

Gloria worked more in the fields than the packinghouse because she wanted steady work. The packinghouse paid more money, but it wasn't consistent; the packinghouses only run when there are orders to fill. But when there was packing to do, she did it. Packing was different then.

"When I used to work packing tomatoes, it was piecework," she explained. "I would make more money doing that than being in the fields. I packed ten, twenty, or forty-pound boxes, putting each tomato in tissue paper. That was before they had gas—in 1964, 1965. The tomatoes were a kind of light pink."

By "gas," she meant a process that is used now for much of the fruit and vegetables sold in supermarkets. I remember this from when I worked at a grocery wholesaler, SuperValu. A natural gas, ethylene, ripens products like tomatoes and bananas. The fruits themselves produce it when they start to ripen. If you can keep the gas away from them, they can be stored and shipped while they are still green. Then, before they are delivered to supermarkets, they are put into special rooms with the gas that begins the ripening process. When I met my husband, Barry Kotek, he was running Chiquita's plantations in Costa Rica and Panama. Chiquita sent shiploads of green bananas from Panama to the U.S. Barry said that if one ripe banana gets on a ship, the entire cargo can ripen and spoil before it reaches New York. That's why today you don't see many pink tomatoes wrapped carefully in tissue paper. Most of them are picked green, and boxes are filled from a conveyor belt.

The main job of the female packinghouse workers is to pull out bad vegetables as they pass by on conveyor belts. The men load the boxes after they are filled. Back when Andy and Gloria worked there, in the 1960s, the boxes were loaded into trailers that sat on railcars, called "piggyback." Ice was shipped with the produce, to help keep it cool. At SuperValu, the train tracks ran right into the yard by the warehouse, and piggyback trailers were transferred directly from the trains onto trucks, without unloading.

I asked Andy what happened to the railroad in Immokalee. He said that eventually the trucking industry came in. It was cheaper and faster to ship in trucks, so they didn't use the railroad anymore. They pulled the tracks out from Immokalee to Copeland, about fifteen miles south of Immokalee.

Getting back to my eternal questions about different groups and when they came, I asked if Andy and Gloria had noticed any black women working in the packinghouse when they first got to Immokalee. I was thinking of the story Albert Lee had told me about his wife. They said at Six L's there were black women, but they didn't remember seeing them at the other packinghouses.

Incidentally, back then it wasn't only Blacks who experienced discrimination, although Blacks had it the worst. Andy said that in 1963 he had to go through a lot, just to talk them into letting him pump gas. There were many places where they could not go.

"When we first got here, we were not allowed to go into any of the businesses," Gloria said. "The only place we could go was the clothing store, and the only grocery store was Fred's Barn. Where McCrory's used to be, on Main Street, there was a hang-out for white teenagers with music, but we couldn't go there."

It took until the late 1960s before they even took down the "Whites Only" signs. But the *Tejanos* learned to live with it, just like the Blacks did.

One of the people in Immokalee I have known the longest is also a *Tejana,* named Lesvia Martinez. She is too young to have experienced blatant discrimination like "Whites Only" signs, but she is aware of the prejudice some people feel toward Latino farmworkers today. Lesvia has worked at the Guadalupe Family Center since I first started volunteering there. One day I asked her where she came from and how she ended up in Immokalee. Her story is very much like Andy and Gloria's.

"My family came to Immokalee on New Year's Day in 1970. We came to see some other relatives," she said as she smiled and shrugged her shoulders. "Thirty years later, we're still here."

Lesvia's family was field laborers in the Raymondville area of South Texas. She said they liked Florida because it was a different kind of agriculture. She described fieldwork as skills that families acquire, specific to each type of agriculture.

"We knew cotton, onions, and cabbage when we got here," she explained. "In Florida we added citrus, tomatoes, cucumbers, and bell peppers."

When they were first here, Lesvia and her family traveled part of the migrant stream between Immokalee and South Carolina. They also spent time on the East Coast of Florida.

"We went to one place and did a lot of planting," she said, "then we'd go to another place and do the tying of the crops, then we'd turn around and do the harvesting of the first field."

Lesvia and I talked once about people today who complain because the Mexicans are here, because they don't speak English, because they come across the border illegally, etc. Lesvia, who clearly sees herself as both *Tejana* and Mexican, said she doesn't understand this.

"We just want to work," she told me. "*You* don't want to do those jobs!"

There is one more *Tejana* story I want to tell you, because it is interesting, and also because I want to tell you more about Lucy Ortiz, who married Tali, the Puerto Rican baseball player. Lucy goes to Our Lady of Guadalupe Church. She helped me with this history by introducing me to immigrants she knows, helped translate their stories, and gave me her perspective on Immokalee. Lucy works for the Shelter for Abused Women. One time when Lucy was holding a support group for battered mothers at the RCMA building, I sang with their children who were cared for in a separate room by a volunteer named Susan. Singing with them was sad, because the children were sad. Lucy works with their mothers to help them adjust to our culture, to be more independent, and to stand up for themselves.

Lucy understands something about their lives, because she was a field worker once herself, but she did not get into fieldwork the way most people did. Lucy was an educated *Tejana*, on her way to college, who later became a migrant worker.

Born and raised in San Antonio, Lucy is the second of seven children born to Gabriel and Carmen Vielmas. Her first name, Maria de la Luz, means "Mary of the Light." But Maria de la Luz is not easy to say, so they called her Lucy for short. Her last name, Vielmas, is really a French name, not Mexican. Lucy and I shared stories about our fathers, who are both dead now. Lucy's father was a third-generation Texan, born in San Antonio.

"My father was a great man," she told me. "He had a third-grade education, but he was a self-made man. He had forty acres of land outside of San Antonio and four houses that he rented. He also ran a grocery store and taught me the grocery business. Later, he had restaurants. He also was very handy and could fix anything!"

Her mother died of an epileptic attack when Lucy was ten years old, so she was raised by her father and grandparents. She graduated from high school in 1964 with a GPA of 3.5. She said she loved school and was active in clubs and sports, and she had dreams for her future.

"I remember taking aptitude tests in school before I graduated that showed I would be a good social worker or lawyer," she told me, "but I thought social workers only took children away from bad parents, so I did not want to do that, and law school was too expensive. So I decided to be a scientist—a pathologist."

She had a scholarship to a Catholic university, but the year she graduated from high school she went with her father to spend the summer in Ludington, Michigan. On the Fourth of July in 1964, Lucy watched some young men playing baseball in a makeshift field next to an old school yard. It turned out she was watching Tali Ortiz, the Puerto Rican who had come to the U.S. in 1959 to play baseball. Tali had by now turned down his AAA offer and had been working in the fields up and down the migrant stream for five years. He was content playing baseball with his friends from the fields.

Tali did not know this pretty young woman who was watching him play, but after the game she went over to talk to him.

"I was attracted to Tali because he was (and still is) good-looking and exciting to me," Lucy told me. "I had never met someone from Puerto Rico before. And he lived in Florida! I thought of Miami Beach, and the Jackie Gleason Show!"

Lucy and Tali fell in love quickly. This was an unhappy thing for Lucy's family; her father had not raised her to be with a migrant farmworker.

"After one month," she said, "Tali asked me to marry him and go to a new and different life. So I did."

I was shocked by this story, and felt a need to confirm it, so I asked, "You had a 3.5 GPA in high school and were headed for college on a scholarship, and you became a migrant worker?"

"Yes, because I loved him," she answered happily. "Also, the life seemed exciting to me. And everyone was so nice. After our wedding, the people in the labor camp in Michigan had a celebration party for us with a cake and presents."

Lucy and her new husband worked in the fields that summer. They arrived back in Immokalee, Tali's home base, so to speak, in late September, because the growing season in Southwest Florida starts up in October.

"We rented a small room and worked in the fields. That year we went to spend Christmas in Puerto Rico, and I met his family."

Lucy's family also got to know Tali, and they ended up being happy with the marriage, but it wasn't long before reality set in for Lucy. Farm work was not what she wanted to do.

"I worked with Six L's Farms on Highway 41," she said. "I discovered that fieldwork was hard, hot, dirty, backbreaking work. I made $5.00 a day. I didn't want to stay in the fields too long."

Lucy had their first child, and the baby had thirteen different baby sitters while Lucy and Tali worked in the fields. Later, Tali became a pinhooker for a few years—a term that refers to people who pay the farmers for the right to go out and glean leftover vegetables from the fields, and then sell them. No one seems to know the origin of the term "pinhooker," but Lucy said she heard it originally came from the way they hung tobacco on hooks to dry it. Others say "pin" comes from "pink," since once tomatoes are pink on the vine, they can go bad before they reach the stores, so the pinhookers were allowed to take them.

After a while Lucy got a job at a local bank, where she worked for twenty-one years, and then for a few years she worked with an immigration project called IRCA that we will talk about later. Lucy finished college and went on to get her master's degree in Social Work, which is what her high school tests showed she would be good at in the first place. Today she works as an advocate with the Shelter for Abused Women in Immokalee and Tali manages the irrigation systems at one of the larger citrus growers. They have two children, three grandchildren, and three great-grandchildren.

I asked Lucy if her husband ever regretted his decision to turn down the AAA baseball league offer. She said he always says he has no regrets.

"If I had done that," he often tells her, "I wouldn't have been there the day I met you."

One of their favorite things to do together is to go to nearby Fort Myers to watch spring training baseball games.

Tali and Lucy settled down in Immokalee just as agribusiness was really starting to take off in Southwest Florida. Tomato production in Collier County almost quadrupled from 4,510 acres in 1966–67 to 20,289 acres at its peak in 1992. Citrus acreage nearly doubled during roughly the same time frame, from 5,321 to 9,101 acres.

I mentioned in the Introduction that the Cuban Revolution was the reason winter vegetable production expanded in Southwest Florida. American-owned businesses in Cuba were taken over by Castro's government in 1959. In 1962, the U.S. government instituted a trade embargo against the purchase of products from Cuba. Jamie Williams of Six L's Farms told what happened from the perspective of a Florida grower.

"Basically what created this was Cuba," he explained. "When Castro took over, he kicked everybody out. They seized assets and that was the end of business with Cuba. Well, somebody had to fill that void. It started in the 1960s and it got stronger and stronger through the early 1980s."

Max Lipman, one of the first production growers in the area, started Six L's. He was a European immigrant who came to New York City and moved to Florida in 1942 to become a vegetable-buying broker. Max's three sons and three sons-in-law became partners in the Six L's Packing Company, and by 1952 Six L's was a grower, packer, and shipper. Almost all of the people I talked to in my interviews had worked for Six L's at one time or another.

Joe Procacci, owner of Garden State Farms headquartered in Philadelphia, confirmed what Jamie told me. Joe Procacci worked in produce since he was eight years old. When he was twelve, his father would wait outside his grammar school with a cart of bananas. He would tell his son, "OK, Joseph. Don't come back until you're sold out." In 1948 Joe and his brother Michael founded Procacci Brothers and sold tomatoes in Philadelphia. I asked Joe specifically about the effect of Castro on agriculture in Southwest Florida, and he said Jamie Williams was correct.

"We used to import boatloads of tomatoes and citrus from Cuba every day," said Joe Procacci. "Then Castro confiscated assets of farms in the 1960s, and kept all the proceeds."

After Castro's takeover, Procacci formed a joint venture with Carl Glidden to grow tomatoes around Immokalee. That partnership grew to be the largest U.S. fresh tomato operation. One of their old fields is now the Vineyards Country Club, where my husband and I are members. I always thought "Vineyards" referred to grapevines, but it turns out the name comes from tomato vines.

The workers in the fields noticed the shift from small production to agribusiness. Andy said there were only small growers here when he first arrived in 1960. He saw the big growers come in the 1960s. He described them as "majors."

"That's when the bigger ones, the majors, came in—the ones with big money," said Andy. "The other growers had just come here from other states, like the Roberts and other pioneers came with their cattle."

Technological innovations were also developed at that time. The first challenge they had was how to grow vegetables in infertile, sandy soil. The solution came in the early 1950s in the form of "culture beds," where vegetables were produced in raised beds of nutritious soil cultures. The second key was to control the water. Advanced drip irrigation was developed that allowed production of high quality crops with only half the water that was needed before. "Fertigation," an offshoot of drip irrigation, allowed growers to deliver liquid fertilizer to plant roots instead of spraying. In the mid-1960s plastic mulching was added, adapted from a system for strawberries developed by the University of Florida. It wasn't long before tomatoes moved out in front as the dominant crop.

In the 1950s and early 1960s, *Tejanos*—Mexicans from Texas—were the main Latino group in fieldwork, and they kept coming. But when agribusiness really started to take off, Mexicans came from Mexico—the newest group of "last heres." I asked Andy and Gloria when they first started seeing Mexicans from Mexico.

"It was maybe 1965, but they didn't live here in the town," they said. "They were in camps on the farms. They lived in barracks out there. They didn't come into town."

"But," I persisted, "you must have seen them. Where did they shop?" They both shook their heads.

"Maybe they brought them in at night. We didn't see them."

But then agriculture grew to a point that more workers were needed than could be housed in migrant camps on the growers' properties, so Mexicans from Mexico started coming directly into Immokalee's town center. One of the biggest proofs that they were there is that in 1967 an order of nuns called "Guadalupana Sisters" came from Mexico to teach religion and prepare people for church sacraments. The Guadalupana Sisters stayed in Immokalee for twenty-five years. Surely the Guadalupana Sisters would not have come unless there were Mexicans from Mexico there.

Now there were two Latino populations that needed services. Immokalee Child Care Center provided child care, but as more and more *Tejano* and Mexican farmworkers came to the area, additional help was needed.

Father Jerry Singleton, pastor of Our Lady of Guadalupe Church in the early-seventies, saw the plight of the farmworkers, many of whom were sleeping on the church grounds in their trucks or in the palmettos. Father Singleton worked with the Collier County Housing Authority to get a subsidized housing development created for farmworkers, called "Farmworker Village." Several of the people I interviewed for this book live there today.

Father Singleton also realized that additional child care services were needed for the *Tejanos* and Mexicans, because most were taking their children to the fields with them. He had heard of a group that provided child care services for farmworkers in other parts of South Florida, so he contacted them and asked if they could come to Immokalee, and they did.

The group was called "Redlands Christian Migrant Association" (RCMA), started in 1965 by a small group of Mennonite Missionaries near the agricultural community of Homestead, Florida. The RCMA organization had experience serving farmworkers that was important for Immokalee, because they had learned something from their initial efforts in Homestead. When they started there, they had trouble getting the migrants to take advantage of their services; very few workers brought their children to RCMA centers. Wendell N. Rollason, a well-known advocate for farmworkers in the region, identified the problem; people were afraid to leave their children with white, middle-class strangers who did not speak Spanish.

"They saw their children as being safer with them in the fields," Rollason wrote in one of his reports. "Our challenge was to change this. Fields and groves were and are dangerous places."

The RCMA solution in Homestead was to hire Latino migrant mothers to work at the center. The fieldworkers could relate to these women, because they spoke Spanish, understood their culture, and had lived the lives of migrant workers.

Barbara Mainster of RCMA in Homestead, a Peace Corps veteran who was fluent in Spanish, came to answer Father Singleton's request for help in Immokalee. She is the executive director there today.

"What is unique about RCMA is that we hire people from the community we serve," explained Barbara. "So almost all the people who have ever worked for us were farmworkers in this town."

RCMA started its first childcare facility at Farmworker Village, a few miles south of Immokalee's Main Street area.

"Things were very poor then," Barbara told me. "Our facilities in Homestead were nothing great. You had to watch where you walked so you didn't fall through the floorboards, things like that. But Immokalee was a tough town, too. One of the women who worked for the state, who had a Russian accent, told us that her husband knew Immokalee, and said to her, 'If you have a flat tire, just keep driving.' It had that kind of rough and tumble reputation then."

In about 1974, when kindergarten began in Collier County, Father Singleton put out the call to RCMA for additional help. Kindergarten at that time was only half days, and fieldwork was all day, so the children had nowhere to go for the other half day. RCMA got the funds to offer childcare in town, taking one group in the morning and another in the afternoon. Their first location was the United Methodist Church on Roberts Road. Later, RCMA also moved its state headquarters to Immokalee because it was a major agricultural area that was centrally located. The state office was built on another church site on Main Street.

RCMA contributes more to the children and families than just quality childcare. It also provides support services for the families, increases public awareness of the lifestyle of migrant and seasonal farmworkers, provides opportunities, and encourages the professional development of the staff. Rollason is quoted on the RCMA web site about the importance of preparing the children for school.

"It's no big deal that we keep the children safe, no big deal that we feed them nutritious food. That's obvious," he said. "That's our obligation. But we are putting these kids into a situation where, from day one they are doomed to failure. This is our biggest challenge at RCMA: to get our kids ready for school, to make sure that they enter kindergarten ready to compete in an environment stacked against them."

Another organization that we mentioned earlier helped the workers and other poor in ways that are more diverse: Immokalee Neighborhood Services. Started in July of 1977 by a group of local Immokalee churches, it still functions today, providing food and other support to those in need. Ruby Chavez, one of its volunteers, said there is no paid staff; they operate with between six and eight volunteers. Ruby told me they had not been able to give out much financial assistance since 9/11, because they were not getting the donations they used to get, but they still gave food that was donated by Publix Supermarkets and by the food drives of the postal service and the Boy Scouts. Ruby described their work by saying, "We're just running along in the ministry of the Lord."

Immokalee Neighborhood Services became involved with much-needed housing when missionaries Bob and Amy Olson came to Immokalee to work, supported by Brethren Volunteer Services. They invited Rev. Bob and Myra Gemmer and Millard and Linda Fuller to come and establish a Habitat for Humanity affiliate under the name Immokalee Fund for Humanity. This affiliate was incorporated on March 20, 1978, two years after the first Habitat began in Americus, Georgia.

The Gemmers' approach was firmly rooted in their belief in the gospel.

"If a man has two shirts," they reasoned, "does that not mean that he should give one to his brother?"

So Bob and Myra sold their Northern home and gave the fifty thousand dollar proceeds to Immokalee.

Each family selected for the Habitat homes made a down payment of five hundred dollars and contributed a minimum of two thousand hours of labor. Thereafter, they made monthly payments of one hundred dollars per month. Housing would become increasingly important in Immokalee as agriculture expanded and more immigrants came to fill its labor needs. Habitat housing, in particular, would help the farm workers as they moved from the fields into Immokalee's middle class. We will learn more about this in Chapter Six.

Acreage devoted to agriculture increased through the 1980s and early 1990s, and Immokalee's immigrant population increased along with it. The timing was perfect; the growers needed labor, and the immigrants needed work.

The largest group was, and still is, the Mexicans. Immokalee's Mexican immigrants left poverty and corruption in their home country as their lives got worse and worse, and for many of them, there was no hope left. They were, and still are, "rural poor," but being poor in Immokalee is better than being poor where they came from.

These workers were valuable to Immokalee's growers because they knew agricultural work and they desperately wanted to work. Most of the Mexican people I talked to had just a few years of school, and they did not speak English, but education and language are not important for working in the fields. They had the things that were needed: experience and drive. They just wanted to work and make a better life, and there was work in Immokalee.

3

The Mexicans

"We had food, but I still say we were poor. My father had to work every day of the week just so we could survive."

—Eduwiges Alvarez

Juan, Maria, and their five children lived on the outskirts of Michoacan, Mexico. They worked in fields, picking cotton, strawberries, chilies, and tomatoes. They told me the same story I would soon hear repeatedly; no matter how hard they tried, they could barely earn enough money to survive.

It was 1979 and Yolanda, their oldest child, was twelve years old. She had worked in the fields alongside her father and mother since she was seven. At first, the picking was part-time after school and on weekends, but after she had completed four years of school—at the age of nine—she started full-time work. She never went back to school.

That's how it was in many places in Mexico. All the Mexican people I talked to in Immokalee worked throughout their childhood. Their education was limited, and therefore so was their ability to get better jobs when they got older.

Juan loved all his children, but especially his firstborn daughter. She was very pretty and very smart, and it broke his heart to watch her stooped over in the hot sun, picking or planting, every day. He felt the worst when they were picking cotton. They picked cotton "clean," meaning her small fingers had to pull the soft cotton from between the spikes in the plants. She was quite skilled at doing this, but often she stuck her fingers and they bled. She never complained. She always told him, "*Está bien, Papá. No duele.*" ("It's all right, Papa. It doesn't hurt.")

She was so beautiful, and he had not pictured this life for her when she was born. He had dreams for her to go to school and meet a nice man and marry. They would live in a nice house in the city, and she would never have to work in the fields again.

Juan wanted everyone in his family to be happy. He wanted his children to be able to play. He never played when he was a boy. All he could remember about his own childhood was working in the fields next to his father and mother.

Though he had no education himself, Juan understood its importance. He knew education offered a chance for a way out, but he could not give his children that chance. Everyone in the family had to work just so they could eat and pay their rent.

The most relaxation and entertainment they had came when they paid to watch a neighbor's television, and most of the time all they had to eat was beans and rice with tortillas they made at home. I heard stories about that kind of poverty from my mother when she remembered the Great Depression. Sometimes she or her brothers would ask their father, "Where's the meat?" My grandfather would point to their plates and answer, "Move that pea. Your meat is under that pea."

I asked Juan if he made jokes about their poverty. He said no, because there were no memories of better times. Their situation was too hopeless for jokes.

One day, as he stood in the fields watching Yolanda picking cotton, he decided he had to go to the United States to make money. He also decided that some day he would take his family there, too. He had heard about a place in Florida where there was work—a place called Immokalee.

So the family scrimped and saved for over a year until they had $500, enough for Juan to make the journey. The money was for a smuggler to guide him across the border. They call these smugglers "*coyotes.*"

Coyote is the same as our word "coyote," but it is pronounced the Spanish way: "*coy-OH-tay.*" Lesvia, my *Tejana* friend who works at the Guadalupe Family Center, spent many years working in the fields and heard many stories.

"They call him *coyote* because he is like a wolf," she said bitterly. "He's a thief and he steals. He charges people money to bring them over, and he brings them here with no housing or place to live. The people come with all their things in a little bag and they have almost nothing. But the *coyotes* have already made the money."

I was curious about the need for *coyotes,* because people often say, "Why don't these people come here legally?" as if coming legally were an option. Sister Maureen has been an immigration attorney in Immokalee since 1984, so when I needed a simple explanation to the question, "Why don't they come here legally?" I went to Maureen. A simple explanation is difficult for an attorney to do sometimes, but she surprised me with her first answer.

"They don't come here legally," she told me, "because they can't."

I looked at her a little sideways. "What do you mean they can't?"

"To come here legally means you have a visa," she continued. "There are two types of visas: non-immigrant and immigrant."

I was right in the first place; this wasn't going to be easy.

"Non-immigrant means you come and visit temporarily as a tourist. The state department person will look at the person to determine if they are likely to return to their home country or not return. That usually comes down to an analysis of what they have in their home country for business, income, land, and also what their purpose is for coming here. You can't get a non-immigrant visa if you're poor, because U.S. officials at the consulate would never believe that you were going to go back."

"So what about an immigrant visa? Why can't they just say right up front that they want to live here and come in that way?"

Maureen said they can't do that either. They need a sponsor—either a company or a close family member who is a permanent resident or a U.S. citizen to petition to bring them in. If they don't have relatives in the U.S., there is no way to come legally. Even if they have a sponsor, it can take years, because there is a control on the number of immigrant visas available each year.

Joe and Charo, my friends from the choir at church, recently brought Charo's sister here from Peru. Because of the control on the number of visas per country, per year, per category, it was twelve years before a visa was available.

That is why Juan came illegally across the U.S./Mexico border. Fortunately, he found a good *coyote* and made his way safely across the river to the United States. Like many Mexican men who come here, he stayed in the U.S. for ten years. Eventually, some of these men save enough money to go back to Mexico and make a better life there, but Juan knew that was not possible for him. He knew that if he went back they could live well for a few years on the money he had saved, but after that they would face the same poverty again and Yolanda would work in the fields for the rest of her life.

Juan saved for the time when he could bring his family. He worked in Immokalee during the winter growing season, and in the spring he "went up the road" on the migrant stream through Georgia, the Carolinas, into New Jersey and back down again. Saving was slow and sometimes he thought he would never have enough. He sent money home every week to help the family with food and to help pay their bills, plus he needed $200 a month to share a trailer with four other men, and of course he had to eat. The men saved money by cooking meals together and sometimes they would buy a six-pack of beer. One of them had a guitar, and he would play and they would sing together. Sometimes, especially on holidays like Christmas or on Mother's Day, they would drink too much. My father used to tell us how poor he was during the Great Depression and how he said he saved every nickel and rarely even bought a beer. I have a feeling Juan and his friends were like that.

Juan called home every week, and every one or two years he went back over the border to visit. During these years, Yolanda grew from a child into a woman. He worried that she and the other children would forget him, but of course that did not happen. Each time he came home, Yolanda and her younger brother, Tito, would wait until they saw their father walking from the place where the bus dropped him off, and then run to greet him with tears of joy. Yolanda, more than any of the other children it seems, missed her father terribly.

My own father was often gone "out to sea," in his job as an engineer on ships. We missed him terribly, too, but it became part of our lives. Once, when we were older, I asked my sister Kathy how it felt when he left. She said, "It was like a sigh." Children in Mexico, Haiti, and Guatemala wait for their fathers like we waited for ours. But we only waited for a month or two at a time; they often wait for a year or more. Getting back to the home country is not difficult; it is the return trip to the U.S. that is costly and dangerous, so they don't do it often. I wondered if these fathers make up for their absence by being as wonderful to their children as my father was to his. My conversations with Juan, and later with his daughter, showed me that he was.

When Juan came home, he would stay for a few weeks, working in the fields with his family during the day and at night telling stories about life in Immokalee, and listening to stories about their lives. But he always had to return to the U.S. When that sad day came, he would once again take the bus to the border, where he would pay a *coyote* to guide him back to the United States and get him a ride to Immokalee. The *coyote's* fees increased each time he crossed.

It took Juan ten years to save the money to bring his family to join him. By the time he had enough, it was 1989, and the cost to cross the U.S./Mexico border had gone up to $1,000 per person. They were a family of six people, so he had saved $7,000. He put $500 toward the rental of a house in Immokalee, bought a plane ticket home, and took the rest of the money with him—to pay the *coyote*.

Yolanda was already twenty-two, and she and several of the other children were old enough to marry, but they had not because they were focused on joining their father in the United States. After Juan arrived home, he stayed for a week to take care of unfinished business. Then he and his family took a bus from Michoacan to Reynosa, on the border. It was a twenty-hour bus ride. There were other people on the bus with them, all headed to the same place. Juan looked for the *coyote* he had used before. He told me this *coyote* was a nice man, with a nice family. The coyote took them into his home until the day came to cross the river to Texas.

Juan and his wife knew how to swim, but their children had never learned how, so the *coyote* had inner tubes for them! I heard many stories about border crossings made in inner tubes; apparently it is fairly common. The *coyote*, Juan, and Maria, swam and pushed the others across, four at a time. It took only twenty minutes to get across. On the other side, they hid the tubes behind some bushes and started walking. Juan said they walked through bushes where he knew there were snakes—snakes he was familiar with from previous trips. He knew how fast their bite was, and how quickly you could die from it, and he was very afraid of them.

Yolanda was visiting her father the day I interviewed him, and I asked her what she remembered about the border crossing. Was she afraid? She said no, all she thought about during the trip was how happy she was to be back with her father.

The rest of the story was like many others I would hear. The *coyote* took them to a tire repair shop and told them to hide behind the tires so no one would find them. He brought them food and water, and they waited for two days until a car came and took them to Houston. There they stayed with a family for one week until another car came and brought them to Immokalee.

When they got to Immokalee, the family went to the house Juan had rented and Juan, Maria, and the older children all went to work in the fields. They worked for Pacific Growers planting tomatoes, chilies, and pumpkins. They had to work because there was rent to pay and food to buy. But at least here they lived better than in Mexico, and here the younger children could go to school.

Juan and his wife still live in that house and they both still work in the fields, but here their work gets them something. Yolanda is working at a small grocery store as a cashier, studying for her GED diploma at night. She married a man who works in construction, and they are raising three children. She proudly told me that the nine-year-old and the seven-year-old are in school now, and they know English very well.

When agribusiness started to really take off in Southwest Florida, it created such a demand for workers that tens of thousands of immigrants came in from Mexico. Some came here legally, but others like Juan and his family crossed the border illegally—"without papers." I asked people who have lived in Immokalee for a long time how these new immigrants knew to come to Immokalee. Often the answer was, "They started bringing them in." But who is this "they," and how did they bring them in? Are "they" the smugglers who bring people over the Mexican border? Or are "they" the crew leaders who bring busloads of workers to the growers? I never found out for sure. Maybe they just meant that the availability of work attracted the new immigrants.

In the 1960s and 1970s, most of the new immigrants were Mexican. So many Mexicans came that today Mexicans account for fifty to sixty percent of Immokalee's population. As agribusiness grew in the area, more and more workers came from Mexico because the word had spread beyond our borders that "There is work in Immokalee."

The Mexicans who came then, and who come today, are from many areas all over Mexico. In the 1960s, 70s, and 80s, most of them were from northern and central Mexico. In the 1990s, more indigenous

Indians started coming from the southern states of Chiapas and Oaxaca.

Mexico has three ethnic divisions. About ten percent, most of the wealthy elite, have predominantly Spanish blood. About one third, mostly in the southern states, are full-blooded Indians. The rest of the population is *mestizo*, a mixture of Spanish and Indian.

The country is about three times the size of Texas, with a population of over one hundred million. In the last half of the twentieth century, many of Mexico's rural poor people moved to the capital—Mexico City—to avoid starving. Because of this, the population in the area around Mexico City alone is over thirty million.

If the Mexicans make it past early childhood, their life expectancy is 70.8 years, compared to a life expectancy in the U.S. of about 76 years. The infant mortality rate in Mexico is quite a bit higher than ours. About two and a half percent of the babies who are born in Mexico die when they are still babies, while in the U.S. the infant mortality is much lower, just over half a percent.

One of the people I know in Immokalee is named Eduwiges Alvarez. Her mother lost a child who may not even have made it into the infant mortality statistics. Eduwiges told me, "He came out feet first, and my mother was having the baby at home, so he died." She said it calmly, as though it happened all the time. And it did happen all the time. In Mexico, poor people have their children at home; they cannot afford doctors or hospitals.

Eduwiges works in Immokalee at Even Start, a program that provides adult education, child care, parenting and life skills classes to needy immigrant families. She and her co-workers teach and care for preschool children while the mothers are learning English. On Wednesdays, when I am finished at the Guadalupe Family Center, I go to Even Start to sing with the children and their mothers together.

I asked Eduwiges to tell me about her life in Mexico. She was born in 1958 and grew up in Bejucos, in the state of Mexico, where Mexico City is located. There were ten children in her family: six girls, four boys, and she was the second youngest. Eduwiges said her family's life was hard when she was growing up.

"We had food, but I still say we were poor," she told me. "My father had to work every day of the week just so we could survive. He worked in the fields planting corn. Sometimes he kept some of the corn. He brought it to us to eat, or some he sold to buy shoes and other things because it was the only way to get extra money. My mother made clothes for us, and sometimes she sold them. We didn't have toys to play with. We didn't have anything."

She went to school through the sixth grade, but her parents could not afford to send her beyond that. "At that time only my father was working to support us. My older brother was married and had his own house, and my sisters couldn't find jobs. My father had to work a whole week to pay the fees for even one of us to go to school, so we couldn't go anymore."

Then Eduwiges' older sisters moved to Mexico City to try to make money so Eduwiges and the other younger children could stay in their town and go to school. This move to the cities was becoming more common all the time. Tens of thousands of Mexicans moved to "shantytowns" on the outskirts of the cities every year because there was no work in the rural areas. This is how Mexico City became the most densely populated city in the world, quite changed from the time when torches blazed on top of the Aztec's great pyramids.

In its early history, before the Spanish, Mexico was occupied by a number of different Indian tribes. The greatest of them, the Aztecs, dominated Mexico's Central Valley from the early Fourteenth century until 1519. They settled on an island in Lake Texcoco where they built the Aztec capital, Tenochtitlan. The ruins of the Aztec's huge pyramids are still standing.

At first the Aztecs were a small tribe, but they were brutal fighters, and they soon conquered and subjugated other tribes. They oppressed the people they conquered, demanding labor and tribute. The other

Indian people both hated and feared them because the Aztecs were also a bloodthirsty people; almost all the young men captured in their constant wars were sacrificed to the Aztec gods.

I have read that the Aztecs believed in five world ages, with multiple births in each, and that each of these eras was called a Sun. Because of this belief, they were known as "The People of the Sun." Moral standards and piety declined with each age, and at the end of each age different types of disasters would destroy the world. At the end of the last age, the one in which Montezuma ruled, the world was destined to be destroyed by earthquakes. But the Aztecs believed that sacrifices could delay this ending, so they sacrificed young men. They also believed that if their people got too proud the disaster could come sooner.

The Aztecs did, in fact, become too proud, and their world was destroyed; but not by an earthquake. Instead, it was the Spanish, led by Hernan Cortez, who entered Mexico in 1519. The last great Aztec king, Montezuma II, initially welcomed the Spaniards, but not long afterwards they killed him and destroyed the Aztec temples and religious symbols, imposing a new form of life that included Christianity. Soon the Spaniards enslaved all the indigenous people, not just in Mexico, but throughout what they called the "New World." The Spanish conquest of Mexico was a sign to the indigenous people that their God had been overthrown and had abandoned them. They began to perceive themselves as subjugated and worthless. The Benedictine Sisters in Mexico wrote a description of these events that said "The People of the Sun now became a poor people."

Not long after the conquest of Mexico, Our Lady of Guadalupe appeared in a remote area to a poor Indian named Juan Diego. The year was 1531. The Lady told Juan Diego to go to the Bishop to tell him of this vision, but Juan Diego asked her to send someone else, someone important, someone worthy. He was certain that he himself was not worthy of anything. Mary repeatedly told him she wanted him as her ambassador to the Bishop, so he finally went. As he expected, the

Bishop did not believe him; he wanted proof. Juan Diego went home by a different path because he did not want to run into the Lady again; he was afraid. A few days later she appeared to Juan Diego again and questioned him about why he had not come back. He told her his uncle was sick and that's why he had not returned to her. That is when she said these words:

"Let not your heart be disturbed. Do not fear that sickness, nor any other sickness or anguish. Am I not here, who is your Mother? Are you not under my protection? Am I not your health? Are you not happily within my fold? What else do you wish? Do not grieve nor be disturbed by anything."

The Virgin told Juan Diego to pick roses from the top of a hill. It was not the season for roses, but he found them blooming there, so he took them to the Bishop. This time the Bishop was impressed. As he and others examined the roses, the image of the Virgin appeared on Juan Diego's cloak.

A key part of this story is the Virgin's appeal to Juan Diego—the lowest and poorest of the Indians—so she has great appeal to the poor. Her skin is bronzed by the sun, like someone who works in the fields, and her head is inclined toward her right shoulder, as if she is carefully listening. Her womb (this Mary is pregnant) is highlighted with a four-petal flower. Its petals are joined in the center to form the meeting place of heaven and earth—the human and divine. Supporting her is a poor indigenous Indian, changed into a person with dignity.

Our Lady of Guadalupe soon became the religious Queen of Mexico, and her influence spread throughout the New World. In 1910 Pope Pius X declared her the Patroness of Latin America. The Indian who saw her, Juan Diego, was canonized a saint by Pope John Paul II on July 31, 2002, the first Indian saint in the Americas.

The Latinos in Immokalee are very devoted to Our Lady of Guadalupe. It is the name of the Catholic Church there, and for years there was a large painting of her over the altar. (The painting was moved in 2000, replaced by a sculpture of Jesus, but the painting remains in the sacristy.) It says some of the words she said to Juan Diego: *"Acaso no estoy aqui que soy tu Madre?"* "Am I not here, who is your Mother?"

Father Ettore Rubin, pastor of Our Lady of Guadalupe Church, said it is important to remember that she and other visions of the Virgin are all the same Lady: "There is really no difference between Our Lady of Guadalupe and Our Lady of Perpetual Help. They are only different depictions that help us bring the Virgin into our lives."

The devotion to Our Lady of Guadalupe is common throughout Latin America. In Immokalee, you can see it best beginning at 4:00 a.m. on December 12. *"Las Mañanitas"* ("Little Mornings") is a special church service for singing "Happy Birthday to Our Lady." It is deliberately scheduled early, because the celebration and the songs refer to the rising sun and the coming of the new day. The early hour also allows field workers to attend services before they go to the buses in the morning.

The second year I was getting to know Immokalee, Sister Judy suggested I come with her to *Las Mañanitas.* She invited me to stay at her house the night before because it takes me about forty minutes to drive out there, and the service started so early. Judy lived in the residential section on the north side of Immokalee, the part few people ever see.

Judy said I could sleep in one of her guest bedrooms where volunteers for Guadalupe Center usually stayed. She asked if I wanted air conditioning, or would I prefer to sleep with the windows open. Windows open? I don't do that in Naples. I sleep with windows and doors locked, and an electronic alarm system. Here I was in Immokalee with no security system, no locked windows, and no problems. She laughed at the thought that I had to come to Immokalee to sleep with the windows open!

The next morning when we arrived at 4:00 a.m., the church was already completely filled, mostly with Mexicans and Guatemalans. But the Feast Day of the Virgin of Guadalupe is a celebration of the whole parish, so Latinos from other countries, some Haitians, and some U.S-born white people were also there. The altar and the steps leading up to it were completely covered with flowers, most of them roses. I have never seen so many flowers in a church anywhere in my lifetime. The congregation sang three songs, and one of them was "*Mañanitas Guadalupanas.*" It means "Little Mornings of Guadalupe."

> *Oh, Virgen, la mas hermosa del Valle del Anahuac*
> *Tus hijos muy de mañana te vienen a saludar*
> *Despierta, Madre, despierta, mira que ya amameció*
> *Ya los pajarillos cantan, la luna ya se metió*

(Oh, Virgin, the most beautiful of the Valley of Anahuac,
Your children come to salute you in the early morning.
Awake, Mother, awake, look how the sun has risen.
Already the little birds sing, the moon is already gone.)

The people sang and prayed for an hour and a half. After the celebration, local school children performed Aztec dances in full costume in the church parking lot, then everyone left to go to work or school. In the evening there was a Mass in three languages, followed by traditional Mexican folk dances and songs. This happens every year on December 12. The celebration is an example of the fascinating culture of Immokalee.

The Spanish oppressed the indigenous people of Mexico for three hundred years, until Mexico won its independence in 1821. Even after independence, not much changed for the poor people, as government corruption and exploitation of indigenous Indians and *mestizos* continued.

In the late 1800s, export markets for mineral and agricultural products brought an opportunity for Mexico to bring new land under cultivation. While it seems that this would have been good for the country, it actually made conditions worse for the working classes because most of the land was taken from the poor. By 1910, ninety percent of the rural poor in central Mexico had their land taken away, and without it they could not even grow enough food to keep themselves alive. Many of them ended up in "debt peonage" to their employers, forced to work to pay not only their own debts for money and supplies but also to repay debts their parents had incurred before them. Realistically, it could never be paid off.

In 1910 Francisco Madero, Emiliano Zapata, and Francisco "Pancho" Villa took up arms to lead the Mexican Revolution. It lasted ten years, and a million people died. The revolution resulted in the Constitution of 1917, which still governs Mexico today, and with this constitution, Mexico began distribution of land to poor farmers. For a while there was great hope among rural poor Mexicans.

The antecedents of what became the Institutional Revolutionary Party (*Partido Revolucionario Institucional,* or *PRI*) first formed in 1929, and became the most important political force in the nation. The party looked like a democracy, but it became a kind of political "machine" in which elections were controlled by fraud and corruption. Voters were sometimes given "ballet tacos," or several ballots stuffed into one so they could cast multiple votes. People were bussed to different voting places so they could vote several times. In general, however, things in Mexico functioned. Roads were paved, schools were built, and many of the people had jobs, but many others were still very poor.

From the 1940s to the 1970s, the Mexican economy grew, helping Mexico's upper and middle classes, but providing few benefits to poor Mexicans. Hundreds of thousands of poor people moved from the rural areas into Mexico City, hoping to find work there. Many of the Mexicans who live in Immokalee today were born during this time, and several of the people I interviewed moved with their families to Mexico City before coming to the United States.

By the 1960s, Mexico was facing runaway population growth, a political structure that was falling apart, and an economic situation that got worse every day. By 1968 most Mexicans were wretchedly poor, with no hope for a better future. Many of their families were starving and there was no work. The people were tired of the fact that their government seemed to be doing nothing to help them. They wanted jobs.

The late 1960s were a time of protests in many countries, but the reasons for the protests differed. While I was in the United States protesting the Vietnam War and segregation of black people, Mexican students were protesting about jobs and a future. On October 2, 1968, ten thousand students demonstrated at the Plaza of the Three Cultures in Tlatelco, Mexico. Soldiers and police opened fire, and three hundred twenty-five people were killed. Hundreds of other students were wounded and thousands of them were put in jail. It was later called a "military massacre."

The Mexican government did try some positive steps to help the people, such as declaring wage increases in some areas and distributing land to about nine thousand peasants. It was a start, but nine thousand is very few people compared to Mexico's total population. The effort barely made a dent.

The wage increases did not reach Eduwiges and her family, and there was no work at all in her hometown of Bejucos, so she and the rest of her family followed her older sisters to Mexico City. It was 1971.

"When I finished school, we moved to Mexico City so we could be together. At that time I had thirteen years," she said, translating her age literally from Spanish. I asked what they did in Mexico City.

"We stayed there working. For two years I helped my sister, because she sold *artesanias* (crafts). I helped with her house and taking care of two of her girls for two years. Later I started working in a factory to sew clothes. I like to sew. I tried to go to *secondaria*—like middle school—but it was hard for me because I had to be working and going to school in the afternoon. And anyway, we didn't have the money for school." Many families could not afford the fees, called "subscriptions," and also they needed the children to work.

A few years later, in 1976, oil was discovered in Mexico and the people were happy. It was hoped that this would provide jobs so at least some people would have money, and they might spend that money on the clothes that Eduwiges made or other things that would help the family, but it did not work out that way. In the end, the oil made things even worse for the poor people, because people with money spent too much. Between 1976 and 1982, inflation rose dramatically and the real income of the lower classes was even further reduced.

Finally, in 1979, the same year Juan made his decision to come to the U.S., Eduwiges' family also gave up trying to make anything work in Mexico.

"We were trying to make a home in Mexico City," she told me, "but we saw that we couldn't make it."

Usually the families decide who can make the most money in the United States. Eduwiges could sew, and her older brother was young and strong, so they decided that she and her brother should go. The plan was that the two of them would make money in the United States and send it home to help support their parents.

One of her uncles had gone to the U.S. in the late 1960s and lived in a place called Immokalee. Eduwiges' father contacted this uncle and he arranged for a smuggler to take Eduwiges and her brother across the border. The more stories I heard about border crossings, the more real it became and the more I understood the passion these people have for coming to the United States.

"My uncle called us in Mexico and told us to come to a place called Piedras Negras," she explained. "It's a town right on the river. Another cousin was coming with us. He knew the *coyote* and would recognize him. We stayed in Piedras Negras for two days, then the *coyote* found us."

Back then, in 1979, the *coyote* charged $500 per person, but Eduwiges and her brother did not pay it directly. Her uncle paid it after the *coyote* brought them to Immokalee.

She said she and her brother and cousin walked with the *coyote* to a little house close to the river and there was a man with a boat; a little boat, like a canoe. Eduwiges was very frightened. It was the first time she had ever been away from her parents, and she said the river crossing seemed very dangerous to her.

"We crossed the river at night," she remembered. "We went in that little canoe, two or three at a time. It took two hours. Me, my brother, and one other person were together. There were eight people all together in the group. They crossed us to the other shore and then went back for the others. When they crossed everybody we started walking."

The job of the *coyote* is complicated, and the good ones actually do a great deal of work. They arrange for places to stay in Mexico and transportation to the border; they figure out how to avoid immigration officials; they escort the immigrants across the border; and they pre-arrange a place to stay in the U.S., plus transportation on this side of the border. It reminds me of the Underground Railroad that Harriet Tubman used to help slaves escape from the South. Of course it is more of a business at the Mexican border, but the planning is equally thorough.

"After we got across the river, we walked for about two hours and they took us to a trailer in the woods. We slept there," Eduwiges continued. "Early in the morning, like 3:00 or something, it was still dark, they told us to go sit close to a road that was there. We hid in the bushes. Then a car stopped right there and they drove us to a town. We stayed at some people's house for three days. Then someone came and got us in a van and took us to Immokalee. About six people from the group went to Immokalee, where we stayed with my uncle."

She could not make money sewing in Immokalee, so for seven years, Eduwiges worked in the fields picking tomatoes. But she saw there were options for a better life, so at night she started to study English. She also "got her papers" through a law called IRCA: The Immigration Reform and Control Act of 1986. Eduwiges could not remember the English word for how she qualified, but she said the Spanish is *"amnistia"*—amnesty. Sister Maureen explained amnesty and IRCA.

"Through IRCA, immigrants could get amnesty, which meant they could live in the U.S. legally if they could prove they had been here since January 1 of 1982. There was also a provision that said farmworkers could get their papers if they could prove they did ninety days of farm work in the U.S. between May 1, 1985 and May 1, 1986."

Eduwiges qualified through the farmworker provisions of IRCA. With the help of the Catholic Church in Immokalee, she was able to prove she had done ninety days of farm work within the specified dates. At first she got her employment authorization, then temporary residency, followed by permanent residency—or "green card." Five years later, when she was eligible, Eduwiges applied for citizenship. Today she is very proud to be a United States citizen.

Another Mexican woman, Enriquetta, crossed the border the same year as Eduwiges and her brother, but much farther west. She came with her Guatemalan husband, Francisco José, in 1979. The Guatemalans I talked with have similar names, so I will call Francisco by his last name, José. They crossed the border at Tijuana, on the border of Mexico (Baja California) and California.

The interview was set up by one of my friends from church. I went to see Francisco and Enriquetta at 1:00 p.m. on a Sunday, after Mass and after breakfast. They lived in a nice neighborhood where the houses had small lawns and a few trees, in a house built by Habitat for Humanity. Most of the homes had a pick-up truck in the driveway.

When I knocked on the door, Enriquetta greeted me warmly in Spanish and asked me to sit down.

Their home was modest, simply decorated, and very comfortable. When I arrived, José was not home from work yet, but their teen-aged children came in. It was common for the children to listen when I did these interviews. They were always curious about what I was doing there. The fact that the children joined us was also helpful for me, because most of them speak perfect English, as well as Spanish. The children helped me translate their parents' stories when I got stuck on a word or a phrase, or confused when the parents became excited and talked fast.

I asked Enriquetta to tell me about herself as we waited for José and about her life before she met her husband. She said she couldn't do this. She said, "It is the same." She and her husband have been together almost as long as she can remember, because they met when she was twelve and eloped when she was only fourteen years old.

Enriquetta was raised in Mexicali, a town on the border between California and Mexico. Her aunt owned a ranch where they grew cotton.

"My mother cooked for the workers and they paid her," she told me. "My mother and father worked together. We had cows, pigs, turkeys and roosters."

Enriquetta took care of the cows. She went to school until the sixth grade. "After six years you have to pay, and we didn't have the money. When I was twelve, I started working full-time in the cotton fields."

After I had heard a few of these stories, I understood something Peggy Diaz had told me. Peggy used to run the Even Start childcare/family program in Immokalee.

"We have to teach the parents how to play with their children," she said, "because children learn by playing. Many of the parents really don't know how. Most of them never played when they were children. They just worked."

People came to the ranch where Enriquetta lived to make money so they could go to the U.S. One of them was José, a Kanjobal Guatemalan from the town of San Miguel Acatan in the northern Guatemalan highlands. He had been working in Mexico and Baja California. Enriquetta was twelve years old when José came to the ranch, and two years later they fell in love. Not surprisingly, her parents did not approve, because Enriquetta was fourteen and José was twenty-five, but the young lovers did not care. They saved money until they had $350 each, enough to pay a *coyote* to bring them across the border.

Then one night they secretly left the ranch to find a new life in the United States. The border crossing at Tijuana was easier than that of the other Mexicans I talked to who had to cross a river; at Tijuana you just walk through the desert. However, because Tijuana is a busy place for illegal border crossings, there are many Immigration Border Patrol Agents. Each time the group José and Enriquetta were in started across, they spotted a Border Patrol Agent on the U.S. side and had to turn back. They tried again and again and the same thing happened each time. After nine tries, they finally made it across without being seen.

They made their way to Los Angeles by getting rides with passing Mexicans. In Los Angeles, they stayed with a Mexican man and his family. They knew him because the man had worked on Enriquetta's aunt's ranch before he came to the U.S., but José and Enriquetta could not make enough money to move to their own home.

"We didn't have any money," she told me. "Then a Mexican woman taught me how to use a sewing machine."

They worked together, sewing pants, shirts, and blouses at what sounded to me like a sweatshop, but still they got nowhere. Finally they called Pedro, an old friend of José's from the same village in Guatemala. Pedro now lived in Florida and he said there was agriculture work where he lived, in Immokalee. So José and Enriquetta came to Florida. Later they were also able to get their papers—José through political asylum because he came from the Northwest

Highlands in Guatemala where a war was raging against the indigenous Mayas, and Enriquetta because she was his wife.

They are still clearly devoted to each other and their four children. Enriquetta showed me a family history book they made that tells the story of their lives together. Most of that life took place in the United States.

The people we've talked about so far were lucky to leave Mexico when they did, because just about everything in Mexico got worse in the 1980s. The whole Mexican economy was on the verge of collapsing, and the economy was not the only thing.

On September 19, 1985, at 7:19 in the morning, a devastating earthquake hit Mexico City. It was of a magnitude of 8.1 and lasted three full minutes. A day and a half later, a second earthquake shook the city, registering 7.5. Estimates of the number of deaths range from five thousand to ten thousand people. More than one hundred thousand housing units and many of the city's public buildings were destroyed. The government's response was slow and inefficient. The people became more frustrated with the PRI.

The only positive thing about the earthquake was that it created work. I talked with a young woman named Juanita whose father got a job cleaning up after the earthquake.

Juanita invited me to her home for the interview. It was typical of all the homes I visited, modest but clean and very comfortable. This one was half a duplex in Farmworker Village, big enough for Juanita, her husband, and their four-year-old daughter. I went to see her in the morning, before she went to work at her job as a cashier in one of Immokalee's Mexican supermarkets. She made me some tea and asked if I wanted some food. I was not hungry, but I appreciated her offering. We talked as she cooked the family's dinner for that evening. Most of the women I met cook their evening meals in the morning because they work during the day, and if they cook in the morning they just have to heat the food up in the evening. Juanita speaks rough but understandable English, intermixing Spanish and English words, so it was easy for us to communicate.

Juanita was born in 1978 in Hidalgo, about three hours west of Mexico City. She only got to the second grade when, like so many other children, she had to help make money. She worked with her father in the fields, picking corn, green beans, squash, and gourds. Juanita helped him fill the buckets, but as time went on, there was less and less work available, until finally he could not make any money at all. Juanita's mother worked in a medical clinic.

"She knows how to do IV and give shots, *ayudando los enfermos* (helping sick people)," Juanita told me, speaking partly in present tense. "Some people can't walk, so my mom went to their houses and gave them a shot or an IV, and people paid her."

As the Mexican economy got worse, her mother's patients had less and less money. Soon she started taking care of people without charging them anything. When they were starving, she brought them food. I thought back to Elizabeth Murphy, my mother's grandmother, the "Saint of Manning Avenue," going to collect rent that no one could pay, and then buying groceries.

I started to talk with Juanita about the earthquake. She does not actually remember it, because Hidalgo is far enough away that they did not feel the tremors, but she remembered what happened after it; her family moved to Mexico City so her father could help with the cleanup. This work appeared to be a blessing, but it turned out differently. She told me about it, using the Spanish word for earthquake.

"You know the *terremoto* in Mexico in 1985? In 1986 my dad worked in construction to remove all the rubbish. Everybody was happy because he was making money and now we had food. But he was down on the first floor and somebody by accident dropped a big thing, like a table or something. My daddy, he tried running, but the thing dropped on his legs and his feet, so he had a piece of metal in his foot."

Juanita's father and mother went home so he could heal. Juanita was eight years old at that time.

"It was so hard for our family," she remembered. "My mom left me with my aunt and she went home to take care of work and the other children. I stayed with my aunt on her ranch, with my little brother. We didn't have water like here. I had a thing, you call it horsy, for carrying buckets of water."

I did not know this term, but she described a heavy wooden pole that she carried across her shoulders. Two pails hung from it, one on either side.

"The water was maybe a mile away, and I had to go back and forth to bring water for my aunt," she complained. "I carried the water and I ground flour and corn for tortillas. My aunt would say, 'You want to eat? Grind your own.' Later my father had surgery, and after a year he could walk pretty good, but it was very hard for my family."

By 1987, in many Mexican small towns and cities, it was common for forty percent of the people to be unemployed. More and more Mexicans moved from rural areas into cities, hoping to find work, but many times, in the city, things were only worse. After her father could walk again, he and Juanita's mother came back to Mexico City where they bought a lot and built a small shack. He did not actually buy the land, but rather he paid to live as a squatter in one of the shantytowns. Juanita, though, called it a house.

"Not a real house like the one I have now, but a little house," she said. "We lived in a little *arroyo*, like houses built on the side of a ravine, on top of each other."

This living situation was precarious, due to the location and also the construction.

"The roof was made of metal," she explained, "so if a *tormenta* (storm) came and it rained and everybody was sleeping, it would wake us up and we could run."

They had to run because of the makeshift way the houses were built in those slums. They were built on the sides of ravines, loosely constructed with no foundations, so a heavy rain would wash the houses down into each other.

Juanita's parents told her the reason their new home had a metal roof was to warn them when a *tormenta* came, but more likely it was the cheapest material available, or maybe it was the only material they could get. I remember seeing the shacks of poor people in the South when I was a child; they all had metal roofs.

"In that year a *tormenta* came, and all these blocks fell down on our house," Juanita continued. "The only thing that helped was that our roof was on an angle. The other roofs were all broken. Neighbors came and helped us get out the window because the door had a lot of blocks and we couldn't open it. So my mom decided we should move back to Hidalgo."

Soon after, at different times, most of her brothers, sisters and cousins migrated to the United States. Only Juanita and her parents remained in Mexico. The other relatives sent money home, and life became a little easier.

In the 1990s, the income disparity between the rich and the poor in Mexico grew larger. The North American Free Trade Agreement, NAFTA, passed in 1996. It appeared to be a boom for Mexico, but shortly after, international investors wanted repayment of their loans. They forced President Enersto Zedillo Ponce de Leon to devalue the peso, and in the process Mexico lost 1.6 million jobs. In the first year and a half after NAFTA, the number of Mexicans living in "extreme poverty" went from seventeen million to twenty-two million. New jobs were created to replace those that were lost, but most of the new jobs paid lower wages.

I visited Mexico on a business trip in the early 1990s, working with coupons in my consulting business. One of the companies took me on a tour of their coupon processing plants in Acuña, about an hour south of the U.S./Mexico border. Most people in the U.S. do not know that almost all the paper coupons accepted in supermarkets are sent to Mexico to be "processed." Hundreds of Mexican people work in each of about thirty-five plants, counting and sorting the coupons so the manufacturers of the products can pay the supermarkets back for accepting their coupons. Acuña seemed like a nice town, and I thought Mexico didn't look too bad. The people who worked in the coupon plants were among the highest paid in that area.

We took a trip to a nearby smaller town, however, and there, for the first time, I saw Mexico's poverty; the poverty the people in Immokalee had lived. The town was dusty and dirty, and the stores were filled with cheap clothing and uninteresting souvenirs. The people did not smile much. They looked tired, and they walked slowly, with sagging shoulders.

An old woman sat on the sidewalk with two children, begging for money, and she looked up at me pitifully. I considered walking by her, because something told me it was not a good idea to enable this kind of lifestyle. But almost immediately, I thought to myself, what do you know about her "lifestyle"? This was not a "lifestyle." This was not what she dreamed her life would be when she was a little girl helping her parents pick cotton and corn. It was not what she envisioned when she got ready for her first days in school, not knowing how few days of school there would ever be for her. Not once did she see her future on a dirty sidewalk with two hungry grandchildren, begging for money so the children could eat.

I gave her ten dollars. She looked down at the dusty sidewalk and said, "*Gracias, Señora,*" more to herself than to me, as I walked away.

Juanita's family was not as poor as that, especially because Juanita's older sisters and brother had gone to the United States. Her family had food now, but not much else. Juanita envied the lifestyle she read about in her sisters' letters.

Her parents said she was too young to leave. She was only fourteen, and she was the only child they had still with them. Her mother wanted her to stay at home in Mexico, but Juanita pushed her.

"I tell my Mom a lot of people are coming here, making money, having nice clothes. I begged her to let me go." Juanita was persistent. "Please, Mommy, please, please. I want to go to the United States. I just want to go for one year and work, and I'll come back in time for you to celebrate my 'fifteen years' *(Quinceañera)*." (It is pronounced a little like "keen-seen-YEAH-rah," with a rolled "r.")

The *Quinceañera* is a coming out party for young girls, but more religious. They have them in Immokalee today, and I was invited to the *Quinceañera* of Isabel Ayala, who goes to our church. The celebration consists of a Mass, during which the young girl sits on a special chair in the front of the church, facing the altar and the priest. All the attendees dress as if at a formal wedding. The priest talks to the girl at various times during the ceremony, beginning with these words: "Before her mother knew she was there, God knew her and called her by name." He then continues to talk about the girl, who is becoming a woman, and later a wife and mother. Then her parents and godparents come up, one at a time, and present the girl with gifts. Isabel received a tiara, a necklace, a bracelet, and a Bible. Afterwards there is a party. It is a major event in a young girl's life. Of course Juanita's mother wanted to have her home for her *Quinceañera*.

One day a family friend came for a visit and to say good-bye. She had been in the United States before and was headed back across the border. She would use one of Juanita's cousins who was a *coyote*. Juanita's mother knew this cousin would take care of her daughter, so she finally gave in to Juanita's pleading and let her go with the friend.

I loved talking to Juanita. She was still quite young, in her mid-twenties, and she got very excited telling me this story. She had been here for ten years when we talked, but was still so happy to be living in the United States.

I asked her how it was to cross the border. I was thinking she might have been afraid, especially because she was only fourteen, but she said she had no fear at all; she just wanted to get to the United States. Juanita described her journey in detail.

"We left Wednesday at five in the morning. We took the bus, driving two hours. Then I took another bus, maybe four or five hours. And there I waited and took another bus to Matamoros. I was there around 6:00 a.m. on Thursday. I slept in the bus. My cousin was there, so at 6:00 I was at the terminal, and my cousin the *coyote* was training everybody. He told us, 'I will walk first, and one or two of you follow me. Just don't make a big line, because immigration will see us. Just walk very casual.'"

They walked in the street and her cousin called two taxis that came and took everyone, then they stopped so the group could buy some large plastic bags and food. The bags were used for crossing the river, to keep money and clothes from getting wet.

"Then I saw the river," said Juanita excitedly. "It's big!"

She said the *coyote* asked everyone, "Do you want to swim it or do you want to pay for an inner tube and float across?"

Juanita knew how to swim, but she decided to pay 20 pesos for the inner tube. She put one hand over her head to show me how she sat in the tube.

"So I crossed," she said, "holding my things in a bag over my head with one hand and moving the tube through the water with the other. I had no shorts to cross the river, so I crossed in underpants and a tee shirt. I got there and went in the bushes and I took off the wet clothes and put them in the bag, still wet."

I asked her if anyone was there along this border, wondering about Immigration officials.

She said, "No, nobody seeing us." She grinned, excitedly, as she remembered the feeling.

"And now, I don't stay in Mexico anymore. I'm in the United States!" She said it with the accent on the middle syllable of United.

"I'm in the United States!"

After they crossed the river, Juanita's group hid in the bushes all day until about 6:00 p.m. She helped her cousin keep the people quiet.

"I heard the immigration helicopter running, but I just said to the other people, 'Shhh. Be quiet, lay down.' Then we are walking down a road, but my cousin he hears a truck and he says 'Lay down, lay down.' Then we are walking, walking, walking through the fields. Until about 2:00 in the morning."

The *coyote* stopped at someone's house and made a call to arrange a pickup later that morning, a few hours walk from where they were. Then everyone walked the rest of the night. They stopped in a bushy area alongside a road where they hid and waited for the van that would take them to Houston.

Juanita's description made it obvious that there were several groups of immigrants waiting to be picked up, all hiding in different parts of the bushes in the same small area, all waiting for the rides that had been arranged by their *coyotes*.

Juanita heard one person calling, "Alberto, Alberto."

"Yes?" answered someone in Juanita's group.

"Are you Alberto?" said the voice.

"No, I am not Alberto."

"Then why you answer me, fucker, you fucker, mother fucker?"

Juanita raised her eyes to the ceiling and then looked down at me as if she were scolding her daughter. "People from Matamoras talk very nasty!"

Soon someone else came and called to them in the bushes.

"Are you the ones who called me who need a ride to North Carolina?"

"No," answered Juanita, "But I saw some people laid down over there. Maybe it's them." The stranger went away to find the group going to North Carolina.

Juanita's *coyote* left to find the man who was supposed to bring their van. First he gave specific instructions to the group.

"Nobody should answer anybody anymore," he told the group sternly. "I'm gonna come back with the van and I'm gonna say 'Nikko' and beep three times. If somebody comes and says 'I'm here, come on,' don't you dare go, because sometimes it could be Immigration. You wait and stay quiet until you hear 'Nikko' and three beeps."

In the next couple of hours, four different cars came and said, "I'm here, come on," but Juanita's group remained hidden in the trees and did not answer, following their *coyote's* instructions. Finally they heard a voice say "Nikko" and three beeps, and everyone got in the van. Only four people were allowed in the front of the van sitting up, because if there were too many people maybe the police would stop them. They did not sleep. They were lying down in the back, one on top of the other. As she told this part of the story, Juanita's face beamed with happiness, as if she were back there again.

"I was so happy to be in the United States," she said with a contented smile. "I was just laying there, smiling, watching the lights."

Juanita ended up in Houston, staying with an aunt, and got a job in a restaurant cleaning dishes. She sent letters and money to her mother: $100 or $200 whenever she could. Her mother was happy for the money, but she wanted her daughter home for her celebration of fifteen years, so she asked Juanita's brother to get her.

When he arrived, Juanita told him, "I don't want to go home, I want to stay."

"You better not live alone," he warned, "or with some crazy boyfriend or something."

He stayed with their aunt and kept trying to convince her to go home, but Juanita was not going home. She loved the United States, but she needed to get away from her brother.

"So a new friend I met in Texas had a boyfriend in Florida. She was going there, and she said I should go. She said I could make fifty dollars a day picking tomatoes. So I put all my clothes in a bag, went and got my check, and said I'm going to Florida."

Some of Juanita's family was in Immokalee, too—a cousin and an uncle. When she got to Immokalee, she went to her cousin's house. Her brother followed her later, and eventually gave up on the idea of bringing his sister home. He now lives and works in Immokalee, too.

I talked to another Mexican man because I was scheduled to interview a Guatemalan woman named Ana. It happened that her Mexican husband, Manuel, came with her to see me because they were in school together learning English. We did the interview in Spanish, but Manuel could see that it was difficult for me to understand when they talked fast, so he helped me by speaking *despacio y claro* (slowly and clearly). He was educated through high school, so he spoke Spanish the way I learned it in textbooks, making it much easier to understand.

Manuel was one of the few people I talked to who did not particularly want to come to the U.S. One day in 1995 one of his friends, Umberto, came to see him. Umberto had decided to go to the United States, and he wanted Manuel to go with him, but Manuel was happy in Mexico. He was doing well, making what he called good money, working construction in Mexico City. He had no reason to leave, but Umberto persisted.

"He would come, all the time," Manuel told me, "saying, '*Vámonos, vámonos*' (Let's go, let's go). I kept telling him no, but finally one day he came again and said, '*Vámonos.*' So I went."

I asked about his family. Wasn't it hard to leave them? Manuel does not remember his father, and his mother died when he was six. He does not know why or how she died. He has no brothers and sisters, just a few cousins.

"I really didn't have any ties." He shrugged his shoulders. "And Umberto kept bugging me, so finally I went with him."

The two young men took a bus from Mexico City and crossed the border at Acuña. Manuel said they did not even look for a *coyote*; they just swam across.

"It was just a short swim because the river was low," he remembered. "Nobody was there."

After they crossed to the U.S., they walked for six hours. Then Manuel started to worry because things looked very familiar.

"This is the same place we started from!" he said to Umberto, but Umberto was sure they were on the right course. He insisted they keep going.

"No, this isn't the same place," he told Manuel "It's not the Rio Grande. It just looks like the Rio Grande. This is the Rio Pecos."

Umberto even showed it to Manuel on the map, but finally they realized they had walked for six hours in a complete circle!

When they finally figured out where they were, they went to see a friend of Umberto's who lived in Plainview, Texas. The old friends caught up on their lives for a while, and then talked about work. There wasn't much available in Plainview at that time, but this friend had worked recently in Florida.

"There is work in Immokalee," he told them, "in oranges and tomatoes."

Manuel had never done fieldwork, but he figured he could do it, so they asked their friend to drive them to Immokalee. After they arrived, Manuel, Umberto, and the friend from Texas moved into a trailer with three other men. They went the very next morning to Miner's Grocery Store, where they waited for the buses that take workers to the fields. Manuel is a strong young man, so he got on a bus easily, and that day he learned how to pick tomatoes. It was not long—just a few months—before he decided it would be much easier to be the one selecting the workers, to be a *Jefe* (boss), so he saved money and bought a truck. Then he talked to the farm managers and told them he was going to bring his own crew. They worked out a deal, and he has been a crew leader ever since.

Manuel was happy enough in Immokalee. Eventually, he planned to go back to Mexico, but there was no rush. Then, late in 1996, he met Ana from Guatemala.

"I loved her as soon as I saw her," he told me. "She had such beautiful eyes."

Manuel never went back to Mexico. He married Ana and adopted her three children. He has two trucks now and works with his crew in the fields, and in the off-season he works in construction in nearby Naples. He likes working in the fields and being a crew leader.

"When there are tomatoes," he said, "I prefer tomatoes."

The only other thing Manuel wishes for is to be able to go back and forth across the border easily.

"I want to work hard here in the U.S., but I would like to see my friends and my cousins in Mexico City."

It is such a simple request.

"So if God permits it, the U.S. government will allow me to get my papers and my residency."

It almost was permitted. When he was first elected, George W. Bush was working on a plan for this with Mexican President Vicente Fox. But then the 9/11 attack on the World Trade Center changed our world. It changed everything, especially for immigrants.

The situation in Mexico seems to get worse all the time. Mexico's President Vicente Fox took office on July 2, 2000. I was very hopeful about him because of his background. Fox was a Coca-Cola executive until 1979, and then worked with his brothers managing two footwear companies and a large vegetable farm. As Mexico's president, he promised to end the rebel conflict in southern Mexico and create one million jobs a year. Several years later, the rebel conflict was less violent, but still going on, and Mexico had *lost* hundreds of thousands of jobs. Half of Mexico's people remained dirt poor.

The Mexican people just want to work, and they cannot do that in their own country. They come here because the United States is still a land of opportunity. Many of those who make it here are living a simplified version of the American Dream, and they are grateful for it.

Juan's dream has come true. He brought his family to the United States, and today he is a happy man because his daughter Yolanda and her children will not work in the fields for the rest of their lives. Eduwiges has made a successful and happy life in Immokalee. She is a U.S. citizen and a teacher now, and she still sends money home to her family in Mexico. She and her brother were able to pay for a real wedding celebration for her parents, still in Mexico, on their fiftieth wedding anniversary. Her parents had married as young people in a simple service with just a priest, but on their fiftieth anniversary, they renewed their wedding vows at a large cathedral with more than one hundred guests. José and Enriquetta, the young lovers who met at the ranch in Mexico, are older now, but still very much in love. Enriquetta works in a plant nursery and José at a golf course. They live in a nice house with their children, two of whom have already graduated from high school. Juanita is still bright and bubbly, smiling and working hard to make a good life. Her job as a cashier ended, due to budget cuts, so now she works in the packinghouse until she can find something else. Finding better jobs is difficult, but she is still very happy that she is able to live in this country, where her daughter can go to school. Manuel, the only Mexican I talked to who was doing all right in his own country, is doing better here. He works in construction in the summer and is a crew leader in the winter. He and his Guatemalan wife, Ana, just want to make a home for their children.

Many of the Mexican immigrants are poor here, but here at least there is hope for a future, and their children can go to school. In Mexico there was no hope for any of them. There, no matter how hard they worked, they could never escape the terrible poverty. Thousands of Mexicans continue to risk their lives each year to come to the United States. They just want to work and make a better life.

4

The Haitians

"In Haiti the world is upside down, and there is no progress for this world right now."

—Desilus Nicolas

Natalie said you find people with boats at different ports. She found hers at Port-de-Paix, in northwest Haiti.

"It was one of those race boats," she told me. "We went at night, twelve people in the boat."

The crossing was more difficult than she expected. The boat was supposed to stop in the Bahamas before continuing on to Miami, but it never made it there because the pilot lost his way. On the evening of the third day, as the winds grew stronger the seas got rougher, and waves crashed against the sides of the boat. Natalie prayed for the safety of land—*any* land.

The next morning the pilot announced that their food was gone. During the day, as the hot sun beat down on them, Natalie prayed to stay alive. At night she tried to sleep and thought of her family, as if in a dream. She does not remember for sure how long they were out on the ocean, but she thinks it was eleven days. When they ran out of water she was tempted to drink the salt water, but she had been told drinking it would make you hallucinate and then you would die, so she did not do it.

Three of the twelve people died. She does not know if they drank the salt water or if they just gave up.

"I think they just dropped themselves in the sea because it was too much misery," she said sadly.

The memory is still very painful for her. She lifted her arms, bent over slightly, let her hands droop, and looked down at the floor.

"We saw them in the morning like this, just hanging there, floating face down in the water."

I have seen pictures on television of Haitians who died attempting the crossing, whose bodies washed up on Miami's beaches. Their bloated bodies looked like soggy lumps covered with sand and flies as police stepped over them, shaking their heads.

Eventually, Natalie's boat landed in Miami and she was safe. She found her way to Little Haiti and to a van service run by other Haitians. She needed work, and the Haitians who drove the van suggested she go to Immokalee. There was work in Immokalee. But the image of the people who died on the crossing never left her.

Many Haitians came in boats to the U.S. at the time of the Cuban Mariel boatlift. The situation in Cuba was entirely different from the one in Haiti, but here's what happened and how it affected the Haitians.

On April 20, 1980, Fidel Castro's regime announced for the third and final time that all Cubans who wanted to emigrate from Cuba to the United States were free to leave, but only from a Cuban port called Mariel. Soon the waters between Mariel and Miami were filled with boats of people from the U.S. who went to pick up relatives and friends. It came to be called the "Freedom Flotilla," as the United States welcomed the Cubans with open arms.

The Haitians, living under the oppressive regime of "Baby Doc" and his Touton Macoutes, were suffering as much if not more than the Cubans were under Castro. The U.S. was welcoming thousands of Cubans because of the political situation in their country, they reasoned, so why shouldn't the Haitians be allowed to come too?

Haitians were so afraid to stay in their own country that they got into anything that would float to get to the U.S. or the Bahamas, and they came by the thousands. Once they got to Miami, some stayed there in the city, taking refuge in an area called Little Haiti, and others made their way to rural communities like Immokalee. Greg Schell, who worked at Florida Rural Legal Services in Immokalee, said that the Haitians who stayed in Miami were mostly young men, urban, and political. The ones who went to towns like Immokalee were from rural areas in Haiti. They were older, and for the most part not involved in politics. They were just poor, and afraid of their own government.

When they reached the U.S., however, the Haitians were treated much worse than the Cubans. Cubans were considered refugees, free to be with their families and friends while their asylum claims were processed, but the Haitians were rounded up and put in detention centers. Many of them were held in Krome Detention Center just outside of Miami, the largest center the INS runs in Florida, while immigration caseworkers decided if their case was bad enough for asylum to be granted.

It took a federal case based on equal protection to get the Haitians to be treated like other asylum seekers and released from detention while their claims were reviewed. If they could prove they had someone here in the U.S. to help them get started and that they would be able to get work, they were allowed to live freely while they pursued their asylum claims. But they had to prove it. If they couldn't, they were held at Krome until their cases could be decided. Some Haitians were left in the detention center for months, until the INS could figure out what to do with them. Attorneys like Sister Maureen, Rob Williams, and Greg Schell, all working at that time at Florida Rural Legal Services, helped them with their claims.

The Haitians were the second large group of immigrants to come to Immokalee. They are between eight and ten percent of Immokalee's population.

There is one big difference between the Haitians and the Mexicans. Like the Mexicans, the Haitians wanted to work, but they also wanted to live in peace, and they could not do that in Haiti.

I was able to talk to quite a few Haitians, because a man named Desilus Nicolas took me to them. He goes by his last name, like many Haitian men, because often their first names are difficult for us to pronounce, and sometimes their last names are similar to our first names. Nicolas was a caseworker at Guadalupe Social Services. Brother Jim Harlow was running GSS at that time, and he and Nicolas both took it as part of their jobs to help me. They knew it would help the new immigrants if people had a better understanding of them.

I met Natalie (pronounced Na-TAL-Yeh), the woman who told me her boat story, because Nicolas introduced me to a teen-aged girl named Yves. (They pronounce it EYE-ves.) Yves said her mother came from Haiti in the early 1980s, that she had some interesting stories, and that she would ask her mother if she could tell her stories to me. We made plans for me to visit the following Sunday at 2:00 p.m. when Natalie and Yves got home from church.

They live in a small trailer park where there are six other trailers. On the day I visited, chickens, a couple of dogs, and one cat were running around in the yard. A group of Haitians sat outside at a picnic table under a tree, playing dominoes. Most of the doors of the trailers were open. I was not sure what to do, so I knocked on the open door and called in "Hello."

The young girl Yves came to the door and invited me in. I felt as if I had walked through that door into another country. I had been a little nervous about going there, because Natalie was the first Haitian I interviewed. Not nervous like being afraid, but nervous about how I would act or how Natalie would act, and because she did not speak much English and I didn't speak much Haitian Creole. But I liked her the minute I saw her.

She was sitting on a stool in between her small kitchen and living room, watching a video of the Haitian Carnival with some other

Haitians who sat on the small couch. Natalie had a red cloth wrapped around her head, her skirt was rolled up to her knees, and her bare calves and feet encircled a bucket of dead fish she was cleaning. She gave me a big smile and motioned with her head for me to come in.

The whole group smiled as Natalie welcomed me. One man gave up his chair as she asked me to sit down. "*Chita, soupla, chita.*" ("Sit down, please, sit down.")

The inside of the trailer was neat and beautifully decorated. She had colorful pictures on the walls, bright cloths on the furniture, and shelves filled with knick-knacks. I explained through Yves that I would like to record our conversation on a cassette tape and Natalie said OK. She finished cleaning the fish, washed her hands, and then sat down on the couch facing me. She had a confident air—almost business-like—that I liked very much.

Natalie was born the same year I was, in 1950, in July, one month after me. Her daughter translated as we talked, and I asked Natalie about her childhood. She came from Bainet near Jacmel on the southern coast of Haiti.

"It was very beautiful," she said, smiling. "We used to bathe in the rivers and wash clothes in the river. If we were hungry, we would just take a mango from a tree. You could take a whole bucket of mango and go to the ocean. For water we would make a hole next to the river to take water home to our house. Every morning we took the jars to fill them with water."

The toilet was an outhouse, but she remembered it, laughing. "You could fall in the hole and you'd be stuck in the hole!"

Most of the Haitians I talked to who were born after 1950 went to school for between nine to twelve years, but Natalie was an exception. She had to work at home so she didn't get much schooling. When she was a child, her parents worked in their own field every day. "The whole town planted things," she said.

"It's not like we had to go buy anything," she explained. "Everybody had their own garden—big gardens. We grew sweet potatoes, peanuts, sugar, and bananas. A lot of people had land. We had chickens, pigs, a donkey, and cows."

She told me that when she was little her father would play games with the family to decide what chores each child would do. One of these games was like London Bridge. Natalie stood up to demonstrate. She motioned me to stand opposite her, then took my hands and held them over our heads. I never really did completely understand it, but the game sounded fun.

"The moon or the sun," she said. "Which do you choose? You hold hands and the person asks you 'sun or the moon?' Just two people holding hands. Other people walk through, in a circle. Then you catch the person. If you were the sun, you would stand behind one of the people holding hands."

Does she have other children? Yes, three, all older than Yves. One lives in Miami, one in the Bahamas, and the third, Bernadette, is still in Haiti. Natalie is a legal resident of the U.S. now, and several years ago she applied for visas for Bernadette and her two children, but the visas have yet to be granted. Bernadette tried twice to come illegally, but both times the seas were too rough and they had to turn back. The third time she tried, the children refused to get into the boat.

Natalie and I talked for another hour and then I had to go back to Naples to meet my husband. She kissed me on each cheek and said "Thank you." I didn't want to leave her. I liked this woman. I asked if I could visit again and she nodded yes, absolutely. I said I would try to come the following Sunday.

She smiled broadly, and said, "*Wi, si Dye vle.*" (Pronounced roughly See Deeyuh' Vlay). I had learned a little Haitian Creole by this time, but this phrase was new to me. It is an important phrase many Haitians use whenever they make plans. She said it again slowly and then told me to repeat it: "*Si Dye vle.*" It means, "If God wants."

Because Natalie was so welcoming and because I liked her so much, I decided to bring her a present the next time I went to see her. The present would be a thank you for spending time with me and for being so nice. The following week I went to her trailer again and the door stood open. I called in to her in my limited Creole.

"*Bonjou, Natalie. Ou isit?*" ("Hello, Natalie, are you here?")

She was there, and she got up from her couch and came to the door to welcome me. She smiled, apparently very happy to see me, and invited me to come in and sit down. Her daughter Yves was not home, so our conversation was limited, but it was very pleasant to sit with her. While we were talking, a Mexican man came to her door and she sold him a single can of beer from her refrigerator. I noticed that two of her refrigerator shelves were filled with beer, soda, and bottled water. I would later learn that Haitian women are very entrepreneurial. Natalie definitely is. The man paid her $1.25 for the beer and walked away.

Then I gave her the present. It was a vibrant blue and red sarong that I bought a few years ago when my husband and I were in Tahiti. Natalie liked the colors, but she didn't know what it was. I gestured toward the kitchen table, saying it can be a tablecloth. Or it can be a skirt—and I wrapped the sarong around me as a skirt, or a dress tied this way—and I wrapped the material under my arms. There was one other way to wear the sarong. I put it on her, brought the material around her from the back under her arms, crossed the ends in front up high, and tied it behind her neck. She loved it. We were both laughing.

Suddenly we weren't strangers anymore, from different cultures who did not speak each other's language. We were "girlfriends." As I left to go home to Naples, she kissed me once on each cheek. I would see her again the following Sunday, "*Si Dye vle.*"

"*Si Dye vle,*" explains how many Haitians live their lives, because nothing in Haiti is definite. Everything might happen or might not happen. Part of the reason is that Haiti is so poor. Sister Judy, now living and working in Haiti, told me about it. Some of her stories were heartbreaking and others were simply touching, like the girl with one shoe.

In Haiti, children have to wear uniforms and shoes in order to go to school. Judy showed me a picture of one beautiful little girl, about ten years old, wearing a red shoe on her right foot and a plastic sandal on her left. Her parents have two daughters and they could afford only one pair of real shoes, so the daughters each wore one shoe, qualifying them both for school.

Haiti is a little smaller than Maryland and has 7.9 million people, about three million more than Maryland. The life expectancy of the Haitians is one of the lowest in the world. The average life span is 56.6 years. In the U.S., life expectancy is 76 years, and in Mexico, it is 70.8 years. The infant mortality in Haiti is tragically high, almost ten percent; one out of every ten babies dies.

Haiti's history is filled with oppression, struggle, and prejudice, and Natalie's ancestors have dealt with hard and uncertain lives ever since they were brought to Haiti from Africa as slaves. I imagine that is why, no matter what the Haitians wish for or hope for or plan for; their reality is always *si Dye vle*.

Africans were brought to Haiti not long after Christopher Columbus landed there on December 6, 1492. Columbus claimed the island for Spain, calling it *"La Isla Española"* (The Island of Spain) and later, the name was shortened to "Hispaniola." The Spanish built their settlements on the eastern half of Hispaniola that later became the Dominican Republic.

There were hundreds of thousands of Taino-Arawak Indians on the island when the Spanish landed there. Not long after they landed, the Spanish put the Indians to work at hard labor, forcing them to search for gold and also to work in their fields, just as they would do later to indigenous tribes all over "the New World." Like many other indigenous people, these Indians were not able to fight off the diseases the Spaniards brought with them, and they died off rapidly.

By 1510 there were only 50,000 Indians left on Hispaniola. African slaves were purchased from Portuguese traders, beginning in the 1520s, to replace the Indians as laborers. Some of the few remaining Indians escaped, often with Africans who had the same idea. Together they created maroon communities in the hillsides, much like the Seminole Indians and escaped slaves would later do in Florida. However, in Hispaniola the Africans survived, but the Indians did not. By 1540 there were only a few hundred Indians left, and by the late seventeenth century, it is believed there was not a single native on the island. Maroon communities of Africans continued to exist in Hispaniola for almost three hundred years. No one ever caught them. They later became helpful in the rebellions that led to Haiti's independence.

While the Spanish focused on other areas of the New World, including Mexico and Guatemala, the French began settling the western part of Hispaniola. The Spaniards had lost interest in that part of the island, so they did not object when the French settled there and began to develop the area, creating new sugar plantations. Not long after, Spain ceded that part of the island to France in exchange for other territories.

The eastern part of the island remained under the rule of Spain and was called Santo Domingo, now known as the Dominican Republic. The French renamed their part of the island "Saint-Domingue" (pronounced roughly "San DoMANG").

The French expanded the sugar plantations and turned Saint-Domingue into the wealthiest colony in the Americas. It became known as the "Pearl of the Caribbean." In sharp contrast, Haiti today is the poorest nation in the Western Hemisphere. Sister Judy once visited Mother Teresa's hospital in Calcutta, and she said Haiti is worse—much worse.

Saint-Domingue's planters were the most productive sugar producers in the world because of the way they treated their African slaves. The French were notorious throughout the New World for their cruelty, to the extent that when plantation owners on other islands had problems with their slaves, they would threaten to send them to Saint-Domingue. They viewed their slaves as expendable commodities, finding it most cost-efficient to work the Africans literally to death rather than encouraging or even allowing them to have children. When slaves died, they were replaced by new ones directly from Africa. This method of managing the slave population later had some disastrous consequences for the French planters, because the result was that the slaves in Saint-Domingue were mostly young and male, with recent memories of freedom. This was a major factor in the success of the rebellions and eventual revolution that would come later.

A second reason the revolution was successful was the fact that the slaves spoke a common language that today is called Haitian Creole. Slaves sold to Saint-Domingue were taken mostly from Congo and the Bight of Benin and they spoke four different languages: Wolof, Fon, Mandingo, and Ewe. To communicate with their new masters and with each other, they developed a pidgin combination of French and the African languages that they used for basic, everyday communication. As time passed, it developed into Haitian Creole, that was used for more sophisticated conversations.

I mentioned that I have studied some Haitian Creole. If you like languages, this one is fascinating. It is particularly interesting to imagine how it developed. The slaves received no education from the French planters, so they used French words the way they heard them. "*Bon Jour*," (good day) became "*Bonjou.*" "*Mes amis*" (my friends) became "*Zanmi*" (friend). "*Sil vous plait*" (if you please) became "*soupla*" (please). Also, grammar was simplified. "*Li*" means he, she, and it. "*Te*" in front of any verb indicates past tense. Haitian Creole is therefore fairly easy to learn, but English is very difficult for people who speak only Haitian Creole. Haitian Creole is spoken by nearly everyone in Haiti and by most Haitians in Immokalee, but the language of Haiti's educated classes is French.

The third thing that helped in the Haitian Revolution was a common religion called Voodoo, still the religion of many of the people there. It is more than just superstition and black magic, according to "Our Lady of Class Struggle," written by one of my professors at Florida International University: Terry Rey.

The book says, "As a religion, Vodou satisfies the religious needs of its adherents just as Lutheranism does for Lutherans, Islam for Muslims, and so on. As such, Vodou deserves as much respect as any other religion."

Is there Voodoo in Immokalee? There may be some, but I found very little evidence of it. The practice of Voodoo is forbidden by the Catholic Church and most other churches, and Haitian priests refuse to give communion or other sacraments to its practitioners. But the priests in Immokalee do not worry much about it.

"Most of it is folklore," said Father Jean Woady Louis, the Haitian priest at Our Lady of Guadalupe Church. "If they use it that way, like folklore, then there is no problem."

The priests do occasionally have a problem, however, such as when people steal holy water from the church for use in Voodoo ceremonies.

"You can spot the people who try to do it," said Sister Judy. "They bring small bottles to fill with water. They seem nervous and fidgety during the Mass. The priest will confront them if he sees them."

During one visit with Natalie, a group of her friends stopped by and I asked them all about Voodoo. Natalie, an Evangelical, believes in it, but views it as a very bad practice.

"Voodoo is the most problem of all," she said. "No good. Plenty of problems. It's bad, bad. Voodoo can kill you."

Her friends disagreed, and a lively argument ensued.

"Voodoo isn't real," they said. "You can't hurt anyone with Voodoo."

"Oh, yes you can," Natalie argued. "They can prepare a powder and throw it at you and you can die in an hour."

"You're talking about poison," responded the visitors, laughing. "Poison can kill you, easy. But that's not Voodoo."

But Natalie was not convinced, and remained very serious.

"Some people do Voodoo and after you die, they go to the cemetery and get your spirit and turn you into an animal." She said it as if she had experience with such things.

"Then, even though you are a spirit, you can remember things, so you would know you are an animal. Later they would give you something not to remember your past."

I later discussed Voodoo with another Haitian woman named Celine, a devout Catholic who spent most of her adult life in Haiti. She also viewed it negatively, but not with the fear Natalie exhibited.

"If you believe it, it will happen to you," Celine said firmly. "If you don't believe it, it can't touch you."

The word Voodoo comes from a word in the African Fon language that means "sacred being" or "spirit." It began in Haiti because of a tactic of the French plantation owners that seems to have backfired. The planters deliberately separated Africans who were from the same tribes and scattered them throughout the island. This way, they reasoned, the slaves would lose tribal religious practices and beliefs, making them easier to control. But the re-distributed slaves created a new religion—a combination of all their religions. They took things the African religions had in common—worship of ancestors, singing, drums, dancing, and the possession of the worshipper by the god—and added some elements of Catholicism taught to them by missionary Jesuit priests.

The priests grew frustrated trying to translate African languages, so like priests in many other parts of the world, they used medals or rosaries to explain Catholicism. The slaves took those items and used them to celebrate rituals of their African gods and spirits in a process called "syncretism." Most of the time, the priests didn't even know it was happening, and neither did the French planters. They believed the slaves were being converted to Christianity. It was not until much later that they realized that the slaves had developed a religion that would tie them all together when the rebellions started.

The fourth factor that contributed to the success of the rebellions was the sheer numbers of the slaves. By the late 1700s, Saint-Domingue had a population of roughly thirty thousand Whites and about the same number of freed Africans, but there were over five hundred thousand African slaves. The slaves outnumbered free people ten to one. About four hundred thousand of the slaves were field workers, usually treated worse than animals. Also, there were tens of thousands of runaway Africans in maroon communities in the mountains. There could not have been a better setting for a successful rebellion.

On August 21, 1791, a Voodoo ceremony by a *houngan* (Voodoo priest) named Boukman started slave rebellions that lasted thirteen years. The first rebellion was incredibly violent, as the slaves paid back some of the brutal treatment they had received. They killed more than one thousand plantation owners and workers. White women were raped and murdered, and white children were massacred. One of my classmates at FIU explained it like this, saying each word emphatically and slowly: "They hacked." Rebellions like this went on periodically for six years, until finally, in 1797, a full-scale revolution took place and two leaders emerged: Toussaint L'Ouverture and Jean-Jacques Dessalines, both ex-slaves and two of the Haitian people's greatest heroes. General L'Ouverture commanded the slave army, and Dessalines was his lieutenant.

The next few years in this period of Haitian history are complicated, and involve politics between L'Ouverture, Dessalines, and Napoleon Bonaparte. In 1801 L'Ouverture conquered the other half of the island that today is called the Dominican Republic, and for a brief time he ruled the whole island. He reorganized the government and instituted public improvements. Then in 1802, Napoleon sent a large force under his General Leclerc to subdue L'Ouverture. Napoleon needed control of Saint-Domingue to control the territory of Louisiana, because the colony's location provided access into the Gulf of Mexico.

Also, new provisions could be loaded there, and the French troops could rest before heading on to New Orleans.

In the process of negotiating a peace treaty with Leclerc, L'Ouverture was treacherously seized and taken to a dungeon in France, where he later died. He remains one of Haiti's greatest heroes, and many Haitians view him as a martyr. After L'Ouverture's death, General Jean-Jacques Dessalines continued the fight, and on January 1, 1804, Dessalines declared independence for Saint-Domingue. Given the odds as they were, thirty thousand French against a half million slaves, most of whom were young and strong and had been treated brutally, I can only wonder why it took them so long.

An independent country called "Haiti" was born. It was the name the land was called by the former Taino-Arawak peoples, meaning "mountainous country." A government was established, and the slaves were freed.

After the initial thrill of independence, however, problems arose with how to structure the new republic, and the new leaders fought political battles among themselves and with France. Also, Haiti began experiencing economic problems as the freed slaves rejected the idea of working on the main thing that made their country strong: the plantations. The result was a serious decline in exports. After the revolution, sugar production dropped to a third of its previous level, and within ten years there wasn't enough sugar to even count it as an export crop. Coffee, introduced in the 1700s, dropped to half of its previous output. Without exports, the new nation reverted to a subsistence economy where the people barely grew enough to feed themselves.

Under the government of one of the first rulers, Alexandre Petion, small plots of land were distributed among the newly freed African people. This helped the people individually, but hurt the economy even more. The people who owned these plots of land could produce enough food for themselves, so why should they go back and work for someone else? Especially why would they willingly go back to the same plantations where they had been enslaved?

This attitude carries over to Haitians today. Even in Southwest Florida, Haitians usually do not like fieldwork, and they typically only do it when they first arrive and cannot get other jobs. I have also been told that many growers do not like to hire Haitians because they complain too much when conditions aren't good. It is as if, consciously or subconsciously, they always remember slavery. Instead of working on large farms in Haiti, almost all the Haitians I talked to in Immokalee described working small plots of land farmed by their families. They grew peanuts, sugar, bananas, rice, sweet potatoes, and "petit mil," a small, millet-like plant used to make flour. Today, seventy percent of Haitians depend on agriculture to live, but most of that is small-scale farming. Only one-third of the people have formal jobs.

They did not work for anyone else and they did not pay taxes. This is still true today. Nicolas told me about it.

"Every Haitian family works in their home," he said, "not for the government."

I was confused about this. How can you expect to have roads, schools, electricity, and other things if you don't pay taxes? He explained it in a way that made no sense, either.

"The problem lies in the nature of the government," Nicolas explained. "If the people paid taxes, the government officials would keep the money and nothing would change—except you would not have your money."

Nicolas' comments reflect the government corruption that has existed in Haiti for the entire two centuries since Independence. Its leaders were either fighting about the country's relationship with France or they were working for their own personal gain.

Haiti also had problems functioning internationally in a white world, as the U.S. and Europe refused to enter diplomatic relations with a black republic. Much of the U.S. economy was still dependent on slavery in 1804, the year of Haitian Independence, and the U.S. would continue the enslavement of African people until 1865. Haiti never recovered from the odds that were stacked against it. It seems to me that they never had a chance.

It is important at this point to explain the role of the attitude of the United States in Haiti's later history as well. I have already told you some of the stories of how Blacks were treated when I was a child in Florida. And I mentioned that when Haiti gained its independence from France, the U.S. would not officially recognize it. This anti-Black attitude did not change, even many years after slavery ended in the U.S. In fact, not long after the U.S. Blacks were freed from slavery, individual U.S. states began passing and enforcing laws to discriminate against them: "Jim Crow" laws, named after a Black minstrel singer.

The attitude carried over into our diplomatic dealings with Haiti. U.S. Secretary of State William Jennings Bryant expressed the prevailing view at the turn of the twentieth century: "Dear me. Think of it! Niggers speaking French!"

In 1915, when the U.S. entered World War I, we entered Haiti at the same time. The rationale was that we had to control the strategic Windward Passage between Haiti and Cuba, the major shipping route to the Panama Canal and the Pacific Ocean, so U.S. Marines occupied Haiti. While there, they trained a Haitian military force, and when they left, that force took over the country. It made and unmade Haiti's presidents for years, until a leader came in who figured out how to control it.

His name was Francois Duvalier, and we know him as "Papa Doc." His nickname came from the fact that he had studied medicine when he was young. The Haitians I talked to in Immokalee thought it was amusing when I said, "Papa Doc." They had heard the name, but they do not use it. They refer to him as "Francois."

Duvalier figured out a way to avoid being removed by the Haitian army, the fate of his predecessors. He formed an organization called the "Volunteers for National Security," who were allowed to steal from the Haitian people and earn their pay through extortion and bribes. That was the deal Duvalier made with them; basically, they could do anything they wanted, as long as they protected him from Haiti's own military. There were about ten thousand volunteers, twice as many as there were soldiers in the regular army. Because of their repressive and violent behavior, these volunteers soon came to be known by the people as the Touton Macoutes. *Tontons Makout* in Haitian Creole means "Uncle Bogeyman." They pronounce both words with the accent on the first syllable. (*TONton MAkout.*) The Macoutes dressed in denim uniforms and matching hats, with red bandanas around their necks, and they robbed, beat, tortured, and killed Haitian people. But they protected Papa Doc—that was their job.

Francois Duvalier campaigned for the presidency of Haiti in the early 1950s and became president in 1957. He had practiced Voodoo all his life, and Voodoo became part of his government, as he used it to control the people. He even appointed a Voodoo *houngan* as head of the military. Duvalier himself was a bogeyman-type figure. He dressed in black and wore a top hat in the style of one of the most frightening and strongest Voodoo gods, Baron Samedi. Duvalier reinforced his godlike image with tactics like having his volunteers paint graffiti messages on buildings: "Duvalier is a god."

Duvalier's control was absolute, and his ego was outrageous. In 1960 he exiled the Catholic Archbishop of Port-au-Prince, and in response, Pope John XXIII excommunicated him from the Catholic Church. From that point on, Francois not only controlled the government and the military, but he also controlled the churches. In 1964 he decided to do away with elections and declared himself "President for Life." A government document distributed under his rule shows the extent of his ego. It was called *Le Catechisme de la Revolution*, and included Francois' own version of the Lord's Prayer:

"Our Doc who art in the National Palace for life, hallowed be Thy name by present and future generations. Thy will be done at Port-au-Prince and in the provinces..."

In 1965 Duvalier worked out a deal with Rome that gave him everything he wanted, and he controlled both the Catholic Church and Voodoo until his death in 1971. His government was corrupt and oppressive, and people in power were in constant danger.

In 1969 I went to St. Elizabeth's College in New Jersey; many of the young women in pre-med with me were international students. One of them was a friend named Kathy Cassis, who came from Haiti. She was a very light-skinned mulatto girl, tall and pretty, with straight shoulder-length black hair that she often wore in a ponytail. Kathy explained to me that her father held a very high position in the government in Haiti. I know now that he must have been part of the administrative staff of Francois Duvalier.

Kathy Cassis told me things I could not even believe. She said that the government of her country was very corrupt and that if anything happened to the current ruler of Haiti, Kathy's family would all be killed. If she went home then, she would be killed too. I was shocked at this, of course. What made it even more shocking was that she said it in a casual way, as I might have explained that we had a house in Florida, or that my father worked as an engineer on ships. I left school after a year and a half, so I don't know if Kathy ever went back to Haiti or if she was ever killed. Now that I know some Haitians and have studied their country, I wish I had asked her more questions, because she could have explained it to me from the viewpoint of the elite ruling class. I know the reality of it today only from the perspective of the very poor—my friends in Immokalee.

Another thing that hurt Haiti was the removal of its trees. There is a theory that it began even before independence, with the French, who cleared the mountains to plant coffee but did not know about terracing. They also were unfamiliar with crop rotation, so their replanting techniques depleted the soil. After Independence, forests were cleared to make more land for individual farms. Later, Haiti's stands of mahogany were cut down and sold to foreign markets. Ironically, in the U.S. much of Haiti's mahogany was used to make coffins. Many Haitians moved to the cities, but they still needed fuel and their only source of fuel was the charcoal they made (and still make) from trees.

Before the Spanish arrived, over seventy-five percent of Haiti's land was forested, but by the middle of the twentieth century it was less than ten percent. Without any trees to hold it, topsoil was washed away by the rains. It flowed down the hillsides and was carried away into the ocean.

I wanted to meet more Haitians, and Nicolas said I really should meet Joseph, who was one of the first Haitians in Immokalee. Joseph came in 1974, several years before any other Haitians. Nicolas drove me to meet him.

Joseph lives in a fairly nice building for senior citizens in Immokalee, not far from the Guadalupe Family Center where I sing to the children. He is tall for a Haitian, standing over six feet. When he was younger, he must have had a very strong presence about him. He has some if it still, but it's hard to see, because Joseph had a stroke not long before I met him; he needs a cane to walk and his speech is slurred. It would have been difficult for me to understand him even if he spoke English or even if I were good with Haitian Creole, but Nicolas understood him and translated for us. Joseph's mind wanders, but he had no trouble remembering the past. He had a wry sense of humor. He told me he thinks the Haitians are no good and that's why he left Haiti. Nicolas shrugged this off as if it were a joke, but I am not sure Joseph was entirely joking.

Joseph was born in 1932 in Petit-Goave, a town on the ocean not far south of the capital, Port-au-Prince. He was the first of seven children, and his parents were farmers, like most other Haitians. They also raised pigs, like most other Haitians. He said he was happy when he was young, filled with energy and ambitions. He started out working in a factory, making sisal, and saving money as he planned his own rope-making business.

"When I was born, I was OK," he told me, bitterly. "I had a plan. I thought I would be something, but I was persecuted because of my ambition. When I was young, I would never have left Haiti, because I had enough to survive. I had a future."

But when Joseph was twenty-five, Francois Duvalier took power with his *Toutons Macoute*. Nicolas explained more about the Macoutes.

"If they see you going to school," he said, "or if you're going to get something, or you have some ambition, they would want to take what you have. And Francois gave them power to help discover people who talked bad about him. This made the Macoutes a high authority, because all they had to do was report you. So they could do anything."

I mentioned that Joseph was an impressive man, in spite of the effects of the stroke, so I could understand why the Macoutes would have a problem with him. He was too confident, too capable, and he worked too hard. From the time Joseph was twenty years old until he was forty, he worked harder and harder but had less and less to show for it. He grew into adulthood in the 1960s and 1970s, and watched as the repression from the Macoutes got worse and worse.

Joseph would not tell me details about things that happened to him. Haitians usually do not say much about things that happened in their country, because in Haiti, saying too much can bring big trouble. I understand it, now that I have learned more about the Duvaliers and the Macoutes. They beat, tortured, and imprisoned people, especially people with ambition. They got even worse when Francois died in 1971 and his son, Jean-Claude ("Baby Doc") took over. My impression was that he was much weaker than his father—a young playboy with little interest in government—and the Macoutes grew stronger under his rule. For poor people, living in Haiti was worse than ever.

Finally, Joseph realized that his dreams could go nowhere, and in 1974, when he was forty-two, he and one of his friends bought fake passports and flew to Miami. Joseph did not want to stay in Miami because he didn't like big cities, so they bought a car and started driving. They drove until they found Immokalee, and that's where they stayed. They just wanted to work and live in peace. Joseph was so bitter toward his countrymen that when he got to the United States, he told people he was from Barbados. He spent the rest of his life in Immokalee working in the fields, at first in watermelons and later in tomatoes. He worked until the stroke stopped him just a few years before I met him.

I asked Joseph who else was in the fields when he first came in 1974. He said it was mostly Mexicans. He said, "The Mexican is the Master of the fields."

Joseph's isolation in Immokalee lasted only a few years, because other Haitians started showing up in the early 1980s. He called it "the time when the Haitians invaded Immokalee."

I tried to clarify this comment. Was he actually unhappy that they came?

"Yes. I don't like the Haitians." He shrugged his shoulders. "But this is not my country. I can't decide if they come or not."

Again, I couldn't tell if he was joking or not.

At the end of our conversation, I asked Joseph about his family, and he told me he has fifteen children. I made a light comment, saying his wife must have been very tired, but he didn't get the joke.

He started to drift off at this point, and looked sleepy. He said he never married, but his children live in New York.

"Would you like to hear them?" he asked.

I wondered what he meant, but it turned out that he had left us, mentally, for the moment. He turned on a cassette tape of Spanish music, leaned back in his chair, and closed his eyes. Nicolas shook his head and motioned that I should follow him. I stepped out into the hallway and Nicolas closed the door softly behind us.

In addition to introducing me to people and translating, Nicolas told me his own story. He remembered the Macoutes with bitterness.

"In Haiti, I studied agriculture," he told me. "That's what I wanted for my trade. I wanted to know how to cultivate the soil. After I finished school, I found out that there would be no progress for Haiti because of the system. I couldn't get anywhere in agriculture. I couldn't get anywhere in anything. I didn't like the government, I didn't like the Macoutes, I didn't like the whole system, so I left Haiti."

He left Haiti the same year Joseph did, in 1974. Nicolas is twenty-five years younger than Joseph, but he left for the same reasons: the Macoutes and the government. In spite of them, Nicolas loves Haiti and he loves the Haitian people. He became sad when he talked about his country. He did not want to leave, but he finally decided he had no choice if he wanted to live in peace.

It is not difficult to understand why so many Haitians fled their country; the Macoutes were unbelievably repressive and there was no logic to their behavior. Sister Maureen has heard stories from many of her Haitian clients, and she gave an example.

"If there was a dispute, say one man was upset because another man's cow ate the grass at his house, a Macoute would intervene," she explained. "The Macoute would tell the man with the cow that he had to pay the Macoute a fine. Then he would tell the man with the grass that he also has to pay the Macoute a fine. If the men didn't pay him, the Macoute would beat them, or worse. It didn't make any sense. They could do anything they wanted."

If you got on their bad side, they could punish you forever. As long as they protected Papa Doc, and later Baby Doc, no one would stop them. It was dangerous in Haiti to even talk against the Macoutes.

Nicolas, however, was so angry with the Macoutes and the way they behaved that he bravely talked against them. He actually told one of them to his face how he felt about them. After hearing how he talked, I did not want to use his real name in this book because I was afraid there might still be Macoutes in Haiti who would read this and come to Immokalee to find him. Nicolas said I do not have to worry about them reading this book, because the Macoutes cannot read.

"We call them '*Baba*,'" he told me, using a word that is not in my Haitian Creole dictionary, but that he said means "ignorant." "They don't know nothing, but they have power. They wear blue jeans and the beret, and you have to be careful. I dealt with some of them, but they never really hurt me. The reason I left Haiti was the *Makout*. They never would go to school, but when they see you as a person that has a little education they hate you."

Nicolas, usually a quiet, soft-spoken man, grew more and more angry as he talked about them. It clearly still weighs heavily on his mind. He told me he pushed one of them and glared furiously, very closely, into his face.

"You want to hit me?" he asked as he pushed the Macoute backwards. "Hit me! Go ahead! Hit me! I can become the president because I have an education, but you're not going to be nothing because you are ignorant. And you think you are going to kill me, and you are going to hit me? I am going to kill you. I'm going to chop, chop up you and your family."

In spite of this defiant attitude, Nicolas eventually left his country because the Macoutes started following him and causing trouble for him and his family. There was really no way to fight them.

I asked my new friend Natalie about the Macoutes. She, too, said they were the main reason she left Haiti.

"I saw that the *Makout* were killing too many people," she said, shaking her head disgustedly. "I saw with my own eyes dogs eating a person, and the *Makout* just watched. They just kept killing people."

I wondered, are there Macoutes in Immokalee today? Maureen told me she thinks she has seen a few. She said the posture of the men who were Macoutes is different from other Haitians; they move more arrogantly than other people do. Joseph, the older Haitian who tells people he is from Barbados, also said they are here.

"There are some here in Immokalee who were *Makout* in the Duvalier regime," Joseph told me, "but now they cannot behave themselves like *Makout*. Now they got to just live here like everybody else."

He laughed, a deep Caribbean laugh, with bitter satisfaction, and said, "They got to be cool now."

I am always curious about the immigrants' journeys because these experiences are so different from anything I have ever known. I want to know details so I can put myself in their place and see the journey through their eyes. Getting this level of detail is particularly difficult with Haitians, because as I said, they don't talk much about details, but Nicolas introduced me to a group of Haitian men one day and they told me some things. The stories varied.

They came in small boats, carrying as few as twelve people, and large boats that held up to 364 people. Fees, when charged, were between $500 and $1,800, but many of them paid nothing. Often a group of people just got together and came in a boat. They would each chip in ten or fifteen dollars for food and water. Some went to the Bahamas, and some went to Miami or to the Florida Keys. When smugglers were used, they did not provide all the services offered by the *coyotes* at the Mexican border (places to stay, inner tubes, vans, trucks to take them to final destinations, etc.). All the Haitian smugglers did was pilot the boats. When the Haitians reached Miami, they were left alone to find their way.

One man told me he came to the U.S. in late 1980 with his son. He said they took a big boat to the Bahamas, and then came in a smaller boat with twenty people to the U.S. They left the Bahamas at midnight, expecting to land in Miami the next day. Instead, they found themselves in Key Biscayne at 5:00 a.m. All twenty of them made it, with no problem, but then immigration agents picked them up. I asked how the INS knew they were here illegally. The group laughed as the man, somewhat condescendingly, explained how they knew.

"We were a bunch of Haitian guys walking around," he said, looking at me sideways. "We didn't speak English, and we didn't know where we were going. I don't think it was too hard to figure out!"

I laughed, too, a little embarrassed, but we were really all laughing together.

Another of them went to the Bahamas from Haiti on a Bahamian visa in 1979, then from Nassau he came to the U.S. in a *chaloupe*, which he described as a small plastic boat, like a dinghy with a motor. The boat held twelve people and it took about five hours to get to Miami. The person in charge was a Cuban. Cubans bring people from the Bahamas to Miami Beach as a job.

I was also curious about what happened to the boats when the Coast Guard picked up the Haitians.

"It depends on the boats," one of the men told me. "If the boats are ugly, the Coast Guard burns them. If they are pretty boats, they keep them."

The other Haitians laughed and nodded their heads in agreement.

Sister Barbara Pfarr, who worked in Immokalee during the 1980s, told me a story about boats at Our Lady of Guadalupe's Harvest Festival Carnival.

"I was standing with a group of the Haitian fellows one night as we watched a ride that was set in a huge boat," she remembered. "I asked the guys if they had any interest in going on that ride."

"No way!" they answered quickly. "We've spent enough time on those boats!"

Back in Haiti, life was getting more and more difficult all the time. I mentioned earlier that Francois Duvalier named his son Jean-Claude as his successor before he died. For a short time, he stopped some of the human rights abuses that had taken place under his father's government and in exchange for this, in 1971 the U.S. restored financial aid to Haiti. But the humane side of Baby Doc did not last long after he got this money. Soon the abuses started up again and the Macoutes were once more out of control.

The Haitians I talked to in Immokalee told me that Haiti got much worse under Jean-Claude. They said that at least when his father ran the country there was some sense of order, and that Francois was strongly on the side of the "*Neg*" (dark-skinned) Haitians who are ninety-five percent of the population. But Baby Doc did not share the same feeling, and in 1980 he infuriated the black Haitians by marrying a Mulatto woman. Their wedding itself enraged the Haitian people. In a country where eighty percent of the people lived well below the poverty line, the couple threw a wedding that cost three million U.S. dollars.

I visited Haiti in 1980 and saw the poverty first-hand. I was on a cruise in the Caribbean with my first husband, and one of the day-stops was Cape Haitian in northern Haiti. I have forgotten most of the people in the other islands where we stopped, but I never forgot the Haitians.

A rickety bus picked us up from the beautiful Norwegian Cruise Ship at the dock and took us about five miles on dusty, pothole-filled roads to a place where we mounted tired, skinny donkeys. We rode these poor donkeys, led by local Haitian men, on a three-hour trip up a mountain to see the Citadel, a fort left from the early days of Haiti's history.

Everywhere, there were people wanting money from us. They followed us up the lower part of the mountain, calling out, "Hey, miss, give me money. You got money?" Some were selling little souvenirs.

One young girl stood out. She was smiling and following me as I rode by on the pitiful donkey. Her question sounded more like a statement.

"Hey, miss, you want to buy this from me?"

I don't remember what she was selling, but I did not want it. I shook my head no, and smiled back. She kept following.

"You want to buy this? Good price, very good price."

I said no again, starting to get a little irritated. I looked away. There were just too many of them and they were too pushy. I was just there to take this donkey ride up to the Citadel. She ran to keep up.

"Hey, miss, what's your name?"

"My name is Carlene," I answered.

"Will you buy this from me when you come back down, Carlene?"

I nodded yes, just to make her go away, because I was tired of people badgering me. The mountain trip was an all-day tour anyway, so I did not expect she would be there when we came back down.

We rode on, on the pitiful donkeys, and after a while we were out of the town and the throngs of people were gone. We passed some people living in the woods with a sheet-sized piece of material thrown over a rope, a kind of a homemade tent. We saw others bathing in streams. It was very hot there.

Whenever I lit up a cigarette, my guide would motion to ask for one. He never smoked them, but just put them in his pocket and I found this annoying after a while. I tried to communicate with him, but of course at that time I spoke no Haitian so I did a bad job of it. I usually made it a point to learn at least a hundred words in the language of any country I visited, because I have found that if I know the one hundred most common words and understand the basic structure of a language I can get along quite well. In this case, Haiti was a one-day stop. There was no reason to learn Haitian Creole for one day.

Our guide was sullen anyway, and not at all friendly. And I was hot. I got dizzy at the top of the ride, from the heat probably, and on the way down in the afternoon the heat was even worse. I couldn't wait to get back to the ship—back to our cabin, the air conditioning, a glass of cold water, and then a glass of cold white wine. When we got back to the town I was surprised to see the same young girl there at the side of the road. She not only remembered me, but she remembered my name. Of course I realized that she had probably memorized the names of half the people on our mountain trip, but it touched me when she said mine.

"Carlene, Carlene, do you remember me? Buy this from me."

I was too tired and there were too many of them. I shook my head no, much less patient now. She followed me and persisted for some distance, but I ignored her. Finally she gave up.

The ship's tour guide had told us that we should give the Haitian donkey-guides about two dollars as a tip. He said that was a lot of money for them and explained that they could live for a whole month on about twenty dollars. I didn't think two dollars was very much money, but the tour was expensive, so I figured the Haitian men made part of that money as a wage for guiding our donkey. I also had it in my mind, based on the tour guide's comments, that it wasn't right to give too much. When it came time to tip, because I didn't want to upset the natural balance, and because I was so hot and tired, I only gave the recommended two dollars.

"That's it," I said, and handed him the two dollars. I didn't even say "Thank you." I was just irritable.

"That's it? That's it?" He looked at me as if I was crazy. He looked angry, as if he couldn't believe this was happening, but I didn't care. I was tired and hot and I just wanted to get back to the ship. I pointed to my husband, indicating that he had our money. Part of me was hoping he would give more, but he, too, held up empty hands. He had already given his two dollars.

We made our way back to the rickety bus. When we arrived at the docks, there were more Haitians, all asking for money. One came up to us and in broken but understandable English asked where we lived.

"In Minnesota," we replied.

"Does it snow there?"

We said "Yes."

"Everywhere?" he asked.

"Yes, everywhere."

"In the mountains, yes?" He was amazed. "But not in the city."

"In the city, too," we answered. "Everywhere."

He started to ask more questions about Minnesota. I was actually enjoying this talk, but suspected that it would end with yet another request for money, so we hurried onto the ship.

That was my only exposure to Haiti, except for knowing Kathy Cassis in college. I felt disturbed about this visit to Haiti for years later. The image of the poverty, and also of the pushiness of the Haitians stayed with me. I wished I had been nicer to the guide who took me up the mountain. Instead of one at a time, why hadn't I given him the whole pack of cigarettes? Instead of two dollars, why hadn't I given him twenty dollars or even more? What did that money mean to us? Nothing. It was just that I felt that I wasn't supposed to give them money. I most of all wished I had bought something from the little girl who remembered my name, and that I had spent more time talking with the Haitian man at the pier. He just wanted to learn about the world outside of Haiti. He just wanted to know about snow.

The poverty in Haiti got even worse under "Baby Doc," and other things happened that hurt the people. One of the worst was the killing of the Haitian pigs. It started in 1979 when there was an outbreak of African Swine fever in Haiti. The U.S. government was afraid the disease would spread to livestock in our country, so in 1983 the U.S. government, along with Canada and Mexico, pressured Jean-Claude into killing all the Haitian pigs. I asked the older Haitian, Joseph, about them. Although he had left by then, he heard about what happened.

"That is what killed Haiti," said Joseph, bitterly. "The U.S. gave the Haitian government money to kill our pigs."

The killing of the scrawny, black Haitian pigs was a huge blow to the poor Haitian people. Because the people had so little to begin with, their pigs were a significant part of a family's assets; pigs were even left to children as part of their inheritance. Over eighty percent of Haiti's rural households had them. Greg Asbed, with the Coalition of Immokalee Workers, wrote his Master's Thesis on the Haitian pigs.

"A piglet could be purchased for $US 10, raised at minimal expense by leaving it to forage on its own and sold as a mature hog a year and a half later for as much as $US 180."

Money was supposed to have been provided by the government so the Haitian people could buy replacement pigs—big white pigs brought in from the U.S., from Iowa. But there were a few problems with the plan. One, often the people never got the money. Two, the replacement pigs were ten times as expensive as the Haitian pigs. Three, the Iowa pigs had special needs.

Where the Haitian pigs ate little and had been satisfied with mango skins and garbage, the Iowa pigs ate too much and required special, expensive food. The Haitian pigs did not need much water, while the white Iowa pigs drank a lot of water—important because fresh water is scarce in Haiti, due to its limited infrastructure. The Haitian pigs lived comfortably outside in the heat and the dirt, and the white pigs required a sty or other kind of housing that the Haitians did not have. The new pigs got sick and died, and the money paid for them was wasted.

The loss of the pigs had a devastating effect on the poor people. Before the Haitian pigs were destroyed, people could cover any unexpected bills by selling a pig. Without the pigs, people were forced to borrow money from loan sharks, or sell their land. The effect of the loss of the pigs was so great that it sparked an economic crisis in the country.

Celine Simeus lived in the poverty of Haiti before and after the crisis of the pigs. She was an older Haitian lady who came early for the Haitian Mass at Our Lady of Guadalupe, therefore joining the last part of the English Mass. A girl named Evelyn and her little brother Marvin came with her. Evelyn was eight years old when I first met her, and we have become good friends. Evelyn told me Celine comes to the end of the English Mass because she likes to hear me sing.

Celine lived in a tiny apartment in a building on Immokalee's south side, not far from the Indian Casino. The first time I visited her, Natalie's daughter Yves came with me to be my translator. Celine had been in Immokalee for twenty years, but like Natalie, had never learned English. There was no need. Everyone in the packinghouse where she worked spoke Haitian Creole, and she lived in a place where most of the other people were Haitian.

She greeted Yves and me with a delighted, happy smile, apparently thrilled that we had come to visit her. The room she lived in was about ten feet by twelve feet. There was a small hot plate on a counter in the back, serving as a stove. A refrigerator stood next to the counter. She had a bathroom, but I did not use it, so I could not tell if it had a shower or not. A double bed filled most of the room, and there was a dresser where she had placed a small fan. There was no air conditioning and I doubt that there was heat.

When we arrived, Celine asked Yves to position three chairs between her bed and the wall. Two of the chairs were small, like those used in schools for students in first or second grade, and the third was an adult-sized card-table chair. Celine put one of the pillows from her bed on the card-table chair, and motioned me to sit on that one, then she and Yves sat on the child-sized chairs, facing me. There was very little room to move in there even without visitors, and we were close enough to touch the whole time. I was facing the side of her bed, looking at the wall behind it. Hanging there were her dresses for church, and her hats.

While I like to bring something when I visit people in their homes, I had been told that Celine was diabetic, so I could not bring anything sweet. I brought some vegetables, and three scarves that I had at home and never wore. I realized when I got there that she would have liked a hat better, but I didn't have any hats. She took these presents from me and gave me presents, too: a watermelon and a large bag of tomatoes.

I protested about taking them because she was so poor, but she insisted. I realized later that people brought her produce all the time. Celine was very well-liked and the other Haitians took good care of her. The produce they brought her allowed her to give gifts to friends who visited.

Celine asked Yves to bring me a pot that was sitting on the little hot plate on the counter. The pot contained something left over, made of pork and some kind of green vegetables, like turnips or something. It was her way of serving her guest something to eat. I took one bite from the pot, using my fingers, because she had not offered a plate or a fork. It was good, but a little bitter. I smiled and told her I liked it and Yves put it back on the stove.

Now we had completed the formalities of the visit. She had given me the best chair, we had exchanged presents, and I had eaten some of the food she offered. Celine sat facing me on the little grade-school chair, with her hands folded in her lap, and I asked her about her life in Haiti.

She was born on June 28, 1928. June 28 is my birthday, too. *Watch for signs.* I told her we would have to sing Happy Birthday to each other in church on our birthdays. She loved that idea. We have done it every year since.

Celine was born in Il de la Gonave, a 37-mile-long island off the coast of Port-au-Prince—very rural, and very poor, with no paved roads, no electricity, and no running water.

So Celine went to live with her "other family," an aunt and uncle in Port-au-Prince. She said she went there because she wanted to be Catholic and her birth parents were a different religion, but it may also have been that Celine's parents could not afford to raise her. Orphanages in Haiti are filled with children who have both their parents, but the parents can't even afford to feed them. The parents visit and bring clothes and food when they can. Celine was lucky to have her "other family," otherwise, she might have been in an orphanage, too. Education was not a priority for them, however, and

Celine was taken out of school after a short time. She made money by selling food to schoolchildren.

She told me she had five children, but never married. I asked Yves to tell her, "You are very intelligent," but she didn't seem to get the joke. She would not talk more about her children, in spite of my persistent questions. I mentioned earlier that the Haitians don't usually say much about personal things. They learned in their turbulent country that the less you say, the better.

As we talked, neighbors came by and peeked in to make sure Celine was all right, or just to say "hello" to me. My new Lexus, conspicuously parked in front of her poor small room, may have attracted them, but I suspected they checked on her, in any case. The little girl Evelyn, who came to church with Celine, came and stood in the doorway. She spoke very good English and proudly told me she knew her times tables.

Celine said she left Haiti because she was not happy there anymore. She was poor, and she couldn't find any work. One of her daughters, who had married an American man and lived in Miami, had been sending Celine money to support her, but Celine was very independent and wanted to support herself. I asked what she liked best about living in the United States, and she answered without hesitating.

"When I got here, I could make my own paycheck."

Her daughter told her about a place called Immokalee where there was work. She petitioned for her mother, and Celine came to the U.S. and to Immokalee in 1983. Celine left her other children, at that time in their late teens or early twenties, by themselves in Haiti. Their sister in Miami could easily petition to bring Celine because she was her mother, but the same rules don't apply to brothers and sisters. Brothers and sisters often have to wait twelve years, if they are allowed to come at all. I asked Celine about her children.

"After I left," she said, with surprisingly little emotion, "things happened and they died."

She said one of them died of an illness, and that the Macoutes killed two of the older boys. That's all she would say about their deaths.

Celine asked if I would like to see some pictures. When I enthusiastically answered yes, she asked Yves to help her pull out a single book of photographs. She showed pictures of her entire extended family, including the two sons who were killed by Macoutes. One of them had a tattoo of a snake on his arm. I asked her what it meant, but she said it meant nothing; he just liked it. She changed the subject quickly and I never found out if the snake tattoo meant something or not.

She also showed me a letter from our Bishop John Nevins in Venice, Florida. It was a form letter thank-you for the forty dollars Celine gave to the Bishop's Fund. Celine gave forty dollars to the Bishop's fund? She barely had any money. She believed Bishop Nevins sent her the thank-you letter personally and was very proud of it. She said she loved the Bishop.

She repeated many times how happy she was that I had come to see her. Yves finally got a little exasperated, translating that repeatedly. I offered to teach Celine English, but she said that I should learn Haitian. She was in her late seventies then, and I did not think she would be learning much English. I told her I would learn some Creole, and I did. Since then, she and I have become good friends.

It took days to absorb the experience of my first visit to Celine. The culture shock I felt when I was first in Immokalee, after the Thanksgiving parade, hit me again. I compared my life to hers, and wondered who was happier. I knew that I was happy she was in Immokalee and not Haiti. Life in Haiti would be too hard for her now. Here she could live in peace.

When she talked about her life, Celine seemed to feel only gratitude. I could only figure that her little room in Immokalee was nicer than where she lived in Haiti, but later I found out that the living accommodations were not important to her. Here's how I learned this.

One day after the English Mass, I looked for Celine but she was not there. She usually came into church at the end of our Mass, but I did not see her at all on that day. I stopped by her apartment, and the little girl Evelyn told me Celine was in Naples in a nursing home. Evelyn gave me a telephone number, and I called there. It was in an expensive part of Naples. Apparently Medicare puts people where there is room. I went to see her, and the place was spectacular, with marble floors and countertops, freshly cut flowers everywhere and soft music playing in the background. I thought she would never want to leave this place! A Haitian nurse's aide brought me to her. Celine was in a room by herself, lying in bed. When she saw me she gasped, she was so surprised to see me. She was very flustered. She motioned that I should wait a minute, outside the room, and she asked the Haitian nurse's aide to help her as I waited in the hall.

A few minutes later the nurse's aide asked me to come in. Celine was sitting up in bed with her hair combed, wearing a light blue cotton robe. She had gotten flustered because she did not look good enough to receive visitors, but now she did. I asked her how she ended up in this place.

She explained that she had gone to the hospital in Naples for an X-ray of her leg. Whoever took her home dropped her off a block away from her home, a strange thing to do because Celine needed a walker to walk. She fell, trying to make her way to her room, and damaged her knee much worse than it was before. The ambulance came and took her back to Naples and she ended up in this nursing home for therapy. Then she started to cry. She was so unhappy! She missed her friends, her apartment, her church, and her priest—especially her priest. She meant Father Woady, the Haitian priest at Our Lady of Guadalupe. Celine was very worried that Father Woady would not know where to find her. She searched frantically through her purse to get me his telephone number. I kept saying I could look it up, but she insisted on finding it. She insisted I had to call him and tell him where she was. I did, of course, and he said he would visit her.

A few weeks later her therapy was done and she was allowed to go home. I have never seen anyone so happy to go back to a tiny one-room apartment. She loved her life in Immokalee. It amazed me.

A few years after Celine left Haiti, a foreign exchange crisis created a gas shortage there, and without transportation, food deliveries were cut off for most of the country. This was the final straw for the Haitian people's tolerance of Jean-Claude Duvalier. In November, 1985, there were protests all over the country and a popular movement called *dechokaj* (uprooting) organized Haiti's peasants against Baby Doc. By 1986, the instability in Haiti was so bad that the Reagan Administration feared the problems might spread to other Caribbean nations, so the U.S. helped force Jean-Claude into exile.

Now, for the first time in their history, the Macoutes were afraid. They had lost their supporter, and angry people turned on them. Many Macoutes were imprisoned or killed during this time. A popular method used to kill them was called "necklacing," where a tire filled with gasoline was placed around a person's neck and then lit. In many ways, Haiti became more dangerous after Baby Doc left because violence in the streets got worse. The whole country was in chaos, and streets blazed with fire as the people rioted.

That violence caused the second large wave of Haitians to come to the United States. Haitians who could no longer stand the violence got into almost anything that would float and sailed away, hoping to find freedom and peace in the United States of America.

During the three years after Jean-Claude left the country, five different governments ruled the country, all military or military-backed. These rulers were as brutal as their Duvalier predecessors were. The people longed for peace and a government that cared about their needs, but all they saw was violence that would never end.

There was one presidential candidate whom they thought could save them. His name was Jean-Bertrand Aristide and his political party was called *Lavalas*, meaning "cleansing flood" of promised reforms.

Aristide was a priest who was known as a defender of the poor people, an advocate of Liberation Theology, a movement of Latin American Catholics that became popular in the 1970s and 1980s. Liberation Theology says that if you believe in the Bible, then you must support the struggles of the poor for freedom and economic justice.

Aristide won the hearts of the people through years of speeches given in his church and over Haitian radio stations. He survived the efforts of the military government to get rid of him, although his life was often threatened and his church was bombed. When it became too dangerous for him to appear in public, he provided speeches to *Radio Soleil* (Radio of the Sun) via cassette tapes. On December 16, 1990, over sixty percent of registered voters turned out to vote, and they overwhelmingly elected Jean-Bertrand Aristide president of Haiti. His victory came in the first free and fair election in Haitian history.

The Haitians in Immokalee were very pro-Aristide when I first talked to them. They followed Haiti's politics closely through a Haitian radio station in Immokalee, and most believed that Aristide would save their country. Nicolas's comment was typical.

"Aristide was a priest, and became the president of Haiti," said Nicolas. "I believe he loves the poorest population, and he loves to see everybody survive."

Celine even had a picture of him in her photo album, along with her family and friends. She told me she loved Aristide. Natalie felt the same way.

"Very good president," said Natalie, in her limited English. "He's a cool man. Good man."

But Aristide's first term was short. He was sworn in in February 1991, and on September 30 of the same year was ousted by a military coup. More than two thousand civilians were killed during the first six months after the coup, and many more were imprisoned and tortured. Haiti's streets were filled with bloody violence, and tens of thousands of them fled in boats. Sister Maureen talked about this.

"There are a lot of people in Immokalee who are here because of the bloody coup of 1991," she remembered. "They saw their family members with a price on their heads because they were Aristide supporters, and they had to hide. They saw a lot of rape and murder, so they got in boats—anything that would float."

They came seeking safety and freedom. Some of them were returned to Haiti while others were taken to the U.S. military base in Guantanamo, Cuba, where they lived in a camp. One Haitian man I talked to was picked up in a boat in 1991 and was kept in Guantanamo for two months. He said there were over 50,000 people there, including Cubans, Chinese, and people from the Dominican Republic. Over 11,000 of them were Haitians.

"They were interviewed there by a whole cadre of people the INS enlisted," explained Maureen. "If they could show a credible fear of persecution, based on their political activity for Aristide, they were allowed to get on a plane and come into this country to file for asylum."

Some of the Haitians who made it to the U.S. came to Immokalee. Maureen said she had four or five books worth of the persecution stories she heard as she helped them with their asylum claims.

The Haitian military defied the U.S. and United Nations' attempts to help, and finally twenty thousand U.S. troops were sent to occupy Haiti. Aristide was brought back in to finish his term, but by now the Haitian military was in shambles. Aristide, aided by the U.S., started training a new police force, but by April 1995 there was a general breakdown in law and order.

When elections came in December of 1995, Aristide was prevented by Haiti's constitution from serving two consecutive terms. He supported Rene Preval, one of his close aides, and Preval won, but then the U.S. got distracted with its own presidential race and paid less and less attention to Haiti. In the meantime, the UN peacekeeping force was the only thing keeping order, as Haiti's new police force was still not ready to take over.

In 1996 the U.S. government changed its mind about allowing the Haitians to come to the U.S. Apparently it was decided that Haiti was no longer dangerous because the UN peacekeeping force was there.

"The asylum claims were getting adjudicated positively until June 1996," remembered Maureen. "Then the U.S. government turned on a dime and decided it was safe for them to go home. We saw a great number of denials of asylum claims."

Maureen was working on the claims of many Haitians at that time.

"No it isn't safe," they told her. "There might be some kind of a multi-national protective force at the airport, but not in my little town or rural area. Where I come from, nobody has even heard of the multi-national peacekeeping force. The same thugs who exploited and murdered at the time of the coup are still in control."

The rural sheriffs, for example, called "*Chef du Sections*," (Section Chiefs) had enforcers who were from Macoute backgrounds.

Aristide ran again for president in 2000 and won, but things were different. This time it looked as if the elections may have been rigged—by Aristide himself. But still, the Haitians in Immokalee who had been inspired when Aristide returned in 1994 after the coup, were also hopeful when he won his second election. I asked Nicolas how he felt about Aristide then. He told me that Aristide said to the people of Haiti, "We don't have any room in our jails for these people, so *you* do justice."

It was basically a zero-tolerance edict that encouraged street justice. At first, Nicolas thought this was a good thing.

"So now people are able to do anything," he said, "and they're not afraid anymore of the thieves." But as it turned out, the directive just increased the violence in Haiti.

Gradually, many Haitian people in Haiti and in Immokalee became disappointed with the man they thought would be their country's savior. There was a sign of his changed personality in 2001 when he gave his acceptance speech in French, the language of the aristocracy, not Haitian Creole, as he did when he won his first election.

In response to criticism of the electoral process, the United States, the European Union, and other lenders held up some $500 million in aid and loans, charging that Aristide's government and *Lavalas* party had failed to reach a compromise with opposition parties.

As time went on, it appeared that Aristide may have become as corrupt as the dictators who ruled before him. There were also human rights issues. Speaking out against Aristide or his political party, *Lavalas*, was no longer permitted, and he had supporters called *chimeres* whose behavior very much resembled that of the Touton Macoutes. An article in the *Naples Daily News* on April 28, 2002 told the stories of two women who appeared to have encountered the *chimeres*. The Coast Guard had picked up one of them just off the coast of Miami. She told the reporter that because she supported a political party that was against Aristide's *Lavalas* party, men with machetes beat and raped her in the street, screaming political slogans. Another woman was beaten when she tried to vote for an opposition candidate in local elections.

"I would prefer for them to get me a coffin than to send me back there," she said.

By 2003, many of Aristide's promises to reduce poverty, feed the hungry, and provide jobs had not taken place. The country remained filled with poverty, starvation, unemployment, and lawlessness. In late 2003, anti-Aristide demonstrations began in Haiti's major cities. Soon after, old enemies, including a former police chief and former military leader, staged uprisings in the north that spread throughout the country. In the end of February, 2004, at the urging of the United States, Aristide left Haiti. Several of Immokalee's Haitians told me that Haiti was actually better off under Francois Duvalier—Papa Doc. At least there was some sense of order then.

Still, all the Haitians I interviewed seemed to love their home country, though none of them had any plans to return there to live. Nicolas said the Haitians are like the Cubans.

"It is their desire to return to their homeland," he told me. "But because of the problems over there—political problems, economic problems—they feel they cannot go. They know it is important for them to remain in the United States while they wait patiently until the problems over there are resolved. Everybody would like to go and invest and do business in Haiti, but they are afraid, because there is no security, no nothing. I went to see my mother, and the violence is terrible there. I cannot understand where it's coming from. The world is upside down and there is no progress for this world right now."

Nicolas said many of the Haitian people have no respect for human life. The Diaspora—Haitians who have left their country and live in the United States—send money that helps many people in Haiti survive. Nicolas said this generosity and perceived success actually makes it dangerous for them to visit their homeland. The Haitian Diaspora is a particular target for criminals.

"A lot of the Haitians have more respect for foreigners and white people than for those of us who left," he told me. "They think we pick up money from the floor here in the U.S. They think money grows here, like leaves on the trees. If we go to Haiti and take a taxi, we don't really know where they'll take us. They might just take whatever we have and then kill us."

Some people believe that there is no hope left for Haiti, but this makes no sense to me, based on my impressions of the Haitians I know in Immokalee. They are kind and loving people.

It remains to be seen if Haiti will ever be a safe country again where people can live, work, and raise their families without fear. Somehow someone must also find a way to restore the land and make the trees grow back so that Haiti will become a tropical island again, the way Natalie remembered it.

"It was very beautiful. We used to bathe and wash clothes in the river. If we were hungry, we would just take a mango from a tree. You could take a whole bucket of mangos and go to the ocean."

If only the qualities we see in Natalie, Nicolas, Father Woady, Joseph, Celine, Michelle, and other Haitians in Immokalee would somehow transfer to Haiti's rulers, the violence there might end. But until then, more Haitians come to us. They just want to work and to live in peace, *Si Dye vle.*

5

The Guatemalans

> *"He told us about a place in the United States where the indigenous Indians were free, and not persecuted. He said that in this place, there was even a town named in the Indians' language, and that it meant 'my home.' The name of the place was Immokalee."*
>
> —Pedro Lopez and Andres Mateo

Andres Mateo stayed in San Miguel Acatan longer than many of the others. He said the situation was tense, but bearable, and he did not want to leave his mother. She had lived there all her life, and despite what was happening, she refused to leave her home. It was 1980.

"It was a problem between the army of the government and the Guerilla Army of the Poor," explained Andres. "There was a lot of fighting between the guerillas and the government troops in our town, San Miguel. People were killed. Some of the houses were burned, and a lot of people left, becoming refugees."

The time came, however, when Andres and Maria had to leave. Not long after he started his first teaching job, guerillas came to their home and threatened to kill Andres if he did not quit teaching and join them in their fight against the government. The guerillas felt that teachers were legitimizing the oppressive government system. When Andres refused to stop teaching, the guerillas burned their house. The couple ran to the home of some friends, and that night they left for the United States. They took nothing with them, because they had nothing left.

They worked their way north through Mexico, then headed for Tijuana. Andres had a brother in California who could help them. They crossed the border by walking through the desert, paying the *coyote* $300 in advance plus $300 on arrival for the two of them. Andres' brother paid the money that was due on the U.S. side and Andres promised to repay him later, but Andres had a hard time making money in California. The only work they could get paid very little. He called his nephew, who had already made his way to Devil's Garden—the remote, rural area about thirty miles from Immokalee—and the nephew said there was work, so in December 1981, Andres and Maria came to Southwest Florida.

"My nephew paid for a ticket for me and my wife," he told me. "A supervisor at the place he was working for came to Miami to pick us up. I got a job easily, because there was a lot of work. I went to work the very next day. We had a tiny little house in Devil's Garden, with three other families."

Andres said the work there was difficult and the hours were long.

"We worked seven days a week. If you didn't work seven days, they would cut you. We were cutting flowers—gladiolas—at Zipper Farms out there. The big boss man lived in Ft. Myers. He had his own big plane because he had farms in Colombia. He was a good boss, but the supervisor who lived here made us work eight to ten hours a day, every day, even if it was raining. Just keep working."

He said it was bad, but not as bad as Guatemala. "We made $3.25 an hour in Devil's Garden. In Guatemala we made $.25 a day."

Not long after Andres left San Miguel Acatan, guerillas seized the town for six months, and out of fear the townspeople agreed to hang a guerilla flag. Soon after, the Guatemalan Army "liberated" the town and literally chopped people up with machetes. They murdered over fifteen percent of the people who lived there: about twelve hundred people. Many others fled north over the border to Mexico.

Then Brig. General Efrain Rios Montt, head of Guatemala's Army, began one of the most terrifying parts of the war against the rebels: the army's counterinsurgency offensive known as the "scorched earth policy." Guatemalans call it *la escoba* (the broom) because of the way terror swept over the country. *La escoba* targeted the northwest highlands, particularly the Departments of El Quiche and Huehuetenango, the original home of most of Immokalee's Guatemalans.

Rios Montt and the other military commanders did not know who the rebels were, but they did know generally where they operated, so they decided to destroy those areas. They burned large parts of the northwest highlands so the rebels could no longer hide and organize there. The environmental damage and ecological effects alone were devastating, but the killing was worse. Government soldiers pulled women and small children from their homes, burned the houses, and then threw the people back into them. They shot some and hacked others to death with machetes, even small children who were screaming for their mothers. Many of them fled and made their way to the United States.

When the Guatemalans first came to the Immokalee area in the early 1980s, they lived out in Devil's Garden. They liked the isolation, especially before they got their papers. Later, in the mid-1980s, the Guatemalans got legal help and were able to file asylum claims because of the war in their home country, and they moved into Immokalee. Today they make up between five and ten percent of Immokalee's population.

I talked to seven Guatemalans, four of whom are from the same town in Guatemala, San Miguel Acatan. There are many Guatemalans in Immokalee who come from that town. First I met Pedro Lopez at a meeting of an inter-faith movement to support the Coalition of Immokalee Workers, an advocacy group for farmworkers. I was at that meeting to gather information for my research. I talked to Pedro afterwards and arranged to meet him the following Sunday for an interview at Our Lady of Guadalupe Church, at 11:00. We were having our monthly breakfast for the people who come to the English Mass, and I would meet him when it was over.

Pedro brought his friend, Andres Mateo, whose story we just heard, with him. I was not confident enough at that time to do the entire interview in Spanish, so I asked a young volunteer named Brian Payne to help me translate. Brian was very fluent and was a great help. The last time I saw him, he was working with the Coalition of Immokalee Workers.

The first thing I did was to thank Pedro and Andres for taking the time to talk to me. They said they thought it was the reverse, and that *they* should thank *me*.

"We think it is important that you write this history," they told me. "It is important that our children and grandchildren know what we went through to get here, and how we fought for our rights. This book will tell them our stories; the stories of immigrants. When it is written, we will look forward to having it to show to our children."

This statement, from two people I had just met, really moved me. It is one of the reasons I started writing this book. It is why I kept on writing it when I would rather have been playing tennis or riding my motorcycle or playing the piano or even working—because Pedro and Andres wanted to have this book to show to their children.

I had saved some food for them from our after-Mass breakfast: a few donuts and some eggs, sausage, rice, and tacos. They didn't touch it, and I was embarrassed to have given them food that was almost cold. I should have invited them to come earlier, when the food was still hot, but when the interview was over, I realized I was mistaken. They carefully wrapped the cold food, thanked me for it, and said they would take it home to their children.

Pedro and Andres both came from San Miguel Acatan in the remote northwest highlands of Guatemala, a good-sized town of about eight thousand people. Andres said it was very beautiful, located in the mountains, surrounded by forests of pine trees, and a river ran through the middle of the town.

Andres and Pedro were both about fifty years old when I talked with them. When they were growing up in San Miguel Acatan, both their fathers grew corn, beans, and sugar. Pedro's father also worked a machine that made women's blouses. Their mothers cooked, cleaned, took care of their home and the younger children, and helped with the family's *milpas* (small plots of corn). Pedro and Andres both worked in local cornfields from the time they were six years old. They went to school in the morning and worked in the afternoon, earning the equivalent of $.25 per day. The school was run by Catholic nuns who taught the children Spanish, but they spoke their Mayan language, Kanjobal, at home.

They also worked three days a week at *Cooperativo Mikel*. It means the "Michael Cooperative." The word "cooperative" refers to the fact that the people in San Miguel Acatan were part owners of this store. The Mayas shared in the labor and also shared in the profits.

"It was a store where they sold groceries, like milk, sugar, and soap," explained Pedro. "What you use in a week. They also sold animals there, like ducks, for cooking. And clothes."

A "rich American" who came to San Miguel Acatan in the early 1970s started the *Cooperativo*. They did not remember his name.

"This man saw the poverty and that we were just living off beans and rice, so he helped us start the *Cooperativo.*"

This cooperative turned out to be a very interesting thing for me, because I learned about it from two completely different sources. First, I heard it from the perspective of Pedro and Andres, who lived it. Later, I came across information about cooperatives in secondary research I was doing for my Master's thesis. They were one of several different movements to help Guatemala's indigenous people in the 1970s. The Guatemalan government chose to help the Mayas by developing these cooperatives rather than implement land reforms, because land reforms would cause problems with Guatemala's big growers. So cooperatives were started in towns all over Guatemala's highland areas, facilitated by an organized group of volunteers.

The effort was supported by the U.S. Agency for International Development and the Guatemalan government.

I found it interesting that Pedro and Andres thought a "rich American" started the cooperative and I mentioned that to Sister Maureen. She said that the people in San Miguel Acatan, like most of the highland villages, were so poor that they would have thought anyone was rich who had the money to come to them from another country.

Through the experience of the cooperative, Pedro and Andres developed a new kind of knowledge. They said it helped them see beyond the struggles of their day-to-day lives—struggles that had never changed until the *Cooperativo*.

"It woke up the village," said Pedro. "We all became more conscious of the environment around us."

Working there opened other doors for the Guatemalans in addition to the profit sharing.

"It gave a chance for new jobs and a chance to export products from the area," Pedro continued. "New jobs, new money for the people." Many years later, the experience helped Pedro and Andres found the Coalition of Immokalee Workers.

The man who showed them how to start the cooperative had one additional influence on the Guatemalans when he made this suggestion to them: "Why don't you come to America, to a better life?" He told them about a place in the United States where the indigenous people were free and not persecuted. He said that in this place there was even a town named in the Indian language that meant "my home." The name of the place was Immokalee.

Guatemala is divided into twenty-two departments, much like our states, and most of Immokalee's Guatemalans come from the three largest Departments in the northwest highlands: Huehuetenango, San Marcos, and Quezaltenango. San Miguel Acatan, the hometown of Pedro and Andres, is in the department of Huehuetenango. (That's pronounced "Way-way-ten-EN-go." It has a nickname, "Huehue," pronounced "Way-Way"). San Miguel Acatan is about an eight-hour bus ride up mountain roads north of the city of Huehuetenango. The town is named after Saint Michael. Every year in September the Guatemalans in Immokalee celebrate a special Mass on the feast day of Saint Michael. I had always assumed that was because Saint Michael was a popular saint with all Guatemalan people, but I later learned that each small Mayan village in Guatemala celebrates the feast day of the saint the town was named after. For example, a town called San Pedro would celebrate the feast of Saint Peter, and San Miguel Acatan celebrated the feast of Saint Michael.

Guatemala is smaller than the state of Tennessee and over ten million people live there. (Tennessee has about half that many.) Life expectancy in Guatemala is 64.8 years and the infant mortality rate is 45.79 out of 1,000—more than four babies out of every hundred that are born. Guatemala's infant mortality rate is not as high as in Haiti, where it is almost ten percent, but it is almost twice that of Mexico.

One of the things that makes Guatemala unique among Central American countries is that more than half of its people are indigenous. I have read that they do not like to be called "Indian," because the term has negative connotations in their country, so they describe themselves as members of their language group, or more generally as "Maya." There are twenty-three indigenous ethnic groups in Guatemala. The names of their groups are also the names of their languages. People from at least four of these groups live in Immokalee: Kanjobal (also spelled Quanhobal or Konhobal), Quiche, Mam, and Chuj. When they came to the United States, the Mayas chose places where there were people from their own groups. It was part of the networking that helped most immigrants when they first arrived.

Pedro and Andres are Kanjobal Mayas. So is Jose, whom you might remember from Chapter Three, who eloped with the young Mexican girl Enriquetta. The only other place in Florida besides Immokalee that I know of with such a concentration of Kanjobal people is Indiantown, an inland town in Martin County, near Stuart on the East Coast. As I began to research the Kanjobal people for my Master's Thesis, I learned that not much was known about them. I learned an interesting cultural thing from Jose and Enriquetta; behind their homes, all the Guatemalans from San Miguel Acatan had homemade saunas where they heated rocks and sat and steamed after their hard days at work.

The Maya were once a great civilization, similar to the Aztecs in some ways, but usually thought of as more peaceful. They lived mainly in two places: the Yucatan peninsula in southern Mexico, and in the highland areas of Guatemala, where San Miguel Acatan is located.

Mayan science was highly advanced and included detailed astronomical observations and advanced mathematics. They built complex religious ceremonies and celebration areas. Chichen Itza, still standing in the central Yucatan, was one of the Mayas' greatest religious pyramids. They were excellent navigators and did extensive trading in sea-going canoes. The Mayan civilization reached its peak in the early eighth century and lasted five hundred years. In the thirteenth century, it seems to have been destroyed, and by the time the Spanish arrived, all that remained was scattered tribes. Scholars disagree about what caused the collapse of classic Mayan civilization. One theory says their cities grew too quickly and the city people relied too much on the rural poor to support them, but the cause of their demise is not really known.

In 1524, five years after entering Mexico, Hernan Cortes set out to conquer what was left of the Mayan tribes in Guatemala. He sent Pedro de Alvarado, one of his most brutal officers, to conquer and subjugate what would later be called Central America. Alvarado started the persecution against the Mayas that they would suffer for the rest of their history. At first the Spanish wanted gold. When the gold was gone, they moved on to crops, moving the Mayas off their lands and forcing them to work on large farms.

The Spanish introduced coffee into Guatemala in the 1700s, and it grew well in the volcanic slopes of the northwest highlands, but the Spaniards confiscated so many communal Indian lands for coffee production that the Mayas could no longer survive on their own. Forced labor programs were established, as in Mexico and in other countries of Latin America. Tobacco, sugar cane, henequen (rope fiber), and bananas all were related to the enslavement of the indigenous peoples.

Guatemala gained its independence from Spain in 1821, but as in Mexico, the indigenous peoples continued to be abused and exploited. There were three classes of people in Guatemala then: the upper class of pureblooded Spaniards who had decided to stay in the New World; *Ladinos*, a mixture of Spanish and Indian; and the Mayas, at the bottom of the social structure.

Descendents of the Mayas made up more than half the population, which, as mentioned earlier, was unique to Guatemala. Most of these indigenous people have retained their original language and customs, but the related isolation and lack of education have inhibited their opportunities and their freedom. They just wanted to live the way they had always lived, working on their land. Many of the *Ladinos,* on the other hand, became more and more educated in Spanish ways, and as they did, they moved up the social and economic scale. But there are also *Ladino* poor.

Whether Maya or *Ladino*, most of the Guatemalans I talked to in Immokalee went to school for only six years, and they worked when they weren't studying. Everyone worked. At age thirteen, they all left school and started working full time. The educational situation of the Mayas in Guatemala is the same today because children are still needed to work in the fields to help support their families. Two Guatemalan women I interviewed, Ana and Rosalinda, grew up, much more recently than Pedro and Andres, yet Ana went to school for only six years and Rosalinda had no education at all.

Throughout Guatemala's history, almost up until the present day, its rulers were dictators, and very few of them cared about the Mayas. The negative attitude generally held toward the Mayas made them easy targets, and their labor and their land were constantly taken from them.

It was not until the twentieth century that the indigenous peoples began to gain any rights at all, and efforts to change were actually made not by the Mayas, but by poor *Ladinos*. Many felt that the Mayas were not capable of rebellion, that they were too ignorant to even fight for their own freedom, as they stayed in their mountain villages, trying to survive.

Shortly before World War II, United States' businesses increased their investments in Guatemala. The United Fruit Company was one of the most notorious, with its huge banana plantations. Because it was U.S. policy to help governments that supported our big business, we supported Guatemala's government with military assistance. The more I studied, the more I understood why my father only spoke German when he went to Latin America.

In 1944, Captain Jacobo Arbenz Guzman took part in a coup that took over the government of Guatemala. He was on the side of the working class and was even sympathetic to the plight of the Mayas. Later, in 1950, he was elected president and took power in 1951. While he was in office, the Guatemalan Labor Party gained legal status and some progress was made for the working people. Land was given to a half million people—*Ladinos* not Mayas—but some of that progress filtered down to the Mayas in the form of more available jobs.

There were two problems with Arbenz's recognition of the Guatemalan Labor Party: its affiliation with the Communists, and the timing, as this was all taking place during the Cold War when Communism and the USSR represented a huge threat to the United States. When I was a little girl, my father stocked a pantry in our cellar, our "bomb shelter" where we could go if the Russians dropped a bomb. He never really took the threat seriously, but he did stock the pantry, just in case. In our grammar school, we had air raid drills where we would go into the auditorium and kneel down, with our hands covering the backs of our necks. I suppose this was to protect our necks from breaking when the school was bombed and the building collapsed on top of us. I never really thought about it; we just did it.

It was around this time that the Arbenz government and the Guatemalan Labor Party recognized the Communist Party of Guatemala. These political groups were the first to ever really care about the poorest people, including the Mayas, but they represented a threat to the United States. So, while I was in New Jersey practicing how to save my life from a Communist bomb, Arbenz gained the nickname "The Red Jacob."

Arbenz's association with the Communists was the main rationale given by the United States for moving against him, but the real reason was the political power of the United Fruit Company. Arbenz was planning to take over all foreign-owned companies, including the United Fruit Company's huge banana plantations, and have Guatemalans run them. This nationalization was the same thing Castro did a few years later when he took over Cuba, but Castro won his war and Arbenz lost. Colonel Castillo Armas overthrew Arbenz in 1954 in a coup orchestrated by the Central Intelligence Agency (CIA). When the coup was over, Armas took power.

One of his first moves was to increase agricultural exports, good for the upper classes and for the government's relations with the U.S., but the Mayas were not a part of the new economy. Armas' actions resulted in even more land being taken from the indigenous peoples and they had trouble growing enough food to survive. Many were forced to work to pay off debts that were incurred by their parents, while others were trapped in their own debt. The interest payments on both kinds of debt were very high, so the Mayas labored for very little money on coffee and banana plantations far from their homes. Three years later Armas was assassinated and a new dictator took over, but still nothing changed for the indigenous people.

I talked to another man from San Miguel Acatan a few months after I met Pedro and Andres. His name was Andres Francisco but I will call him Francisco, or we will confuse him with Andres Mateo. Francisco was a few years younger than Andres and Pedro, but his life in San Miguel Acatan was not very different. He had three brothers and sisters and two of them had died. For two months out of every year during the school vacations, Francisco went with his father down to a large coffee *finca* (farm) and picked coffee beans. Many of the people in San Miguel Acatan traveled to work on the coffee *fincas*.

"We were very poor," he told me. "There was no money. We went to school from January to November, working in local cornfields when we were not in school. Every November, when school was out, I went with my father to pick and cut coffee to earn money. It took twenty-four hours to get to the coffee *finca*. We didn't have a car, so we took a bus. They had a big house—a long house with no rooms—for us to sleep in."

He drew a picture of this and I could see that he was describing barracks.

"A lot of people slept in there," he continued. "It was just men. We stayed there for two months every year."

While they were gone, Francisco's mother stayed in their home and took care of their animals and the three younger children. She also kept up the small *milpas* on land they sharecropped.

By the 1960s the Mayas had even more to think about than endless poverty and constant work, as big plantation owners supported by the military became more and more aggressive in taking their homes and their land. When the Mayas refused them, these owners would just come into a village and start measuring it for crop use. Then they would go into the houses, order all the people to get out, and do whatever they could to disrupt the ability of the people to live normally. Sometimes the plantation owners would throw out all their possessions: cooking utensils, grinding stones, clothing, what few precious keepsakes they had. They would take their food, and kill their animals. The Mayas would live in nearby fields for a while, but when they tried to go back to their homes the same thing would happen again as the growers and the army that supported them became even more violent.

Soon a war started between the government and the resistance groups who had decided to fight. Some of the Mayas finally joined the guerilla organizations and fought for the rights of the Mayan people. The Guatemalans in Immokalee did not want to talk much about this. I could tell they knew more than they told me, but I decided not to push it. There is still controversy in Guatemala about this war, and it is safer for people not to be quoted about it. They could still be in danger, especially if they were involved. The war is over now, but many of the people who worked to expose the truth about it have been threatened or killed. A report that exposed the thirty-six years of repression and genocide was released in Guatemala on April 24, 1998. Bishop Juan Gerardi, one of the main authors of the report, was beaten to death two days later.

Immokalee's Guatemalans told me some things about how the violence started. They said that not all the Mayas were involved. Most of them were just working to survive, caught in the middle between the government and the guerillas. That's what Pedro, Andres, and Jose were doing—passively living in poverty, caught in the middle. While the young boys were working in the fields, rebel forces were organizing not far from San Miguel Acatan.

By 1962, the Guatemalan government had established a military cabinet whose main purpose was to repress any groups that opposed the government. More leftist groups emerged to fight them. The one that included the Mayas was called the "Guerilla Army of the Poor."

The Guatemalan Army was in complete control and had a formal intelligence agency to gather information about dissenters. They were particularly worried about rural areas where the guerilla movements were strong, areas like the one around San Miguel Acatan. Religious leaders and others who supported the guerillas were assassinated. Meanwhile, the size of Guatemala's military doubled and the police were brought under the control of the military. Urban patrols and "Death Squads" became a regular part of the army.

From 1963 to 1978, the fighting escalated. Guerilla forces grew stronger, and so did the government troops. The military killed, imprisoned, and tortured rebels and their sympathizers, and the rebels fought back. The rebels also killed many of the Mayas, accusing them of working with the Government.

José, who later married the young Mexican girl Enriquetta, was orphaned because of the war. José's mother and two younger siblings had died when he was very young, from illnesses, but later, after the war started, José's father accidentally discovered a guerilla camp. These guerillas wanted him to join them in their struggle against the government, but he refused, so they killed him. That's how it was. If you weren't on the side of the guerillas, the guerillas would assume you were working with the government, and if you weren't working with the government, army troops would assume you were working with the guerillas.

His father was the only close family he had left, and José was devastated with grief. He did not wish to stay in San Miguel Acatan any longer, so at the age of sixteen he crossed over the Guatemalan border to Mexico. He worked in agriculture all over Mexico and in Baja California, following the crops. Eventually he ended up in Mexicali, a town not far from the U.S. border on the West Coast near Tijuana. There he found work at a ranch, where he met Enriquetta, the young Mexican girl who would later become his bride. I explained in the Mexican chapter how this young couple made their way across the Mexico/U.S. border, turning back nine times because of the border patrols but finally making it across safely. They went together to Los Angeles, where they both worked, sewing pants, shirts, and blouses.

That was in 1979, the same year Pedro Lopez first left San Miguel Acatan. Pedro had finally given up trying to pay the debt that never ended, so he went to the U.S. to make some money. Pedro worked his way through Mexico to the Mexico/U.S. border where he found a *coyote* that took him across for $250. He asked the *coyote* about the place the man who formed the cooperative had mentioned—the place called Immokalee. He took Pedro there for an additional $200.

When Pedro arrived in Immokalee, people there told him there was work out in Devil's Garden. It's very remote, they told him, a good place to go if you don't have papers. Pedro got a ride there and started working, planting gladiolas. He called home every week to talk to his wife and parents on the one telephone in San Miguel Acatan, and sent them money when he could.

The following year, José and Enriquetta decided to leave Los Angeles, because they were barely making ends meet, but they were not sure where to go. José called home to San Miguel Acatan to talk to his aunt, who told him that Pedro Lopez had found work near the town called Immokalee—the place with the name that meant "My Home"—so in 1981 José and Enriquetta bought a truck and went to Florida to join Pedro.

The camp where they all lived in Devil's Garden was a group of shacks next to a polluted canal in a remote orange grove. That's where Rob Williams and his wife Lynn introduced Sister Maureen to José and Enriquetta. The couple's first baby, Marta, had to stay in the hospital for weeks just after she was born, and Maureen thinks the baby was so sick because of the conditions out at that camp. Also, none of them were eating well because they had so little money.

"My first memory of José was his long reddish-black hair, that I think was that color because of poor nutrition," Maureen remembered. "Now his hair is so black. I called him Omar Sharif, whom he resembled."

Later Maureen took José and Enriquetta to get married in LaBelle, a town just north of Immokalee. It was important that they marry, because if José was successful in getting his legal residency through a political asylum application, Enriquetta would also qualify, as his wife. Enriquetta was seventeen years old by then, but the judge in LaBelle said she was still too young to be married without her parents' permission. Maureen couldn't really tell the judge that they had run away from Enriquetta's home and illegally crossed the border from Mexico, but luckily, she could explain that they already had a child, and that made their situation an exception by Florida law, so Enriquetta did not need her parents' permission after all, and José and Enriquetta were married. Maureen helped them celebrate.

"I took them back to my house in Immokalee and served my newest specialty…tostadas. Then it hit me. Enriquetta knew how to cook 'real' Mexican food. My paltry effort at tostadas must have seemed like peanut butter and jelly to them. Some wedding reception!"

In the meantime, as Pedro, José, and Enriquetta were settling into their new lives in Devil's Garden, the war in Guatemala escalated. Many people first learned about this war because of a book by a Maya woman named Rigoberta Menchu. In Spanish, the book is called *Yo, Rigoberta*. In English, the title is: *I, Rigoberta; An Indian Woman in Guatemala*. Rigoberta came from the Quiche' people in the northwest highlands, not far from Huehuetenengo. Her book was published in Spain in 1983 at the height of the worst repression and violence in Guatemala, when she was only twenty-three years old.

Later, in 1992, Rigoberta Menchu would be awarded the Nobel Peace Prize for bringing to the world the story of the persecution of Guatemala's indigenous people. Rigoberta told the story that the Guatemalans in Immokalee did not want to talk much about: the story of the power of the military government, and the things the military did. She described how the army kidnapped people, tortured and killed them, threw the bodies all together in some place near their homes, and then told the people in the village to go and get their relatives. Rigoberta's brother was tortured and killed when he was only sixteen years old.

Sister Maureen had been interested in the Mayas since high school, when a Maryknoll priest talked to her class about the poverty and the oppression they lived in. In 1983, she heard Rigoberta tell her story to a small group of clergy and nuns in Washington, D.C.

"When I was in law school, I went one day to a U.S. Catholic Mission group meeting," said Maureen. "Rigoberta Menchu was there, and she spoke to us of what she and her family had suffered. I remember Rigoberta as a soft-spoken woman, but she told us of such unbelievable atrocities! And yet I can't remember crying or seeing her cry. It was like a sacred moment. We were a small group of clergy and nuns and we did it in a prayerful setting, otherwise, I do not think I could have sat through such horror."

Then Maureen did a law-school project where she gathered documentation on the death squads and massacres and other abuses in Guatemala.

"I wanted to make a master exhibit for those filing for political asylum here in the U.S. so they could prove what was happening in their country."

Maureen said she considered going to work in Guatemala, but could not bring herself to do it.

"I knew I was too much of a coward," she admitted. "I knew that nuns had been killed in El Salvador and I was not ready to die. That was one of the reasons I found work in Immokalee so fulfilling. I could assist these immigrants who needed political asylum."

Part of the reason Rigoberta's story was so moving was that her father was one of the people who stood up to the government and organized the people. He was arrested and imprisoned, accused of "compromising the sovereignty of the state," but that did not stop him. He continued to organize and fight from inside the prison until he was released. In 1980 guerilla rebels took over the Spanish Embassy in

Guatemala City. In response, government security forces burned down the embassy, and dozens of protesters died; Rigoberta's father was one of them.

Whole Mayan villages that were even suspected of supporting guerillas were systematically wiped out. The innocent victims of this violence were just trying to work and live, like the people in San Miguel Acatan.

Pedro Lopez, who was living in Devil's Garden as the war got closer to his hometown, called home every week to talk to his wife. She was living with his parents, waiting for him to return. One week he called and learned that both his parents had died. I did not ask how they died, but I do not think it had anything to do with the war. Pedro flew back to Guatemala for the funeral. It was not hard for him to go home, he told me, even though he did not have papers. Nobody stops you from flying back to your home country. It's the return trip to the U.S. that is difficult.

After the funeral, Pedro stayed for a year in his hometown, but soon decided to leave again. Everyone in San Miguel Acatan was talking about the war now, because the army was getting closer. Pedro had been to the United States, so he knew life could be better.

"I realized I couldn't work in Guatemala anymore because of the fear of being killed by the army," he explained. "I knew that in the U.S. there was peace, and you could work without fear."

The problems were mild during that year he stayed in his home. At that time it was mainly curfews and suspicion.

"You would go to your work," he told me, "your normal seven-hour day, but when you came back home you had to stay inside your house. You weren't allowed to come back out. They were organizing in the area for better salaries and wages, and as a poor person, you would be accused of being a guerilla just for talking to them. If you brought food out of the house, anything more than your own lunch, you would be accused of bringing it to the guerillas. No matter what you did, as a poor person you were sucked into the war between the guerillas and the army."

Pedro thought it was obvious that he was not involved with the guerillas because he didn't have any weapons. He became more frustrated as he talked.

"But they kept accusing me."

I got some sense of what it must be like to live in fear like that on a business trip to Colombia in 1996. One of the big scanning companies in the United States, NCR, hired me to go there and work with two of their supermarket clients. First, I spent two days in Bogotá. Two of NCR's managers met me at the plane, and escorted me everywhere; they insisted that I not even leave the hotel without them. Whenever we walked out of a building, one of them stood on either side of me. They looked right and left, trying not to make it obvious that they did it, every time we stepped outside.

Then we went to Medellin, the home of one of the biggest drug cartels in Colombia. What a surprise that was! Medellin is one of the most beautiful places I have ever seen in my life. It sits in a valley between mountains, so we drove down a winding road on the side of the mountains until we got to the bottom. The hotels and restaurants were beautiful and the people were lovely, yet on every street corner there was a soldier dressed in fatigues and armed with an Uzi. I was only in Medellin for a day and a half, but while I was there one of the public buses was blown up and three people died. I read it in the newspaper in the morning, but no one in the meetings I attended even mentioned it. Life just went on, but there was always an underlying fear.

I imagine that San Miguel Acatan was like that as the worst part of the Guatemalan Civil War approached. Things seemed normal, as they did for me in Medellin, but the underlying fear was always there.

Pedro could tell it was getting worse in the Guatemalan highlands, so he decided to leave again. He walked several hours from San Miguel Acatan to a road where he could get a bus.

"I got on the bus and made it to the city of Huehuetenango on May 10, Mother's Day," he remembered. "I wasn't sure where to go or what to do. I was there alone, so I went to the border of Mexico and Guatemala. At that time you could buy a permit to be in Mexico for seventy-two hours. I told them I was going to visit a place called Comitan Los Flores. Of course, I didn't say I was going to the U.S.; I said was just going to visit this area."

Pedro and the other Guatemalans who came to Immokalee had to make two journeys. The first was from Guatemala through the entire length of Mexico, about fifteen hundred miles. They took buses and trains if they had the money, and if they didn't have money, they walked.

At the Guatemala/Mexico border, Pedro bought a ticket to Mexico City. He said it took all night and most of the next day to get there. No bus went north from Mexico City, so he had to take a train. Trains were the preferred way to travel, anyway, Pedro said, because Mexican Immigration doesn't check trains very often. He stopped and did fieldwork on the way, because he knew he would need money to get across the border.

Pedro said it was dangerous to be an immigrant passing through Mexico. You had to watch out for Mexican Immigration, he told me, and *banditos*, but his main fear was of the Mexican police. He said they would steal your money.

He finally reached the border town of Juarez and found a *coyote*. He paid $300 in advance, money he had saved while working his way through Mexico. He would owe another $300 when he got across the border.

"You have to give an address of where you're going in the U.S. and the telephone number, so if you don't pay the money they know where to find you." Pedro gave the number of Zipper Farms in Devil's Garden.

He crossed through the desert and then through a river to New Mexico. This was a different place from where he had crossed a few years earlier. Unknown to Pedro, there were several channels in this river, and he couldn't tell that the water was deep. He hadn't expected to have to swim; he didn't know how to swim. Pedro was the last of twenty people in the group.

"It was a full moon," he said. "It reflected off the water and it was just white, so I couldn't see where I was going. They didn't even tell me there was water there. I couldn't tell if it was deep or just a little water. I went in, because I was following them, but I started to drown! One really tall guy named Pasqual was crossing with us, and he came back and saved me. If it weren't for this guy I would have drowned."

Pedro went back to Zipper Farms out in Devil's Garden and started working there again, planting and cutting gladiolas. He liked the isolation and the fact that there were other Kanjobals there.

I have been told by many social workers in Immokalee that the Guatemalans generally feel more isolated than Mexicans or Haitians, and part of the problem is the language. If they speak Kanjobal or one of the other Mayan languages, they not only want to live and work with other Guatemalans, but they want to find other Guatemalans who speak Kanjobal.

The Guatemalans who lived in Devil's Garden came in to Immokalee for church and to buy groceries. Our Lady of Guadalupe Church sent a bus for them. The pastor at that time in 1981 was Father Richard Sanders. Father Sanders was particularly moved by the situation of the immigrants, and he helped start many of the services that still exist in Immokalee today. The Guatemalans loved him very much. Andres and Pedro both talked about him as if he were a saint. I think the fact that they had all been treated so badly during their lives made them appreciate him even more.

"Father Sanders did almost a miracle for us," they told me. "He would come and get us out in Devil's Garden, a group of ten to fifteen of us. Every Saturday night he would bring us to church in Immokalee in a van. Soon there was a whole bus. The bus also took us to the supermarket! He did so much for us. We didn't have any papers, but it didn't matter to Father Sanders. He still came out and helped us."

Pedro, Andres, José, and Francisco all left Guatemala before the worst part of the war. In 1982 army troops staged another coup. Brig. General Rios Montt formed a three-member governing *junta* that included the head of the President's Special Guard and the Minister of Defense. They quickly annulled the constitution, eliminated political parties, and canceled elections. Rios Montt assumed the title of President of the Republic.

To fight the government, four guerilla groups combined forces and formed the Guatemala National Revolutionary Unity (URNG). The government massacred whole villages of Mayas who were suspected of supporting URNG. *La Escoba* ("the broom") had begun.

Many of Immokalee's Guatemalans lived through horrors during these conflicts and Maureen processed many of their asylum claims. She told me a few stories about them. For example, when one young Immokalee immigrant went home to visit his family, the army was in their village, accusing the people of supporting guerilla activity.

"They had come to punish all young men of a certain age," explained Maureen, "because they assumed they were working with the guerillas. They knew that this particular young man had been in the United States because he was wearing American clothes and he had some money in his pocket. So they didn't kill him, but they made him dig the graves of his friends."

Hundreds of thousands of Mayan men, women, and children fled across Guatemala's northern border to Mexico. But even leaving the country did not guarantee their safety. Maureen said the Guatemalan military followed some of them to refugee camps in Mexico and executed them there.

Francisco was in those camps for a brief time. He said the camps were much worse than the barracks he and his father stayed in when they left home to pick coffee every year. Francisco did not know Pedro, Andres, and José in Guatemala, but their experiences were similar. Francisco left San Miguel Acatan in 1979 and headed for the U.S. to make some money. He was in Arizona doing fieldwork when other Guatemalans said the war was getting closer to his home. Francisco hurried back to San Miguel Acatan to get his girlfriend, Inez.

"I went back in 1981, but my girlfriend had gone to Mexico with her mother," he told me, "so I went to get her. They were in a refugee camp not far over the border. We stayed in the camp for two to three weeks, and then went to live in Comitan Los Flores in Chiapas. We knew that because of the war, we could not go home again. We were in Mexico for one year and my daughter was born there."

Not long after they went there, the Mexican government clamped down on Guatemalan refugees; there were just too many of them. Eventually, all Guatemalans who crossed the Mexican border were placed in refugee camps and detained there. But Francisco and Inez were there earlier in the war, so they were permitted to leave.

Francisco talked to his brother-in-law in Canada and borrowed money so Francisco and his wife and baby could come to the United States. Francisco said it was a very long trip. Their daughter Gloria was a tiny baby then.

"We headed to Los Angeles, because it was the easiest place to cross," he explained. "We found a *coyote* in Tijuana."

It took about eight hours to walk through the desert around Tijuana. There were ten or eleven people—men and women. The cost was $250 per person for Francisco and his wife. The *coyote* didn't charge for the baby, because they carried her. They tried working in Los Angeles for a while, but did not do very well, so Francisco bought a used truck and he, Inez, and the baby took off for Florida because they heard there was work there. On the way, he met some Guatemalan fieldworkers who told him they could get him work in Delray Beach, Florida. It turned out there was work, but there were also bad conditions: pesticides used in the fields that could hurt the baby. Remember, back then parents took their babies to the fields and laid them on blankets between the rows while the mother and father worked. A paralegal named Jeronimo Compeseco went to that camp and then went back to Immokalee and told Maureen about them.

"Sister Maureen came for us in Delray Beach with a truck," remembered Francisco. "She brought us to Immokalee. It was 1985. She said there was a place to rent where we could live, and there was work."

Maureen said she suggested that they come to Immokalee, because it was one way she could assure competent help in their asylum claim.

"My office would help them," she said. "I was also very concerned about the pesticides and herbicides. Immokalee seemed like a better choice to raise a family, because they would not be so remote and cut-off. I remember taking them to the ocean. They were right there on the East Coast of Florida and had never gone there!"

Maureen also knew that Francisco and Inez would probably be happier living in a place where there were other Kanjobal Mayas from their hometown of San Miguel Acatan. They went directly to Immokalee, not Devil's Garden, however, because the other Kanjobals we had met—Pedro, Andres, and José—all had their papers by now and had moved into Immokalee. Attorney Rob Williams, with Florida Rural Legal Services, had helped them get their papers. He filed political asylum applications and obtained employment authorization for many Guatemalans, including Pedro, Andres, and José. They petitioned for asylum on the grounds that going home would endanger their lives. Pedro and Andres told their stories into a cassette tape recorder about the war between the government and the guerillas and of how they got caught in the middle and could not live in peace. Rob

Williams even flew to Guatemala and went to San Miguel Acatan to get evidence of this war to help prove their stories.

"He took pictures of the burned-down buildings and other things," Pedro told me, "then he took our stories to Miami, and that's how we got our paperwork. A judge in Miami approved it."

In 1983, after the Guatemalans we had met so far were safe in the United States, the Guatemalan military finally realized how far they had gone in their criminal behavior. Rios Montt was deposed by his own Minister of Defense, General Mejia Victores, who took over temporarily and then turned a limited degree of power over to civilians. One of the things that prompted this move was that Guatemala's economy was suffering from declining tourism because of the war.

The Guatemalan presidents who followed Rios Montt brought about the Central American Peace Accord of 1987, but human rights abuses continued, and in reality, the war was far from over. There was evidence of this in a letter written by John Witchger in 1988, when he was the director of Guadalupe Social Services in Immokalee. In it, he talked about a young man who had left Guatemala in 1987 and made his way to Immokalee.

"Tomás, twenty-two, told us that the guerillas would throw bombs into their village forcing everyone to leave. These revolutionaries would then pillage their homes. Other times the guerillas would come in a truck and visit every home threatening to kill if the townspeople didn't give them rice, flour, sugar, and supplies for their mountain existence."

Then the government forced Tomás to serve a mandatory twelve hours per week of military patrol to protect his village from the guerillas. Government troops supplied him with a gun and he and others like him had to make a daily patrol. He said it was "kill or be killed."

The situation got so bad that in 1990 the U.S. cut off most of its military aid and stopped selling arms to Guatemala. The CIA, however, unknown to the public, continued to fund the Guatemalan army and CIA agents worked to suppress reports of the army's human rights abuses. President Bill Clinton later acknowledged the U.S. role in the conflict and admitted it was wrong.

When Rigoberta Menchu won the Nobel Peace Prize in 1992, the whole world was exposed to the ongoing struggle for human rights in Guatemala. Despite the international attention, the military still controlled Guatemala, and even then, thirty-two years later, guerillas continued to fight against them. It was not until 1996 that a peace accord was finally signed. The guerillas and the government agreed to work on the problems together, but the government still refused to accept responsibility for many of the massacres. The fighting stopped, but it left thousands and thousands of orphaned children, and the poverty was even worse than before.

I talked to two Guatemalan women, Rosalinda and Ana, who did not personally experience the war at all. They were younger than the people I just told you about, and they came from different towns, but they were both raised in abject poverty. I met them in separate interviews. They did not know each other.

I met Rosalinda through Lucy Ortiz, the *Tejana* who married the Puerto Rican baseball player and became a migrant worker. After they settled in Immokalee, Lucy went back to school and eventually got her Social Worker's degree and license, and began working as the Immokalee outreach advocate for the Shelter for Abused Women. Lucy knew Rosalinda because she used to come to support meetings for battered women. I met her at Lucy's office, and Lucy helped me translate.

Rosalinda was born thirteen years after Pedro and Andres, in 1963. She was from a small town called Malacatan in the Department of San Marco. She was not Mayan, but the story of her life growing up was the same as that of the Mayas. Her father was a coffee picker and her mother worked at their home, growing food to feed their family. Rosalinda was the second youngest of eight children.

The main difference between Rosalinda and the other Guatemalans I talked to was that she had no education at all. At least the others went to school for six years. When I met Rosalinda, she was thirty-eight years old. She could sign her name but could not read or write in any language. Her father did not think it was important for women to go to school because he could not see any future for them beyond working in the fields. Besides, their family needed the money she could earn.

As soon as she could walk, Rosalinda helped her mother work in the family's small garden plot and take care of their few animals. Then, when she was ten years old, she got a job picking coffee and spreading fertilizer on a coffee farm. The farmer sent a truck to take them to work. The farm was an hour and a half away. She made fifty-two cents a day.

Rosalinda knew some of the stories about the guerillas and the army. Her mother tried to keep it from her, but she could not hide her own fear. Rosalinda and her mother were very close, and she said she always knew when her mother was afraid. She wished she could take away her fears, but Rosalinda was only a girl; all she could do was be as good as possible. At the end of a day picking coffee, she helped her mother with the chores of the household. All she ever did was work and then sleep. It was the same every day of the week.

Rosalinda kept working through her teen-age years and her twenties. After a while, the stories of the war between the guerillas and the government army quieted down. She knew it was still bad in other parts of Guatemala, because one of the families that lived near them had a television, but in her town, things were normal. Normal poverty, that is. Rosalinda is very pretty and I asked her why she did not marry. She said there were a couple of men in her village who wanted to marry her, but she didn't want to spend the rest of her life working on a coffee plantation. She hated everything about her life at home, except her mother.

One of her brothers went to the United States and lived in Los Angeles. He would call sometimes and tell her there was work in the United States. He said people could get an education and get a better life, so Rosalinda decided to go to the U.S. by herself. She was in her mid-twenties—old enough to do what she wanted now—but when she told her mother her plan, her mother pleaded with her to stay.

"If you go, you will suffer," she told her daughter. "I know you will. Besides, how will I get in touch with you if I'm sick? You won't even know if I'm sick. Maybe I will die and you won't see me before I am dead."

My sense is that Rosalinda was the only light in her mother's life. Rosalinda said nothing about her father, except that he would not let her go to school, and she said very little about her brothers and sisters. After I got home and transcribed the interview from beginning to end, I realized her father must have died somewhere in her story, but she never mentioned it; she talked only about her mother. She was torn between making a better life for herself and staying at home to keep her mother happy.

Finally, Rosalinda decided she would set off alone to make the long journey to the United States. Her mother was devastated, but Rosalinda promised she would come back as soon as she had some money. I do not know if Rosalinda really believed she would go back; I don't know if either of them believed it. She kissed her mother good-bye and left.

She did not need a passport or anything else to get across the Guatemala/Mexico border, because people in the border towns were allowed to go back and forth to work. She took a bus to southern Mexico and, while she waited for the next bus that went further north, she went into a restaurant. They needed a waitress. She knew she would need money to get across the Mexico/U.S. border, so she decided to stay there and work for a while. The couple who owned the restaurant were very nice, and they let her live with them while she worked there. A Mexican man named Pablo worked at the restaurant, too, as a cook. She told Pablo she was saving money to go to the U.S. and he told her she was crazy.

"Why are you going over there?" he asked, disgustedly. "Don't go there! All the women who go the United States become prostitutes. You're a beautiful woman. You shouldn't go."

She liked this man, and she thought that maybe he was right, so she stayed there in Chiapas, working in the restaurant. Soon Rosalinda and Pablo fell in love, and a year later Rosalinda gave birth to their first child. She was thirty-one at that time, and in the following two years, two more children were born. Because she was still close to the border, Rosalinda went home often to visit her mother.

Not long after the third child was born, the restaurant where Pablo and Rosalinda worked went out of business. Political problems were beginning in southern Mexico and the couple couldn't find any other work. She already knew that there were no options in Guatemala besides the coffee *fincas,* so they made a decision: Pablo would go north to the U.S. to earn some money and Rosalinda would take their children south to live with her family in Guatemala and wait for him. Her mother, of course, was very, very happy to have her back at home. A few weeks later, Rosalinda received a letter from Pablo that said he had found work in a place called Immokalee, in the state of Florida. He said he would save money and come for her as soon as he could.

When Rosalinda was living in Mexico, her mother had started having heart problems. She had lost some weight and was very weak, but she seemed to get better every day with Rosalinda back at home, and Rosalinda was glad to be home with her mother. She told me over and over how much she loved her mother, but she was torn because there was a problem with the children's education. Rosalinda again got very agitated, explaining this to me. She started talking louder, using her hands expressively in a very frustrated way, as if she were explaining something and couldn't get it through to me. As if she were saying, "Why don't you understand?" I don't think I was the one she was frustrated with. I think she was still trying to explain it to her mother.

"They wouldn't let my children go to school in Guatemala because they were Mexicans," she said, becoming more emotional as she talked, "and I couldn't be in Mexico because I didn't have a place to live. Education for my children was very important to me. If you don't go to school, you have to go to work; it doesn't matter how young you are. I couldn't stand the thought of my children growing up like I did."

She had picked coffee all her life and never gone to school herself, and she had a terrible fear that her children would spend their lives picking coffee. She wanted them to have a future.

In 1995 Pablo returned to Guatemala from the U.S. with $3,500, enough to bring Rosalinda and their three children to the United States. They could cross through the desert in Arizona for $700 each, not including the baby. There would be no charge for the baby, because they could carry him. Rosalinda was ready, but her mother protested again, using the same arguments she used the first time.

"You can't go," she pleaded. "What will happen to me? What will happen if I'm sick again? How will I find you? I'll be sick and you won't even know it! I'll die and you'll never see me again."

There were other brothers and sisters, all older now, so it was not really necessary for her to stay. The mother's reaction must have come simply from the fact that she loved her daughter so much. Rosalinda gave in to her and delayed the trip to the United States. She didn't know how long her mother would live, but she figured she and the children could stay in Guatemala until she died.

As they waited, Pablo spent the money he had brought from the U.S. It was more money than most of the people in Malacatan had ever seen. He bought a few things for the family, like a television set, but mostly she said he was just showing off with this money and living like a big man. She said living in the United States had changed him. Even though he said he still loved her, it didn't show as much.

It was not long before most of the money was gone. Pablo finally started working, picking coffee, but he couldn't make much money doing that. Rosalinda worked at home, growing food and raising the animals so she could feed her children. The children helped her the way she had helped her mother, and the more she watched them, the more determined she became that they would have a better life than this.

After two years, her mother's heart condition worsened and she died. Then Rosalinda was ready.

"When my mother was alive, I lived for her," Rosalinda told me. "That's why I didn't push to leave as soon as Pablo came back with the money. But when she died, I decided nothing was going to stop me."

But now there was no money. Pablo had spent it all.

So Rosalinda told Pablo he could stay wherever he wanted to stay, but she was going to the U.S. with the children: she would go to Los Angeles and her brother would help her, but Pablo talked her out of that idea. He said the border crossing was very dangerous, that it would be dangerous for the children if there wasn't a man with them. The argument made sense. The trip through Mexico was long and difficult, and the border crossing was dangerous; it would be safer if they had a man with them. Finally, she agreed that they would all go together.

By mortgaging some land she had inherited from her mother, and borrowing money from two other people, Rosalinda managed to get $2,000, but could not get more. Two thousand was only enough for two people: enough for buses and trains through Mexico, for a *coyote* to take two people across the Mexico/U.S. border, and for transportation to Los Angeles to the home of her brother. I mentioned that they could bring the baby for free because they could carry him, but the other two children, now aged five and seven, were too big to carry. An additional $1,400 would be needed to bring them, and there was no way either Rosalinda or Pablo could get any more money. If they stayed in Guatemala, they would not be able to make enough money to pay back what she owed, never mind saving to bring everyone to the U.S. together.

She made the most difficult decision of her life; she left her two older children with her sister in Malacatan and came to the United

States without them. She could earn money in the U.S. and then she would come and get them. The children cried and Rosalinda cried when she left. She told them she would be back for them very soon and they would all be together again. They would live in a beautiful place and the children would go to school. Her little five-year-old son followed her down the path as they walked away, still crying, until Rosalinda's sister picked him up and brought him back into the house.

Rosalinda, Pablo, and their baby Juanito took buses through Mexico headed for Sonora, a Mexican state just south of Arizona. They went that way because they were headed to Los Angeles, to her brother who she thought would help them, and also because it cost less there than crossing the Rio Grande in Texas. Rosalinda found the *coyote*. She was looking at clothes in a shop when a woman working there asked if she wanted to cross the border. The woman said she knew someone who could take her. I realized as I heard more and more of these stories that this woman in the clothing store was just one of many people who are part of the *coyotes'* networks; she was paid by a particular *coyote* who made his living taking people across at Sonora. The fee of the woman at that store, and the fees of others that helped with the trip, were built in to the cost the travelers pay the *coyote*.

They joined a group of thirty people who met the *coyote* that evening, just as it turned dark. A truck came and took them to the border, and they all walked out into the desert. They walked all night. She said it was raining, with thunder and lightning, and it was very windy.

These desert border crossings are very, very dangerous. In 2000, 491 migrants died, trying to cross the border in the desert. I have heard details of many of them, and I remember reading about four who were struck by lightning as they huddled under a tree during a thunderstorm. These things happen because many of the *coyotes* deserve their nickname; they are "like a wolf." They are involved every time we see a headline that reads like this: "Mexican families mourn migrants who died crossing Arizona Desert." In that particular story by Jo Tuckman, printed in the *Naples Daily News* on May 28, 2001, a group was trying to enter the United States illegally in Arizona and was abandoned by their *coyote* near the border. Without the *coyote*, they didn't know where to go. This group spent nearly a week wandering in the scorching desert, trying to find their way, and twelve of them died.

Some of the immigrant smuggling is highly organized. In October 2000, U.S. immigration officers worked with their counterparts in Mexico, Guatemala, and other Central American nations to arrest some of the large-scale smugglers. They arrested José León Castillo, one of the most notorious, who allegedly brought thousands of undocumented Latinos into the U.S. in five years of operation. During the time of these arrests, 3,500 migrants who were headed for the U.S. were detained and returned to their home countries. Most had paid $3,800 each.

In June of 2001, Mexico and the United States announced a sweeping effort to reduce the deaths of migrants. It included campaigns to warn migrants of the risks they were taking, a crackdown on the smugglers themselves, and the idea that Border Patrol agents might fire pepper gas instead of bullets, but it had little effect. Another story on May 15, 2003 ran with the headline, "Apparent Smuggling Trip Kills 18" (T.A. Badger, Associated Press.) In that particular case, "Seventeen people were found dead in a sweltering, airless trailer that had been abandoned at a South Texas truck stop with more than one hundred illegal immigrants locked inside."

An even bigger idea was that Mexicans could work legally in the United States. President George W. Bush and Mexico's President Vicente Fox started working on plans for this.

"It is a country that was built up by immigrants. I don't know why today immigrants should be rejected," said President Fox, referring to the United States.

Apparently George W. agreed, and it all looked very promising. But that was before the 9/11 tragedy, before our outlook on immigrants of all kinds changed.

Rosalinda told me she saw on television the place where she came across, not long before I talked to her, in a story written by an undercover reporter. She thinks they did the report in the exact spot where she came across. Ever since then, I see documentaries and newscasts concerning border crossings differently, imagining that the people I see on television are Rosalinda or Ana, or Pedro or Francisco. It changes the perspective completely.

Rosalinda's group continued walking through the desert, through the rain and thunder and lightning. Rosalinda covered her head with a shawl and put the end of it over the baby, then she covered both their heads with a piece of plastic to protect them from the rain and the wind.

"We were walking fast, up and down hills," she told me. "If we didn't keep up, I was afraid they would leave us. It was very rocky and the rocks hurt our feet. It was really dark and we couldn't see. We ran into cactus and got the spines stuck in our legs. And there were big lizards. I don't know what kind, but they were much bigger than iguanas. They told us the lizards were very dangerous."

Finally, just before the sun came up, they came to a road, and the coyote told them to hide behind some bushes and wait; he would come back for them in a few hours. At 8:00 in the morning, three trucks came, and each took about ten people. The trucks took them to Phoenix.

When they got there, Rosalinda called her brother in Los Angeles, and his wife answered the telephone. Rosalinda had never met his wife, and she told Rosalinda to call back the next day, that her brother was not home. But when she called the next day, the number was no longer in service. Months later, when Rosalinda finally talked to her brother, he told her that his wife never mentioned the phone call. He said his wife probably did that because she did not want Rosalinda, Pablo, and the baby coming to live with them. The brother's wife was not typical. Usually, families help related immigrants when they come to the U.S.

Rosalinda was devastated about not being able to reach her brother, as she had planned to start work the day she arrived in the United States. Her two other children, still in Guatemala, were on her mind constantly. All she wanted to do was get somewhere where she could work. The only other place they knew about was Immokalee, because Pablo had been there, so they used the two hundred dollars they had left to get a ride to Immokalee.

Rosalinda and Pablo both got jobs in the fields as soon as they arrived. He had made some friends when he was here before, and one of them let the couple stay with them until they had some money. One of the wives took care of Juanito during the day for five dollars per day. Then they were able to rent a small apartment of their own, but they fought much of the time.

"When we first got here," she said, "we would fight about why I brought the baby, and then he would hit me. He said I should have left all of them in Guatemala until we could get all of them together, but I couldn't do that."

Rosalinda started going to meetings for abused women. She was very strong to begin with, and they helped her be even stronger. The meetings helped her stand up to Pablo.

"OK, we're here now, and the baby is here," she told him, "so if you don't like it, get out! I was going to come here by myself, anyway. I don't need you to stay here."

He told her he didn't want to leave her, and that he would get better and not hit her anymore, and he said he would work hard and they would bring the other children. They were married last June. Rosalinda said he has changed back into the man she met at the restaurant in Mexico—the man she fell in love with. She thinks it might be because they are married now, but it seems more likely it is because she stood up to him.

"He told me I should tell him anything I want now and that he will never hit me again," she said. "When I first knew him, he was a nice man, and now it seems that he is a nice man again."

They were making progress paying off the money she still owed in Guatemala and saving to bring their other two children to the U.S. They used Pablo's wages to cover their rent, car payment, and food. She was saving hers. It seemed it might all work out. But two months before I talked to her, the bus bringing Rosalinda and other workers home from the fields had an accident. She said the driver was going too fast around a curve, and the bus turned over. Many people were hurt. It sounds like she must have fractured her skull.

"The doctor told me what happened to me," she explained. "It's like when you're demolishing a house and pieces of it fall. He said that's like my head."

She cannot work now because she gets dizzy. The MRIs and other tests the doctor requested are too expensive, and farmworker jobs do not come with health insurance, so she has not had the tests. The company she worked for paid her $400 the first month after the accident, but that was all. It will be some time before she can work again.

In the meantime, Rosalinda's two oldest children are growing up without her in Guatemala. Soon they will go to work in the *fincas*, picking coffee, and they will do that until their mother comes for them.

I was so sad for her. I always hope that the end of these stories will be happy ones and that the American Dream will work out for everyone. But, of course, that can't always happen.

Rosalinda said all she thinks about is going to get her other children, but there is no money. She started to cry again.

"It is so hard. I talk to my children on the phone, and they can't understand why I can't come to them."

The other Guatemalan woman I talked to made a different decision about her children. Born in 1975, Ana was younger than Rosalinda. The two women do not know each other, but their stories are remarkably similar, except that Ana did not have a man in her life, and she brought her three children with her from Guatemala.

Ana came from a village in the *Departamento* of Huehuetenengo, a few hours from San Miguel Acatan, and her village, La Democracia, is closer to the Mexican border. Like Rosalinda, Ana left Guatemala because she was worried about her children's future.

I interviewed Ana at a school where she was studying English. Her Mexican-born husband, Manuel, came with her and told me his story, too. We met Manuel earlier in this book, in the Mexican chapter. He was doing all right in Mexico City, and he only came to the U.S. because his friend Umberto wanted to come. They crossed the border and then walked six hours in a circle, ending up in the same place. Eventually they went to Immokalee, where Manuel worked in the fields. He said he had often thought of going back to Mexico, that was, until the day he met Ana. He was driving down Main Street and she came out of a store, with groceries in her arms. He was so taken with her that he pulled his truck over immediately and offered to give her a ride home. The rest is history—good history. But the story before that was not.

Ana was the eighth of nine children, and one half of a set of twins. Both of her parents worked in the coffee *fincas,* and so did Ana, since she was a little child. The place where they lived was close to the *fincas,* so at least they didn't have to travel far to get there. She is *Ladino,* like Rosalinda, with only a small amount of Indian blood.

When Ana came to the United States she was twenty-one years old and she had three children: six months, four years, and six years old. She wanted a better life for them than the one they had in Guatemala, so she decided to come to the United States, where she could work and earn money. Her mother offered to keep the children for her, but Ana could not stand the thought of leaving them.

"I know that maybe leaving them might have been the best thing," she told me, "but I couldn't do it. I just couldn't leave them."

She took them on a long and dangerous journey across the Guatemala/Mexico border and up the fifteen hundred miles through Mexico to the U.S./Mexico border. They rode buses, took rides from strangers, and walked, ending up in Sonora, like Rosalinda. Ana had no idea how much it would cost to get across the border, but it didn't matter, because she had used up all of her money just getting that far. She had not realized how much it would cost. She thought about going back to her home. What else could she do?

"In that moment, I wanted to return to Guatemala and give up," she remembered, "but right when I was about to return, someone came. He was a young guy who brings people to the United States. He told me he would help me. He was Guatemalan also. He said he would help me because I was from Guatemala."

Other people she met also tried to convince her to continue her journey to the U.S.

"Don't go back to Guatemala, because you and your children will die on the trip," they told her. "You made it this far. Just keep going. It will be worth it when you get to the United States."

Ana had no plan about where she would go in the U.S. She just wanted to find a place where she could work and make a good home for her children, a place where they could go to school. The young Guatemalan man said he would take her to the town where he lived.

"It is called Immokalee, in Florida," he told her. "I understand that you have no money. When you get there you can get a job and pay me back, little by little. It won't be a problem; there is a lot of work in Immokalee."

The cost would be $1,200 for herself, plus $600 for each child, for a total of $3,000. She is still paying, she told me, "...a little each week."

Ana said a lady at the border felt sorry for her and gave her some food and some prayers written on a piece of paper. The woman said, "While you're crossing the desert, when you rest, read these prayers. You will need prayers."

No doubt this woman gave prayers to many other travelers as they prepared to cross the desert.

There were fifty-six people in Ana's group when they left Sonora. They walked all night, and at dawn they reached the beginning of the desert. They had just sat down to eat when eight men with guns appeared—Mexican bandits. I asked why the *coyote* did not defend them, and she said if the *banditos* knew which one was the *coyote*, they would have killed him.

"They took everything," she told me, reliving the painful memory, "our water, food, milk. I was crying for my children. There were four women and me. The rest were men. The *banditos* didn't take our clothes, but they took the clothes of the men, even the clothes they were wearing. Then they threw the men, naked, on the ground and started beating them with guns and sticks."

Ana thought she was safe—that the *banditos* were just going to beat up the men.

"And then they started with the women…"

As she said that, Ana started to cry. She looked away from her husband and stumbled on her words, but Manuel reached for her hand and held it as she tried to continue.

"They took everything from us…"

Ana's eyes moved to the floor and the tears kept coming. I wondered, but did not ask, where her six-year old boy was while this was happening. The possibility that he was watching seemed more horrible than what Ana went through. I decided to believe that the rest of the group shielded the children from watching, as I tried hard not to picture her repeating the prayers the woman had given her, over and over.

I started to ask Manuel another question about his life so Ana could rest from this painful story, but after a minute she continued.

"After it was over, one of the *banditos* wanted to take me with them," she said, "but another stepped in and said to him, 'You did that once before, remember? The last time you took a woman, later you just left her somewhere.'"

So they decided not to take her. One of them even felt sorry for her and gave her two bottles of juice.

After the *banditos* left, the group walked in the desert for two days, and the two bottles of juice were the only food or drink she and her children had. Immigration flew over in helicopters, looking for people crossing illegally through the desert, but did not see them. The men helped her carry the younger children, but Ana's six-year-old son walked the entire trip through the desert.

"We were so scared," she continued. "When we got to where we were going, the *coyote* counted us, and three people were missing."

No one knew what happened to those three people. I have read stories of people dying in the Arizona desert where the heat reaches over 115 degrees. A doctor was quoted in one article about hopeful immigrants who died from dehydration, who said their bodies actually shriveled up. "Have you ever seen a mummy from ancient Egypt?" he said. "That gives you an idea." Such a horrible thought, especially since Ana is such a beautiful young woman.

She said the group just kept walking and walking. She thought it would go on forever, and still they had no water. During the nights the group made fires because it was so cold, and there were animals, real coyotes, very near them, howling all night. The children huddled near their mother to keep warm and safe. The third day they walked all day, and then finally there was water.

"Thank God, we passed by a dirty watering hole for cattle," Ana told me. "I didn't care if it was bad water. I just lay down on my stomach and drank and drank. It was nasty, but it was good. We filled some bottles, then we went and hid under a tree all night."

Finally, they arrived in Tucson. The children by this time were sick and coughing, a potential problem as the group hid from immigration under a tree. Ana tried to keep the children from coughing when anyone came near, and fortunately no one heard them. They stayed there on the ground all night, until finally, trucks picked them up in the early morning and took them directly to Immokalee. The long journey was at last over.

The stories of Ana and Rosalinda are both moving and heartbreaking, but actually, Ana was lucky that the *coyote* who approached her in Sonora was an honest man. And Rosalinda might be lucky that she did not make the journey alone as she originally planned. One Immokalee woman was not so lucky. The *Naples Daily News* told her story on March 16, 2002, in an article written by Mireidy Fernandez. The woman, Julia Gabriel, had some very frightening experiences when she came across the border in 1992. Two men, one Mexican and one Guatemalan, picked her up in Phoenix and told her there was work in South Carolina. They said they would take her there and she could work to pay off her smuggling debt. Julia lived in a camp, and no one was allowed to leave.

"If someone even just tried to attempt to walk out of the place, they'd beat them," the article reported Julia saying. "They would constantly taunt us and shoot guns up in the air as a way to intimidate us and would say things like 'We own you' and 'You should be grateful to even be in this country.'"

Julia also said the words I had heard so many times from the people I interviewed: "I thought I was coming to America to find a better life…"

After three months, Julia escaped. She worked with the FBI, and they were able to find and prosecute the smugglers. In 2000, Julia Gabriel received one of three "Women of Courage Awards" given by the National Organization of Women. Today she works in street landscaping for the Collier County Government.

As I neared the end of writing this chapter, I had a few open questions about the Guatemalans. At about the same time, we noticed mold growing on the ceiling of our guesthouse, so we called a painter we had used a few years ago named Rudy Lopez. He does good work, and his prices are reasonable.

It had never occurred to me when I met him several years ago to ask where he was from. That was before I got to know Immokalee, before I started working on my Master's degree, before I thought of writing this book, and before I knew very much about Latin America. But now I know more, and I am more curious. I realized I did not recognize his accent.

"Where are you from?" I asked.

"Guatemala."

I was surprised. He was taller than the Guatemalans I had met, and his accent was quite different.

"Really? What part?"

He answered, "Huehue" (Way-Way). *Watch for signs.*

"Huehue! I know where that is!" I was amazed. But the amazement quickly turned to disappointment. Rudy was from Naples, not Immokalee, so his story would not fit with the others in this book.

"It's too bad you live in Naples and not Immokalee," I said with a sigh, "because you could really help me with my book."

"Yeah, too bad," he answered. "I moved out of Immokalee a few years ago."

Do what comes easy. I got my tape recorder.

There were several things about Rudy that helped me. One, he was right there, right when I had questions. Two, he spoke good English. All the other Guatemalans I talked to spoke only Spanish. As I mentioned, I can function in Spanish, but I miss some subtle things. The third thing about Rudy that was helpful was his perspective, because he was an educated man. He was raised in the city of Huehuetenengo—about eight hours down the mountain from San Miguel Acatan—and was just becoming a teacher when he left. The fourth thing about Rudy that was helpful was that he came to Immokalee in the middle of the 1980s, so maybe he could fill in some of the gaps.

I asked Rudy what Mayan language he spoke, but he said he doesn't speak any. Neither do his parents. He called the Mayan languages "dialects."

"Most of the people from Huehue don't speak any other language except those dialects," he said, referring to the entire Huehuetenengo area. "That was one of the problems teaching there."

Rudy was seventeen years old in 1983 when he was doing student teaching. He called it "preview teaching."

"Some of my friends got to do their preview teaching in schools right in Huehuetenengo," he explained, "but I had to go out of town to the little villages in the mountains."

He meant little villages like San Miguel Acatan, where Pedro, Andres, Francisco, and José were raised. Rudy said it was difficult to communicate with the children in those towns because many of the students did not speak Spanish. They could only understand their own Mayan dialect.

I asked him about the war in Guatemala, and he said it came on gradually.

"I wasn't that affected at first," he said, "because I was in school in the city, and most of the massacres and killings were in the smaller villages. That's where the rebels were, and that's where the military was looking for them."

But Rudy had to go to one of those smaller villages.

"When I was doing that preview teaching, I had to take a bus about two hours from Huehue to this village," he remembered. "There were supposed to be between thirty-two and forty-six kids in each class, but as the war got worse, the kids stopped going to school because their parents wouldn't let them go; it was too scary. Also, many of the people had gone to Mexico as refugees. Some of the families had already been killed, and they didn't want to get killed, too."

Rudy said a lot of people wouldn't talk much about what was happening, because they could get in trouble, but he saw things.

"My family had a few trucks, and during the worst time of that war we went to Guatemala City to get supplies from the stores to sell them in our town. On the way, we saw people dead in the middle of the road. You had to keep going, because it was dangerous to get out of your car because of the Army. We just had to drive around the bodies."

"What were you doing?" I asked, cautiously. I knew no one wanted to admit that they were involved. "Were you on the side of the government or the rebels?" He gave the same answer I had heard before.

"We were just caught in the middle of it," he told me. "None of my family got into political things. Mainly, we just tried to make a living and not get involved too much. But when you were in the middle, then somebody from either side could cut you down."

It almost sounded as if it was safer to be on one side or the other. Rudy seemed to agree.

"One of the families we knew left their town because there was so much harassment, so much pressure," he said. "The military was saying they were rebels, and the rebels were saying they were with the government, so they had to move out of there. I heard a lot of those stories. One of the guys I knew said his brother got caught in the middle and they just killed him. They just found the brother dead in a place outside of their town. The family never even knew which side killed him."

I asked Rudy why he finally decided to leave, in 1984. He said there was one last incident that was too close to home, and he just did not want to live like that any longer.

"The rebels blew up a military base right in Huehuetenengo, not far from my house," he explained. "One of my brothers was driving a taxi then, and he came right home. He was afraid, because it turned out the rebels had used taxis to get to the base. My brother just took off in his taxi, going to the other side of the city. They never did anything to him, but it was all too close, and too scary. I finally decided to get out of there and come to the United States. I was only seventeen years old."

Rudy came to the U.S. without papers, but he has them now. He came through Mexico like the other people I talked to, taking a bus from Huehuetenango and ending up on the Arizona border. He was thinking of going to California.

Rudy's stories about the trip through Mexico and crossing the border were fascinating because he told me things I had not heard before. By the time he was making his way through Mexico in 1984, the Mexican government had gotten tougher on Guatemalan immigrants because hundreds of thousands of them had streamed across the Mexican border to escape the war. Mexico finally restricted them to refugee camps in southern Mexico, and Mexican Immigration officials were always looking for them elsewhere. Rudy told me about the bus ride.

"There were all these checkpoints in Mexico," he explained. "At one checkpoint all these Mexican Immigration police came onto the bus: six of them. I was sitting there, surrounded by all these Guatemalan guys—little short guys speaking dialects. The police walked back and forth from the front to the back of the bus. Then they started looking at everybody in the face and saying 'Where are you from?'"

Rudy said all the Mexican guys started giving Mexico addresses. Then the police started asking the Guatemalans, and they told the police they came from Mexico's southern states, Oaxaca and Chiapas. I remember being told it was difficult to tell the Guatemalans apart from southern Mexicans. Rudy paid close attention, trying to overhear an address that he could use, too.

"But then all the Guatemalans started talking in dialect. It was kind of funny." He smiled. "But I guess the police figured it was a dialect from southern Mexico. I kept watching all of the Mexicans, trying to learn what they were saying so I could say it, too."

He did, and the Immigration police believed him. At the next checkpoint the same kind of thing happened, and again, Rudy studied what was going on.

"This time the police started asking for names of items, like a belt, or shoelaces, because Mexican words are different from Guatemalan words. For example, shoelaces are *correas;* in Mexico they call them *aguhetas* or *cintas*. And the belt, they call *cinto*. We call them *cincho*. So whoever didn't know these little words, they would get them right away."

This was just like World War II when the American soldiers asked suspicious soldiers who won the 1938 World Series! Rudy did a good job studying the different answers, and when they got to him he came up with the Mexican words, and the police believed he was from southern Mexico.

Rudy's border crossing was also fascinating. I had not heard anything like it before.

"I got to the border with a group of guys, and we spent the night there, right on the border." He enjoyed relating this story. "We couldn't go across, because it happened to be a place where the American Indians came on the weekends to get drunk, smoke, have a good time and get happy with music and all that. We didn't know what they would do if we came across, so we just sat there, looking at them. There were over 150 Guatemalans and Mexicans sitting there, waiting, looking at the Indians. They were looking at us, too."

I asked him how you could tell where the border was, exactly. He said it's marked with stakes every once in a while, but really, it's like an imaginary line. Somehow, they know. The Indians were on one side of that imaginary line, and the potential immigrants were on the other. Then Border Patrols showed up in helicopters and jeeps, and Rudy and the other Latinos started running. But Rudy said the first thing that came to his mind was that he had no place to hide. He was in the middle of the desert. There was nothing to hide behind or under. There was no point in running.

"So I dug a hole and buried myself."

I tried to get a mental picture of this, but could not, so I asked him to describe it.

"I dug a hole for my face and put my sweater like a bag around my head, and laid face down in the hole, with my hands at my side. Then I reached behind my back and threw dirt over myself."

Rudy said a few of the other guys saw him and did the same thing.

"More Border Patrols came in jeeps, and they caught a lot of guys, but not us. After a few minutes it got quiet, so I decided to come out. I looked over and the Indians were laughing so hard. We were still probably a hundred feet away from the border. And they just kept laughing! I figured they weren't going to stop us, because they didn't tell Immigration we were there. So, I made it across late that night. I passed into the day of my eighteenth birthday right there on the border."

He spent two days in Nogales so he could get his papers.

"One of the first things I did was I went to a lawyer to get the applications for my asylum. That was easy then, because the war in Guatemala had been going on for a while. I didn't have to prove that much, because by then everybody knew what was going on down there."

Then Rudy came to Immokalee.

"I took a ride—they call it a 'ride'—somebody brings you here," he explained. "The guy was going to Immokalee, not California, but I didn't care where I went. I just had to get somewhere where I could work. I told him I didn't have any money to pay him, but he said I could work for him."

It sounds to me like this *coyote* was also a crew leader. Maybe these *coyote*/crew leaders are part of the "they" who brought people to Immokalee. They got their labor source, with built-in debt obligations, by picking them up at the border. Rudy made it to Immokalee and started working the day after he arrived, picking tomatoes.

Most of the Guatemalans who came to Immokalee, including Pedro, Andres, Francisco, and José, had a more difficult time than Rudy or other *Ladinos* or Mexicans, because most of them were

Mayan. The Mayas did not speak Spanish well, because it was their second language; some of them learned it on their way through Mexico. Also, they are physically smaller than *Ladinos* and Mexicans, making them easy targets for muggers. And, perhaps most significantly, they come from a culture where they are considered to be the lowest social class. They are used to being abused, so they tolerate treatment that other nationalities might not.

Anne Goodnight visited Guatemala several times in 1988 and 1989 with her husband, who had taken a position with a honeydew and cucumber company in Guatemala. She told me about the attitudes toward the Mayan people.

"The Spanish were very mean to the Indians," she told me. "The man we worked with had an Indian maid. My husband offered to give her a ride to town so she didn't have to walk. It was four or five miles away. They heard him make the offer and they told him not to take her. They said, 'If you start doing things like that, they'll start to expect it.'"

Those attitudes still exist in Guatemala today, and the low self-image of the Guatemalans carries over to the United States and to Immokalee. Brother Jim told me he could almost tell which people were Mayan by the way they walked.

"They tend to walk a little stooped over, in single-file," he explained. "I call it Indian-file, one behind the other. One person seems to take over as a kind of a leader, and the others just follow him."

Brother Jim said many of the Mexicans think of them as "just Indians." "That is a put-down. These are the subtle things we don't usually see, because we see everyone as Hispanic."

Brother Jim also explained that the poor self-image carries over into their work. That, plus the fact that they are physically smaller than the other ethnic groups, makes them easier to take advantage of. He explained why:

"A Guatemalan guy is trying to find a job he can take some pride in, and what does he do? The only thing to do is 'go pick.' Well, at the end of the day, he's asking for his salary, but he can be treated as a little guy, and a crew chief might say 'This is all I'm going to give you.' You do that, day after day, and there is no pride."

I can see the difference between Mexicans and Mayan Guatemalans in multi-cultural church services. Usually the Mexicans do the first music, then the Haitians, then the English-speaking, then the Guatemalans. The Mayas' low self-image is obvious in their music. They strum guitars, quietly, monotonously, and sing very softly in their Kanjobal language. They always look down at the floor when they sing.

The Guatemalans pray more devoutly than other people, too, it seems. They seem to be completely humble. Sometimes, when the church doors are locked, you will see them kneeling on the concrete outside, praying very deeply. The other place you will see them is at Father Sanders' grave, nearby on the church grounds. Father Sanders is like a saint to them.

In the U.S., many of the Mayas are learning to feel more confident about themselves and their race. Pedro and Andres, for example, were among the founders of the Coalition of Immokalee Workers. They work at Harvest for Humanity blueberry farm where they are learning English and will someday be part owners. José works at a golf course, and his wife Enriquetta works at a nursery. Their younger sons are still in school, and two older daughters have already graduated high school. I never saw Rosalinda again, so I do not know if she ever found a way to get the medical treatment she needed to recover from her accident. If she did, she will have gotten back to the business of saving money to bring her two older children to this country. Ana is happy because her children are already here, and she loves her Mexican husband, Manuel. They are working hard to buy a house so the children have a place to come home to. Rudy has his own business, painting houses, working and living in Naples.

In their home country of Guatemala, political issues are still not settled. It took until December 29, 1996 for Peace Accords to be signed between the government and the guerrilla forces. During the thirty-six-year civil war, over two hundred thousand Guatemalans were killed or "disappeared," and over one million were displaced from their homes. Some of them now live in Immokalee. Most of the families of the people I spoke to never left Guatemala during the worst part of the violence. Andres explained what it was like for his parents.

"They lived in fear," he said. "They couldn't be peaceful. But the danger passed, and now there is no problem."

I hope Andres is right. Today, General Efrain Rios Montt, the military leader who instituted the "scorched earth" policy in the early 1980s, is the leader of Guatemala's Congress. In late 2003, he even ran for president, but he lost.

The poverty is still there. Because of price declines in the international coffee market, many people in Guatemala today are even poorer than Immokalee's Guatemalans were before they left home. Many of the people in the northern Highlands today eat wild bananas and their children beg for food on highways. Mexico will not take them; it has enough problems with its own poor people in the southern states of Oaxaca and Chiapas. But word trickles down from northern to southern Mexico to Guatemala that there is work in the United States. Many who hear that word will come to a place that in the language of the indigenous people means "my home"—the place called Immokalee.

6

Coming Together—The 1980s

"They said, no problem, pretty place, everything is OK. But when we arrived there, we see that is not true; that it's a dirty place. Only one bathroom for about thirty people to go, sometimes two and three people live in one room."

—Haitian man in "Fields of Fear" Documentary

When Southwest Florida's agribusiness really began to take off in the 1970s, the area around Immokalee became more and more crowded with Mexican immigrants. The word had spread: "There is work in Immokalee." Up to this point, crew leaders and *coyotes* had brought workers directly to camps on the farms, but in the 1970s these workers started coming to the center of Immokalee.

Beginning in 1980, after Mariel, waves of Haitians joined the Mexicans, and in 1983, as the height of the war hit the Northwest Highlands, Guatemalans started to arrive.

The new people needed to live close to the parking lots where buses picked up workers for the fields, so the south side of Immokalee became more and more crowded. Thousands of people like Juan, Natalie, Pedro, and Ana came to a place with a name that means "my home," but there was no room for them in this home. Most of them had nothing but a few dollars and some clothes in a bag, and they knew no one. How did they survive?

I try to imagine it. I just came from a tiny rural village in Guatemala. I speak no English. My view of the world is limited to what I knew of my mountain village, the plantations an hour and a half from my home, the trip through Mexico, crossing the border through the desert or on the river, and the ride to Immokalee. I have only a few dollars and some clothes in a bag. I arrive, exhausted, with eight other people. The van drops me off on a corner and the driver points at a parking lot.

"That's where the bus will pick you up in the morning to take you to the fields," he says, and he drives away.

What do I do now? How will I eat? Where will I sleep? When will I find work? How will I do little things, like wash my few items of clothing that are dirty from the long trip?

I asked Rudy, the Guatemalan teacher who spent his eighteenth birthday on the border buried in sand, how it was for him. He nodded his head thoughtfully, as if starting to relive the way it was then.

"That was a problem," he said, "because I didn't have anybody to stay with. Nobody knew me. I slept under a tractor-trailer. You know Main Street and Ninth Street?"

Yes, I know it. Our Lady of Guadalupe Church is on Ninth Street.

"There's a Handy store there, with a gas station. Behind that store used to be tractor-trailers. And this guy who brought me to Immokalee used to have his bus there. I slept under his trailers."

I buy gas at that store. Today there are no tractor-trailers behind it, but there is a vacant lot. I asked Rudy how he could just sleep like that, on the ground. He said he still had his *chamarra* from the border crossing—the thing he put over his head when he buried himself in the sand. He said it's like a sarape, but bigger. "Thank God I had it to keep me warm," Rudy said. "It was January, and it was cold."

I asked what he did for food, and how he cleaned his clothes.

"There was a water outlet right by the trailer I slept under," he told me. "I washed my clothes out there. And I only had a couple of dollars, so I bought a cup of coffee and a hot dog. That's about it."

In the 1980s there were hundreds of "Rudys" sleeping all over Immokalee. Long-time residents could not believe what was happening.

New immigrants arrived in town every day, with no money and no place to stay. The biggest problem was that they were not expected. Anne Goodnight was a Collier County Commissioner during that time, and she lived in Immokalee.

"We had no idea all these people were coming," she said, "but we were expected to take care of them."

The biggest problem was that the immigrants were so poor. They had basic needs, like food and shelter. Anne said many of them lived in the saw palmettos, a plant like a palm tree, but smaller, and sprawling. Favorite habitats of eastern diamondback and pigmy rattlesnakes, the name "saw palmetto" comes from the razor-sharp "teeth" on their stems. The immigrants created special spots of their own in the spaces between the palmettos, sleeping on old blankets or cardboard boxes.

Once they had spent time working in the fields and had a little money, they could rent a place to stay. Because they did not have cars and there was no public transportation, they needed to live as close as they could to Miner's Supermarket, where buses picked up workers headed for the fields. During segregation, this part of Immokalee was where the Blacks lived, and the poor Whites. The buses picked up in that area because those two groups dominated fieldwork back then. This area, the south side, is still the worst part of Immokalee. For years, banks would not extend credit because the condition of the houses was so bad, and since building owners could not get loans, they rarely did much in the way of repairs.

"Slumlords" charged the new immigrants exorbitant rates to share a run-down trailer or a tiny one-room shack with other immigrants.

"The slum landlords were making so much money," said Anne Goodnight, shaking her head. "Even 'mom and pops.' If they had a little land they'd put in a couple of trailers and charge the immigrants by the head. It wasn't that the immigrants didn't care; they just didn't know any better."

"Charging by the head" applied most of the time. Sister Eileen Eppig, SSND (School Sisters of Notre Dame), who came to help the new immigrants in 1980, wrote about a woman named Nena. She came to Immokalee from Guatemala with her three children, very much like Ana, who came many years later. Nena came to join her sister and help care for the children while her sister and brother-in-law worked in the fields. When the landlord found out there were more than four in the trailer, he increased the rent from $120 a week to $240 a week.

"It's the same cost," he told them. "Thirty dollars a head."

Another landlord rented out a trailer with one kitchen and one bathroom to two families who didn't even know each other, and each family's rent was five hundred dollars a month. So, it cost one thousand dollars, in 1980, for ten people to share a small trailer with one kitchen and one bath. There wasn't even any furniture. The tenants put up a blanket to separate the living room, and they all slept on the floor on blankets.

Conditions in Immokalee were a terrible disappointment for the immigrants. They had risked everything, including their money and often their lives, to get to a place where they could work and make a better life.

"I just want to make a home for my family," said so many of the immigrants I talked with. "I just want to make a house for my children."

But in the 1980s, Immokalee wasn't much different from their home countries. According to the 1980 census, twenty percent of the buildings in Immokalee did not have toilets and running water. And 2,121 housing units were classified as "substandard," due to lack of kitchen and lack of complete bathroom facilities. Sister Eileen said they called these places "migrant camps." She remembers one that advertised hot and cold running water as if it were an important amenity, shocked that anyone would advertise hot and cold running water in 1980 in the United States of America.

Some of the early Haitians were interviewed in a documentary about farmworker abuses called "Fields of Fear," part of a 1992 WTVJ

Miami news series by Pam Saulsby. One of the Haitian men in that documentary told how it was in Immokalee in the mid-1980s.

"When we arrived there," he said, "the men told us they got the permit to work there. For all the people to work. They said, no problem, pretty place, everything is OK. But when we arrived there, we saw that was not true. That it's a dirty place. Only one bathroom for about thirty people to go, sometimes two and three people live in one room."

Catholic Sisters from various religious orders came, answering calls for help. The SSNDs (School Sisters of Notre Dame) were particularly committed to Immokalee. Some of them work there, still. Sister Veronica Cohen was one of the early ones. She moved to Immokalee in 1978 to work at Farm Worker Health Services and became well known, as her care for her patients went far beyond nursing; she gave baths, did laundry, brought food, found shelter, and drove people to the hospital. She was an advocate of eye care, arranging eyeglasses for those with poor sight. Someone once said, "Veronica put glasses on every Haitian woman in Southwest Florida."

For eighteen years Sister Veronica traveled with the farmworkers as they followed the crops. One of her most important jobs was ministering to single farmworkers who were dying from accidents or diseases, men who had come to the U.S. without their families. She brought them comfort at the end of their lives, and sometimes Sister Veronica and a few friends were the only ones at their burials.

As thousands of Haitians and Guatemalans joined the *Tejanos* and Mexicans who were still pouring into Immokalee, additional services were badly needed. Our Lady of Guadalupe church became more directly involved because so many of the new immigrants were Catholic—the reason some people refer to the 1980s as "the heyday of the Catholic Church in Immokalee."

Our Lady of Guadalupe was the first place many of the new immigrants went when they arrived. They slept on the church grounds, in their trucks, or in the palmettos, because they felt safer there than in other places in town.

Even before 1980, Immokalee was a difficult assignment for priests. The work, the strain, and the frustration of working with poor immigrants took a heavy toll on them. Consequently, there was a continuous turnover of priests every one or two years.

"Most left broken," remembered one long-time parishioner. "Many lost their faith, the longer they stayed."

One of the biggest problems was the isolation, because usually only one priest was assigned to Immokalee at a time. They lived in very small rooms in the back of the original church that is now Sanders Hall, and were responsible for everything in the parish, including church duties, doing the books, and cutting the grass. But most of their work involved the new immigrants.

"Most immigrants didn't trust anyone in the U.S. except the priest," explained long-time Immokalee schoolteacher Patty Ligas. "They wanted help from the priest for everything."

In the late 1970s, years before the Haitians and Guatemalans came, Father Pedro Jove was Our Lady of Guadalupe's pastor. When Mexican immigrants started coming to the rectory for food, he realized he could not manage this job alone. He asked the SSNDs to send someone to start social services, and Sister Eileen Eppig answered this call.

The first part of her job was to be a liaison between the Church, local agencies, and farmworkers. This included knowing where to send the new immigrants and what kind of help they could get there. She said this was important, because often people got lost in the paperwork and legal technicalities of social service agencies. The second thing she had to do was a "needs assessment" and home-visitations to get a realistic idea of what the immigrants needed. Her visits to their homes also showed the people that someone cared about them.

Sister Eileen got to Immokalee just in time, because in the latter half of 1980, in addition to a continuous flow of Mexicans, the Haitians started coming. Sister Maureen remembered it clearly.

"We saw on our televisions boatloads and boatloads of Haitians arriving on the beaches of Palm Beach and Miami," she told me. "The federal government realized they couldn't keep them all in Miami, so they had people suggesting relocation to places like Immokalee that needed labor."

"There was a flood of Haitians into Immokalee from 1980 to 1982," said Rob Williams, also of Florida Rural Legal Services. "People in Miami would tell the Haitians to go to Immokalee or Belle Glade, not realizing what an incredible strain that would be on a community. They were sending these desperate people to one of the poorest communities in the United States, and there were hardly any social services."

The Haitians who came to Immokalee were mostly country people from Haiti's rural areas. They were older—in their thirties and forties—uneducated, and very poor. They spoke only Haitian Creole and had very few skills, but they knew something about farming, valuable experience for Immokalee.

Sister Eileen said the Haitians were very industrious and knew they needed English to get ahead, but back then the adult education center at the public school only offered English once a week, on Tuesday nights. The class was helpful, but the Haitians complained that once a week wasn't enough, so they showed up every night and sat there with their books, saying, "We need a teacher." Finally, English classes started up every night for the Haitians.

In 1981, a major crop freeze made the immigrants' situation even worse than it was before. To be cold enough to freeze vegetables, the temperature has to get down below freezing for at least an hour or two. Remember that many people in Immokalee were sleeping in palmettos or in their trucks, with very little clothing and no blankets. There was nowhere else for them to go.

But feeling cold was the least of their worries. When temperatures get below freezing, crops are destroyed, and field workers have no work. That means no money, and often it means they do not eat. Sister Eileen's organization, at that time called "Our Lady of Guadalupe Outreach," helped the farmworkers as much as possible, but she had limited funding. Soon, however, more people in nearby coastal towns started understanding what was happening in Immokalee, and they began sending contributions and volunteering.

In March of 1981, at the beginning of the biggest growth and greatest diversity in Immokalee's population, Father Richard Sanders became the pastor of Our Lady of Guadalupe Church. I never met him, but pictures still hang on the walls of many social service offices in Immokalee. He had thick coarse hair, gray on top, dark eyebrows, a thick dark moustache, and a full beard of black speckled with gray. His eyes were intense, but at the same time had a kind of gentle peacefulness. He looked like someone from another time, like a prophet or a disciple.

Father Sanders had challenges beyond those of priests who worked in Immokalee before him. Not only did he have a steady influx of Mexicans to deal with, but also Haitians, and then Guatemalans who came within the space of a few years. He had to help people in three languages—Spanish, English, and Haitian Creole—plus minister to people who spoke Guatemalan Kanjobal. He already spoke Spanish quite well, but after he got to Immokalee he took a trip to Indiana University to study Haitian Creole. Being able to speak to his parishioners in their own languages was an important part of his ministry. All the people who worked with him said he was a wonderful counselor who patiently listened to, understood, and helped everyone who came to him.

His brother, Jim Sanders, told me that Father Sanders saw the need for both charity and empowerment for the immigrants. I can explain the difference between charity and empowerment with the well-known saying that goes something like this:

"Give someone a fish, and you feed them for today. Teach someone to fish, and you feed them for a lifetime."

Giving a fish is charity. Teaching how to fish is empowerment.

Father Sanders made special efforts to ensure ministry to the various ethnic groups. For example, we heard from Pedro and Andres that he would send a bus to the camps in Devil's Garden to pick up the Guatemalans, and would not start Mass until they arrived. The Guatemalans called this a miracle. The van was a good thing, but not really such a big thing. The reason it felt like a miracle to the Mayas is that it showed that Father Sanders respected and loved them enough to send for them—something they had not previously experienced. Sister Eileen told me he focused on the value of each individual person.

"He communicated to them that they were of inestimable worth," she remembered. "This in itself was empowering. When you believe you are somebody, it gives you the power you need to stand up for yourself and take steps to make your life better."

Father Sanders saw the needs of the immigrants, but also understood he did not have time to do it all; his job was to be a priest and do religious things. He made it a point to train leaders in the community, giving each lay leader keys to "their" church and "their" hall. During his four years in Immokalee, Father Sanders recruited and trained sixty-three lay ministers, more than any parish in what was then the Miami Archdiocese, and he did it working with new immigrants in three languages.

Father Sanders also encouraged the multi-cultural congregation to meet weekly to discuss things that were important, not just to Catholics, but to everyone in Immokalee. Whenever there was a meeting at the Miami diocese, he made sure that people of each nationality went with him. He wanted to make sure all groups were represented when decisions were made.

In the meantime, Sister Eileen continued to develop social services. A volunteer named Mike Hughes came from Marco Island, built a database, and taught her how to keep track of donors. Another volunteer,

Bill Mauter, came from Naples three days a week to interview people, bag food, or whatever else needed to be done. When he talked to men who needed shoes, Bill would ask their shoe size, and if the man wore the same size as Bill, Bill would take off his shoes and give them to him. At the end of the day, Bill would go back to Naples in his socks. Eileen said he did this fairly often.

Soon two more SSND sisters came to Immokalee: Jane Burke, and Marie McFadden. Sister Marie had worked in Immokalee before, in 1974, as a social educator at Lake Trafford School, but when she returned with Sister Jane in 1981, they figured out that one of the biggest needs was for food; people were hungry. So they decided to open a soup kitchen. They called their organization "Guadalupe Center."

A soup kitchen technically falls into the category of charity rather than empowerment, and in fact this particular soup kitchen has been criticized as being a form of dependency-creating welfare. I asked Sister Judy Dohner about this, years later when she ran Guadalupe Center. "Isn't it possible that the soup kitchen creates a dependency?" Judy dismissed my question, simply and succinctly.

"Nobody goes hungry."

When I repeated my question, wanting to get into a theoretical discussion of charity versus empowerment, she just repeated what she said before.

"Nobody goes hungry."

Father Sanders provided a building for the soup kitchen on the church grounds. Sister Jane studied soup kitchens, and Marie learned how to raise funds. Businesses from nearby towns contributed building materials and labor. A Naples heating and air conditioning man named Joe Brett volunteered every day and worked on everything from the site development and pouring of the concrete floors to the building of the walls. He continued to work in Immokalee as a volunteer for years, whenever the Center needed to remodel.

One day another man walked into the soup kitchen, a few weeks before it opened. Sister Jane was there, scrubbing the floor.

"Are you one of those nuns?" he asked. When she responded that yes, she was, he said, "Well, what do you need out here?"

She said they still needed a big refrigerator, and a few days later he brought one. Three or four times a year, until he died, that man came back and asked what they needed, and then he brought it. He never wanted credit for what he did.

He must have been just like the man who, fifteen years later, brought me a piano at the Guadalupe Family Center. Here's how it happened. Not long after I had started singing with the children, we were asked to do our first performance. The building was being dedicated to Jim Near, who had died, but his wife, Nancy Near, was among the two hundred or so people who attended. I had prepared the children to sing a few songs, including "Alligator in the Elevator," and "I Believe I Can Fly." That day was my first exposure to people who gave money behind the scenes to help people in Immokalee. Most of them were from nearby Naples, Bonita Springs, Fort Myers, Marco Island, and Sanibel. Those invited to this ceremony had given of their time or their money, or both.

Up to this point, I had been playing my guitar when I sang with the children. It's difficult to teach the basics of music with a guitar, however, and I really wanted a piano. So as we performed for our guests, I looked out at all these people and thought, boy, I bet someone out there would give us a piano. But they had contributed so much already, and this was a day to thank them, not ask for something else. I was allowed to say a few words, however, and I thought I might get away with a carefully phrased request.

"We could really use a piano out here," I said to the audience after thanking them for their generosity. Most of them shuffled their feet, cleared their throats, or looked at the trees.

I clarified. "I'm not asking for anyone to *buy* one for us."

The shuffling stopped and their attention returned.

"But I wanted to mention," I said, proceeding cautiously, "that I know there are many homes with pianos that no one plays." I paused, then finished my point.

"Those are very unhappy pianos," I frowned and then smiled.

They laughed! *I might just pull this off*, I thought to myself, so I kept going.

"If one of those pianos came here, it would be a very happy piano."

They all laughed again and it was forgotten—or so I thought. The following week I received a call from a man who had been in the audience that day.

"What kind of piano do you want?" he asked.

I was so surprised, I stammered, "Uhhh…any kind. Any kind at all." He said goodbye and hung up before I got his name.

A few weeks later, just before Christmas, I was at the Family Center in the middle of a music class with the oldest children, the four-year-old Busy Bees. I was playing the guitar and we were singing "Jingle Bells" when two men came in quietly, pushing a piano on a wheeled platform. I couldn't believe what I was seeing: an old upright barroom piano like the one my father used to play! The children were thrilled. Some of them had never seen a piano before. One of the men asked me to play a song, so I played "Silent Night." He smiled and looked very happy. Then the children came running up to see it, and I explained how it worked. (Little children love to see how things work.) I lifted the front cover and showed them the strings. Big strings, I pointed out, not little strings like the ones on my guitar. They were fascinated. They crowded around, all reaching to touch the keyboard. A minute later, I turned to say thank you to the men who had brought it, but they were gone.

I never found out who they were, only that the man who arranged it was from nearby Bonita Bay. There are people like that; people who want no publicity or gratitude. It is enough to know that they helped.

The man who brought the piano was just like the man who brought Sister Jane the big refrigerator, and later, many other things. Yolanda Buitron, who works with outreach services at the Learning Center in Immokalee, told me that she occasionally gets a request from a family for a washing machine. She said there is a lady in Ft. Myers who, over time, has purchased thirteen washing machines for thirteen different families. Yolanda does not even know her name.

On October 4, 1982, on the Feast Day of St. Francis, Guadalupe Center first opened its doors. Its mission statement was a mixture of charity and empowerment: "Guadalupe Center believes in the dignity of each person as created and loved by God, and is therefore committed to serve the disadvantaged poor of Immokalee with interim help and long-term programs that promote self-sufficiency and social change."

You can see the commitment to dignity if you go to the soup kitchen today. Poor people come, sit at a table, and are served by volunteers from nearby communities. If they want more food, it is brought to them. For many of them, it is the only time in their life they have ever been served.

While the soup kitchen was being developed at Guadalupe Center, Sister Eileen kept expanding Guadalupe Social Services, and decided to do something about education.

"Education is another means of empowering people," she explained. "It enables people to have choices in life."

GSS started a bus to Naples Vocational-Technical School, so some of the immigrants could learn skills and get jobs other than fieldwork. Barbara Widman from Naples' Moorings Presbyterian Church in Naples almost single-handedly raised the money for the project. The van carried hundreds of adult students to the Vo-Tech school for the next ten years.

After a while, Sister Eileen went to Mexico to improve her Spanish so she could communicate better with the people she served. Father Sanders insisted that while she was there, she should visit a town farther north, the original home of many of Immokalee's Mexican people. Eileen was not thrilled with the idea of going to Guanajuato.

"I remember the twelve-hour bus ride," she told me, "hot, dusty, crowded with people and chickens."

She had a hard time even finding a place to stay, but she ended up spending two days in Guanajuato. When she got back to Immokalee, she was able to get much closer to the people because she had been to their town. It made sense. Sister Eileen credits Father Sanders for helping her learn this.

"I learned from Richard," she explained, "that caring for the whole person doesn't just mean caring for the person who is in need now. It means connecting with the reality that the person left part of their life behind, in another country, and that to care about the people of Immokalee was to care about that part of their lives, too."

Caring about the new immigrants was challenging because they had so many different needs. One, for example, was for a secure place to put their money. The problem was that many of the immigrants carried their cash around with them. They still do it today, and it makes them easy targets for muggers. They did not have bank accounts because they were working during banking hours, and because many of them did not have papers.

For a while, an Immokalee grocery store called "Fred's Barn" (later called Pantry Shelf) functioned as a bank. The buses picked up and dropped off workers from the fields at the store's parking lot, and the store developed a service where workers could deposit their money. It even had a teller window and offered printed receipts to customers. It opened early and closed late to accommodate the farmworkers' schedules. Fred's Barn did not pay interest on the deposited funds, but at least the money was safe there—or so the workers thought. The store acted as a post office, too, where migrants could mail letters and pick up mail from home.

In June of 1983, Pantry Shelf abruptly closed its doors. Sister Maureen remembered it, because her office was right across the street. One day she saw a huge crowd of Haitians protesting outside the store. It was not only Haitians who lost their money; hundreds of migrant laborers lost all their savings. When the store collapsed, there was only about one thousand dollars cash on hand. The owners later pleaded guilty to money-laundering charges.

The *Miami Herald* picked up the story and it ended up in newspapers all over the country. People sent money, and Guadalupe Outreach coordinated the effort of returning some of their savings to the farmworkers. Dan Rather of CBS had done a documentary on Florida farmworkers in 1970, and sent a representative to interview Sister Eileen for CBS News. They did the interview in the soup kitchen, with 2,500 letters containing donations piled on the table in front of her. It was not enough to replace all the workers' savings, but at least they got part of their money back.

Sister Eileen accomplished smaller things, too, every day. She sent out a monthly letter to volunteers and donors that explained how their gifts helped the people of Immokalee.

"Despite my early morning prayer," she wrote in one letter, "I feel inadequate as I approach the office and see the line of waiting people—need written in their faces, their clothing, their bearing. Faint smiles, a few 'Good mornings' greet me as I pass. An old man grabs my arm and tries to tell me his story as I go in."

The letter then describes one day's work at the Guadalupe Outreach office.

"Maria comes in. She is pregnant and cannot get migrant health insurance. Ernesto's electricity will be cut off if he doesn't pay the bill today; he could only get two days of fieldwork last week and it paid for some food and medicine for his baby daughter, but not the electric bill. Leonore's family just moved into a one-room migrant housing apartment for $60 a week, unfurnished, and she wants to know if there is any way to get some used beds or mattresses."

The letter goes on to say that on her way home, Eileen brings some rice to Elena and her children. Elena is very grateful, because she cooked her last bag of beans the night before. She stops to pick up Jessie's mail and takes it to her; visits a family living in a gutted trailer to see if she can help; and takes a blanket to Anna who just got out of the hospital. For her work in Immokalee, Eileen later received a state award for "Outstanding Community Leadership."

At the same time, Guadalupe Center expanded beyond the soup kitchen. In 1983, Sisters Jane and Marie added tutoring, getting back to the roots of their order: "School Sisters." The addition of other services gave them the opportunity to hire local people as employees. A year later, a used-clothing program was added in the back of the property, and Maria Rodriguez, a *Tejana* who was previously a field worker, was hired to run it. The following year showers, toilets, and washing machines were added for migrants without plumbing; they could leave their dirty clothes in exchange for clean ones.

In the summer of 1984, Eileen changed the name of her organization from Guadalupe Outreach to Guadalupe Social Services and hired three more people: Sister Barbara Pfarr, SSND, Maria Teresa Gaston-Witchger, and John Witchger.

Sister Barbara and John Witchger organized farmworkers to start a tenant organization to work on concerns in their lives and their neighborhoods. Barbara described the work they did as "systemic change," or getting at the causes of the poverty—different from charity, which helps people with immediate needs. Their work gave the farmworkers and rural poor a political voice and built working relationships between Guatemalans, Mexicans, and Haitians. With the help of Barbara and John, Guadalupe Social Services worked to identify what the new immigrants needed and developed a support system to help them solve their own problems.

The organization soon expanded its goals and got involved with working conditions in the fields. John Witchger and Sister Barbara drove vanloads of migrant farm laborers to Washington, D.C. to advocate national field sanitation laws. They also made many trips to Florida's capital, Tallahassee, to get field workers involved in promoting benefit laws.

Soon more people came to help. One of the more unusual volunteers was Mike Kimble, who photographed Immokalee, and with his photographs, educated people about the needs of the new immigrants. His collections were printed in the *Naples Daily News* and the *Miami Herald*, and he became known in Immokalee as the "picture man." Sometimes he gave the new immigrants copies of the pictures of themselves. John Witchger remembered visiting a man in the flophouse who proudly posted his photograph, taken by Mike, on the wall next to his bed.

I have seen those flophouses; they are still there. I even remember seeing a faded picture on a wall, and it might have been one of Mike's. I saw it because, just before Christmas the first year I was out there, Sister Judy asked if I would help her deliver presents of toiletries to Immokalee's homeless. "The poorest of the poor," she called them.

St. William's parish in Naples provided the gifts. They do it every year. I agreed to help Judy distribute them, intensely curious to learn more about Immokalee. My role was easy: play the guitar and lead people in Christmas carols.

We walked through flophouses and shelters, delivering the bags of toothpaste, deodorant, shampoo, and soap. These places tend to segregate by nationality. Young Guatemalan men slept four or six to a room in tiny one-room houses with no plumbing, while not far away, U.S.-born whites slept in a long building in individual rooms with hotplates. Fifteen to twenty of them shared a single toilet and shower with broken plumbing, and filthy floors and walls. Mexicans stayed in a similar building farther down the street.

We stopped to bring gifts to some of Immokalee's prostitutes, mostly white women living in small, dirty rooms. We left some gifts for them in a tavern on the corner, too.

In one place there were two large rooms, with maybe thirty cots in each room. A drunken white man with missing teeth asked if he could play my guitar. I let him, but he didn't really know how to play. He just pretended he was playing chords and strummed a little, but he enjoyed it. A white woman about my age came up and started to sing with me. She was "worn," but very sweet, and grateful to sing a Christmas carol. I would like to have stayed longer with her.

I was feeling good until we got to a place where there was a group of Haitian men. They smiled and were very happy for the music. They looked comfortable, yet like they didn't belong there. I decided that next year I would learn how to sing "We Wish You a Merry Christmas" in Haitian Creole. These men were very appreciative of the gifts and the music. When I saw them, all the poverty I had seen that night came crashing down on me. I kept singing and playing, but I wondered, what did all these people want in the beginning of their lives? What did they expect to find in Immokalee? They may be happier and safer than they were in the place they left, but couldn't their lives be better than this?

Tears I could not control streamed down my face, but I kept on playing. The men stared at me quietly, and I could tell they felt sorry for me. *They* felt sorry for *me*. The present-givers took over the singing, and we moved on to the next place.

The immigrants kept coming, and more people came to help them. Father Sanders guided and inspired many of them, working tirelessly to help the immigrants make Immokalee a livable home. He spent his days and nights doing both religious and social work, always focused on organizing and empowering people to help themselves.

Then, in January of 1985, Father Richard Sanders had a heart attack. He was only forty-eight years old, overly stressed from the efforts of helping the migrant population, and from working alone. There was no hospital in Immokalee, then or now, so people in Immokalee had to go to Naples Community Hospital in downtown Naples. It is over an hour's drive, and Immokalee's one ambulance was already in Naples with a Haitian woman having a baby, so it took longer than it should have to get medical help for Father Sanders. As a result, there was massive damage to his heart. He was later taken to Mercy Hospital in Miami for surgery, but the damage could not be repaired. He suffered two strokes, and on March 18, 1985, Father Richard Sanders died.

Our Lady of Guadalupe church was filled with people praying for him, and people who were there say that thunder rolled and lightning flashed at the time of his death. The church bell tolled in mourning for twenty-four hours.

An altar was placed outside, between the church and the soup kitchen, for the wake and the funeral, because so many people came that they could not fit inside the church. During the wake service, the night before the funeral, two large white swallow-tailed kites flew in and circled the altar, then flew away. Nearly a thousand people came to the funeral, making a long procession around the church and then down Ninth Street as grieving Mexicans, Haitians, Guatemalans, *Tejanos*, and U.S.-born Blacks and Whites passed the coffin from one to another. Everyone wanted to carry him.

His mother came and was incredibly moved to see how loved her son was. She insisted on personally greeting every person who was there. Remembering this, Sister Eileen said, "It was then that I understood why Richard had such a deep compassion and respect for each human being."

Father Sanders was so loved by the people of Immokalee that he was buried on the grounds of Our Lady of Guadalupe Church, just off to the side of the original church building that is now called "Sanders Hall." Burials on Catholic church grounds are uncommon, and this one required much petitioning on the part of the parishioners.

"It was so clear, such a good idea," said Sister Maureen, "because he was such a giant of a figure in a very humble, silent way."

Each year the parish has remembered him at a special Mass on the anniversary of his death. People frequently come by the gravesite, clean it, and leave flowers. Every year when the migrant workers return from the north, a group repaints the railing around his grave.

After Father Sanders' death, Bishop Nevins made it a rule that a priest should never work alone in Immokalee. Father Vilmar Orsolin, CS (Congregation Scalabrini), pastor of Our Lady of Guadalupe in the 1990s, talked to me about this.

"The church wants priests to live in the community," he explained. "They have to live together so they can assist each other. If Father Sanders had had somebody with him, he would not have died like that. He was all for others, just giving and giving until he gave himself up to death."

In the summer of 1985, a new order of priests took over Our Lady of Guadalupe parish. They were Scalabrinian, an order dedicated to the religious, moral, social and legal care of migrants.

The Scalabrinians were started in 1887 by an Italian bishop named John Baptist Scalabrini, who felt compassion toward the poor Italians who were leaving Italy, bound for a new country where they could work and make a better life. Later he started receiving letters from the people who had migrated to countries all over the world, complaining about the condition of their lives. He started the Congregation of the Missionaries of St. Charles to help them. The people they served were very much like the immigrants in Immokalee in the 1980s.

Father Isaia Birollo was the first pastor to be assigned to Immokalee from their order. Father Isaia worked closely with the new immigrants, helping in the soup kitchen and with other services. He humbly rode around Immokalee on a bicycle to visit people. Later, in 1986, another Scalabrinian arrived. The new priest was Haitian: Father Jacques Fabre. He made his novitiate in Mexico, where he learned Spanish, so he also spoke the three main languages of the Immokalee parish. It was Father Isaia's direction from the beginning not to have Father Jacques there only for the Haitians, so the two priests alternated saying the Sunday Masses in Spanish and Haitian Creole. They wanted the parishioners to know they were both there for everyone. Father Vilmar Orsolin explained this concept to me.

"If you're just here for the Haitians," he said, "you don't help the Haitians. You have to push yourself to learn the language of the country you're in in order to be a liaison from the nation to the immigrants. You have to be the leader that goes to the new culture and new language and enrich yourself so you can help these people mingle into the new culture." In Immokalee, the new culture was not only American, but also Mexican, Central American, and Haitian.

At that time, mingling into new cultures was not a priority. People still needed decent places to live. Not long before Father Sanders died, he heard about money available for housing. John Witchger remembered when, not long after he and Sister Barbara started working in Immokalee, Father Sanders came to their office and gave John the keys to the parish van. He told John to pick up a group of guys in front of the church at 6:00 p.m. and drive them into the County Courthouse for a meeting.

"There's some money available in the county for people in need," he said to John, "and we need that money out here."

John picked up the men in front of the church and drove to the courthouse. John remembered Celestine Pierre, one of the Haitians who was translating for the others, who stood up and explained the biggest problem.

"We need housing," said Celestine. "We live in places that don't even have plumbing."

Not long after the county meeting, with a one hundred-dollar donation, Guadalupe Social Services founded Immokalee Non-Profit Housing, Inc. This organization developed two housing projects of rental apartments: Sanders Pines and Timber Ridge. At one point, the development of Sanders Pines got stalled, but Carl Kuehner, a developer from Naples went out to see John Witchger. He sat down in John's office and asked, "Is there anything I can do to help out here?" Carl looked at Sanders Pines and cut a deal with the general contractor to get it finished, then he worked to get a tax credit program and got loans from state and local banks to develop Timber Ridge. Organizations helped each other, too. Years later, for example, volunteers from Habitat for Humanity spiffed-up Timber Ridge homes by giving them a fresh coat of paint.

The other kind of housing needed was the kind people could own. The first three Habitat for Humanity houses were completed in 1980, and the happy new owners moved in: one white family, one black, and one *Tejano*. The new immigrants would wait a few years before they could qualify, because Habitat families have to provide evidence of stability in this country, including employment data, housing history, Social Security cards for all family members, resident alien cards or birth certificates, three years of tax returns, and rent receipts for the last two months. But it was not long before the Mexicans, Haitians, and Guatemalans had enough history in this country to own Habitat for Humanity homes. By 1988, fifty homes were built, and by 1993 there were one hundred. Several of the people I interviewed in this book own Habitat homes.

Juan Garcia owned one of the first in Immokalee. His story was told in the winter 2003 issue of *Habitat Highlights*. Born in Texas, Juan had worked in the fields from the time he was only four years old.

"Later, when I was nine, I remember filling an eighty-pound sack with cotton," he said. "It was so heavy I could hardly drag it through the rows."

In the summers, the Garcias loaded up their belongings, migrated to Illinois, Michigan, Indiana, and then went to Florida to pick fruit and vegetables. Juan's family found steady work in the fields around Immokalee when he was eleven, and Juan was able to go to school. He graduated from high school, then earned a scholarship to Edison Community College in Fort Myers. While there, he married Maria, who worked in the fields to help support them while he studied and worked odd jobs.

In 1978, when their son Noel was three years old, the Garcias heard about Habitat for Humanity. They went to a meeting, made an application, and were chosen as one of Immokalee's first Habitat families. After contributing the required two thousand hours of sweat equity alongside Habitat volunteers, they moved into their home in 1981.

Today, Juan works at a wholesale tropical fish company in nearby Naples. Maria graduated from floral design and nail-technician school and is a manicurist in Immokalee. Their son Noel graduated valedictorian of his High School class and today has a Bachelor's Degree in Communications. He works at his alma mater, Southeastern College in Lakeland, Florida.

In the winter of 2003, Juan paid off the twenty-year mortgage. He explained the importance of the Habitat effort.

"Our house had an important role in our lives," he said. "It gave us a whole new future...it's *our home.*"

Sam and Mary Ann Durso, Collier County Habitat's president and executive director, received Governor Jeb Bush's Points of Light Award in 2002. They said Habitat for Humanity offers the "American Dream" of home-ownership that people would never have experienced had they not become legal residents of the United States. Habitat for Humanity continues to provide the most single-family, owner-occupied housing for the working poor of Immokalee. The Dursos felt this area was the ideal place for the concept to work.

"We have a hard-working immigrant population," they explained, "combined with a large number of prosperous retired volunteers and donors willing to work side-by-side to provide a simple, decent place to live."

Another area critical to the immigrants was legal help. In the early 1980s, Florida Rural Legal Services in Immokalee was staffed by attorneys Rob Williams and Greg Schell, plus others who were litigating farmworkers' employment cases. In 1983, Sister Maureen joined them for the summer as a volunteer. It was right at the height of the war in Guatemala.

"It was a summer of long hours doing political asylum claims for Kanjobal Mayan Indians from the highlands," she explained. "I spent the summer writing clients' stories about the army's machine gun strafing from helicopters; aerial bombings of mountain hamlets; and selective killings by guerrillas when local leaders would not cooperate."

Their stories captivated her so much that she came back to Immokalee in 1984 as an employee. At that time the only way she could help people seeking legal immigration was if they were eligible for political asylum.

"That meant they had to be able to prove a well-founded fear of persecution based on race, nationality, social group, religion or politics, in their own countries," she explained.

In 1986 new legislation was passed that added an additional dimension to Maureen's work: the Immigration Reform and Control Act (IRCA). We mentioned IRCA briefly earlier because Eduwiges, the Mexican woman who originally came with her brother from Mexico and who now works with children at the Even Start program, got her papers through IRCA.

IRCA said that immigrants could get amnesty if they could prove they had lived in the U.S. since January 1 of 1982. There was a specific provision in IRCA that helped farmworkers—a provision supported by agribusiness. It said farmworkers could get their papers if they could prove they had done ninety days of farm work in the U.S. between May 1, 1985 and May 1, 1986.

Getting this proof was a difficult task, especially for farmworkers who were often paid in cash and for those hired by crew leaders who, at best, kept records in scribbled notebooks. Immokalee's Catholic Church became one of the active offices that assisted thousands of people.

According to Sister Maureen, the INS initially demanded more proof of farm work than IRCA actually required. She said that Rob

Williams "went into high gear," along with Miami attorneys, and they basically sued the federal government to change the way the INS was insisting that IRCA be implemented. The case went all the way to the U.S. Supreme Court, and it changed the lives of thousands of farmworkers, not just in Florida, but all across the United States.

Joe Brueggen became the director of the IRCA Project at Our Lady of Guadalupe in Immokalee, and he hired Lucy Ortiz to help him organize the office and the volunteers. They told the immigrants to bring every piece of paper they could find that proved how long they had been here and how long they had worked, and then the staff would go through it all and try to establish a case.

"They had to prove either that they had been here since before 1982 or else that they had worked for so many days in the year starting May 1, 1985," explained Joe, "so you had to establish that consistency. They sometimes came with names of employers, check stubs, rent receipts, and utility bills. We literally went through bags of bits and pieces of paper, stuff written on the backs of this and that. We flattened it all out, taped it on paper, and made binders for people."

About five thousand people applied, just in Immokalee, but not all of them could find the required proof.

"Unfortunately, there were many times we couldn't complete the trail," continued Joe. "A lot of people qualified to get their papers under IRCA, but they didn't get processed because they just didn't have the pieces of paper they needed."

Lucy told me that the other sad thing was that there were people who knew about it but did not apply because they thought their relatives would be able to sponsor them, or that there would be some other way. Many people still live in Immokalee today "without papers" who would have qualified under IRCA.

Maureen said that the farmworker provisions of IRCA came about because of agriculture's need for labor. She explained that our country's need for labor has historically been the thing that determined whether there was a generous immigration policy or a tight one. At some points in our history, the word was out all over the world that there was work in the United States. That is what made the U.S. the "land of opportunity."

By the early 1990s, over 120,000 Florida farmworkers received their permanent residency through IRCA. More than 2,500 of them were in Immokalee.

In the meantime, more and more immigrants kept coming, still sleeping in their cars, under trucks, behind buildings, and in the palmettos. There was a need for temporary shelter, so Sister Marie at Guadalupe Center formed a committee with other church leaders in Immokalee and developed Immokalee Friendship House. On cold nights Marie would go out in a van, pick people up, and bring them to the shelter. After Friendship House was built, people like Rudy, who were in need of a bed, could stay there instead of in the streets. So can people who have temporarily come on hard times and need a safe place to stay for a few nights.

In early 1988, there was an organized effort by the churches to improve the quality of life, not only in Immokalee but also in all the poor areas of Collier County. Sister Barbara Pfarr organized this group, and the first problem they tackled was the abandoned lots in Immokalee. Pedro Lopez worked with her on this effort, because he said Guatemalans were often mugged near the abandoned lots. The organization was called "Collier United for Rights and Equality" or CURE. A church bulletin explained the problem and the action.

"The abandoned lots are ugly and dangerous. Rats, snakes, and other dangerous things breed in them. Also, robbers and muggers hide in them. The CURE Action Committee is planning a strategy to get the county to clean them up."

Other community actions followed, including a free trash-dumping day to help with efforts to clean up neighborhoods; security lights in the main areas of town; and regular transportation from Immokalee to the Naples hospital. Through the efforts of CURE, an emergency room was added to the Immokalee Clinic, along with a doctor, nurse practitioner, and an aide.

Despite all these efforts, life for the new immigrants of Immokalee was far from ideal. Let's go back to Rudy, the Guatemalan painter who came to fix the mold in our ceiling, to see Immokalee in the 1980s from an immigrant's perspective.

When we last mentioned him, it was 1986, and Rudy had left "Way-way" after the guerillas blew up a military depot near his home. He made his way to the U.S./Mexico border and waited there with one-hundred-fifty other immigrants, afraid that the Indians on the U.S. side wouldn't let them cross. He spent part of his eighteenth birthday buried in the sand to avoid immigration's Border Patrol, then he got a "ride" to Immokalee, a place he knew nothing about. He had less than ten dollars, so he bought a hot dog and a cup of coffee. The soup kitchen and the showers and laundry facilities at Guadalupe Center had opened by the time he came, only a few blocks from where he slept, but he did not know about them. So he ate his hot dog, drank his coffee, and washed his clothes in a water outlet near the trailer.

The next day he started working in the fields, picking cherry tomatoes and learned how difficult fieldwork was. Remember that he was becoming a teacher when he left Huehuetenengo.

"I never did that kind of work before!" he told me. "At the end of one day my hands were full of blisters, and they were swollen. And my back hurt so much!"

Rudy learned about fieldwork and how to be productive from some people who were very good at it: the Mexicans. At first Rudy worked with the Guatemalans, but he said it was a problem because he couldn't understand them. They talked in Mayan languages, that Rudy called "those dialects," and he did not know those languages, so he started working with the Mexicans and was amazed at how fast they were.

"These guys were so good, and I saw them pass by me so fast, so many times! We got paid two dollars a bucket. The guy who picked the most that day, he picked forty-two buckets. By the end of the day, I had picked eight. The next day I couldn't even get up. I slept so bad because I had a fever, my hands were so swollen, so I missed a day of work. The third day I went back and got two more buckets—I picked ten."

I was reminded of Joseph, the older Haitian man who told me, "The Mexican is the Master of the Fields." Rudy eventually got into better shape for fieldwork, and learned some of the tricks for faster picking.

For a while he continued to sleep under the tractor-trailer, but then he made enough money to pay back his ride and rent a place to live. He got a small trailer in one of the migrant camps that cost $320 a month. I assumed he shared the trailer with other guys but he said no, he lived alone.

"I had to get it alone because nobody wanted to go in with me." He meant the Guatemalans.

"Everybody goes with the guys with the dialects. None of them wanted to live with me."

The Mexicans didn't want to live with him either. "The Mexicans have their own little groups, like the Guatemalans have their little groups. I was, like, in the middle again."

It wasn't long before Rudy decided he did not like fieldwork, so he started going to night classes to learn English at Immokalee Middle School.

"I went usually two or three times a week," he explained. "I skipped a lot of nights. By the time you get out of the fields, you feel like you are dead! I had to make something to eat, and wash clothes. There was always something to do. So I could speak a little English, but not very well."

But the little bit of English he could speak helped him get to the next step. One day he started talking to a couple of older white men on the street. They had just started building Friendship House, the homeless shelter, and they hired Rudy to do various kinds of labor. Then Rudy met one of the volunteers from Naples, named Edward.

"Edward helped me a lot," Rudy told me. "By working on Friendship House, I learned about electric work, and carpentry, the way it's done here. In Guatemala, it's totally different, so everything was new for me. Then I helped with the painting, and I learned about painting, too." Another volunteer told Rudy that he should go to Naples to look for work.

"You're doing good work," Frank told him. "You could make more money in Naples than here."

Rudy discussed it with Edward, who told him that if he wanted to go to Naples he should work for an electric company, because electricians made more money than painters did. Rudy liked that idea, but he didn't know anyone and didn't know how to pursue it. Also, because his English was still rudimentary, he had trouble asking questions and understanding the answers. So he continued to work on his English, and started going to school every night. Then one day he talked to Edward again.

Edward said, "Rudy, I have a friend who has an electric company in Naples, and he's willing to take you on."

So Rudy came to Naples and talked to Charlie, the father of a father-and-son company, Bentley Electric. They hired him, but Rudy was disappointed in the work.

"At that time," Rudy told me, "they had me digging ditches to put in pipelines. I was working in the hot sun, doing backbreaking work. It wasn't much different from the fields!"

But after a while, Rudy got to work inside and learned how to do some basic electrical conduit and wiring. After a few months, Chuck—the son in the business—offered to send Rudy to school to learn electrical work. He paid for the school and the books.

Rudy went to school and worked the Bentleys for a few years. Later, when electrical work slowed down, he had to look for another job. He remembered that he had liked painting, so he decided to start his own business.

"So here I am," he said, contentedly. "I have my own business, a wife and family, and a nice house. Some good people helped me out, and I am very grateful to them."

As the 1980s ended, Immokalee was much improved from the beginning of the decade. Social services, housing, health care, and legal aid had been provided to thousands of new immigrants.

Those immigrants, like Rudy, are grateful to the people who helped them: people who gave out food, provided health care and eyeglasses, comforted dying men, brought blankets, paid healthcare or electric bills, built houses, organized workers, inspired community improvements, taught English, provided childcare, and offered legal counseling. They are also indebted to the many volunteers who came—like Mike Hughes, who developed a fundraising database; Joe Brett, who helped build the soup kitchen; Barbara Widman, who provided transportation; Mike Kimble, who documented the immigrants in pictures; and Bill Mauter, who gave away his own shoes.

And finally, Immokalee's own saint, Father Richard Sanders, who gave up his life helping the new immigrants make Immokalee their home. His legacy is carved on his gravestone: "Love one another, as I have loved you."

7

Stepping Stones

"First, I pray that God keeps us healthy. Second, that my children grow up to be good men. And third, I want to get a nice, small house for my family."

—Ana

In the 1990s, the huge influx of immigrants settled down to a more steady flow. There was still work in Immokalee, but the demand for labor was not quite like before. Florida had lost part of the winter vegetable market to Mexico due to two factors: NAFTA (the North American Free Trade Agreement), and the devaluation of the Mexican peso, both of which made it easier for Mexican growers to compete with growers in the U.S. Tomatoes alone illustrate the changes. After NAFTA, Florida's tomato revenues dropped forty-three percent, acreage dedicated to tomatoes in Florida went down twenty percent, and some tomato companies in the Immokalee area went out of business.

Still, there were hundreds of thousands of acres dedicated to agriculture, almost three hundred thousand acres just in Collier County. The migrant stream was still in need of workers and Immokalee was one of the main "jumping off" places, so it was still one of the first places new immigrants came.

Juanita, the young Mexican girl who came to the United States alone when she was only fourteen years old, was one of these. She moved from Texas to Immokalee in the early 1990s, and worked in fields for the first time in her young life.

"I was planting bell peppers," she told me. "I don't remember the company. They paid about four dollars an hour. The first day was OK; I was just walking and replacing plants that died. But the second day I had to plant all day. The next morning my cousin I was living with said, 'Wake up wake up, go to work.'"

But Juanita couldn't even get up, because her back hurt so badly. She said, "Ay, ay, ay, I can't go! My back hurts!"

Other workers heard about this and made it a point not to let her forget it.

"So the day after, I went to work again and everybody said, 'Look who's coming: 'Ay Ay Ay!' It was my nickname after that."

She soon found other work, picking bell peppers instead of planting. She said that for each bucket you picked, you got a ticket.

"After you finished at the end of the day they paid you ten cents per ticket. They paid in cash." Next she worked in tomatoes and then in the packinghouse.

A few years later, her brother asked a friend named Carlos to give Juanita a ride home from the packinghouse. Carlos quickly fell in love with this excitable, vivacious young woman, and it was not long before he asked her to marry him. She did not have to tell me why, because she was delightful. Now they have a beautiful little daughter, they rent a small but comfortable home, and Juanita is very happy. She was laid off from her job as a cashier and now works in the packinghouse, like she did when she was younger, but she is trying to find a different job. The only thing that would make Juanita happier would be to go and visit her mother. Since she doesn't have papers, she can't go—not because she can't get home, but because it would be too expensive and too difficult to get back. If another law like IRCA were passed, many of the immigrants who came illegally in the 1990s could get their papers, and then they could travel back and forth. Juanita could take her daughter to Mexico. Juanita never made it back home for her own

Quinceañera, but when her daughter gets older, maybe she will celebrate her *Quinceañera* with her grandmother.

Workers in the fields today are different from those working when Juanita picked vegetables. The ethnic composition of the field workers is one change; the Haitians have, for the most part, left fieldwork. The other is that there are fewer women and children in the fields, because many women now stay home maintaining steady jobs, and the children go to school.

If the Haitians stay in fieldwork, they tend to work more in the citrus groves. I've been told the reason is that the Haitians like steady work, with regular days and hours.

"Orange picking is usually five days, sometimes six days a week, but never seven days," one of the vegetable growers explained. "And it's steady, at least five days a week. Also, the citrus takes the cold and other conditions much better than the vegetables, so the pickers are rarely out of work. The only thing that will stop orange picking is flood rain."

The Haitians told me the main reason they changed jobs was the amount of money they could earn. One of the men I talked to did fieldwork for four years in tomatoes and peppers, working seven days a week to make three-hundred-fifty dollars.

"Now I work in construction," he said, "where I work five days and make eight-hundred dollars."

Paul Midney suspects that the Haitians' quick shift from fieldwork also has to do with the fact that Latinos dominate the fieldwork.

"The crew leaders and the bosses, mainly, are Mexicans," he told me. "The farmers are used to dealing with the Spanish-speaking people, so it is harder for Haitian crew leaders to get established. The Haitians, therefore, have to work for crew leaders who are Spanish-speaking."

Also, I've been told by many growers that they don't like to hire Haitians for field work. Sister Maureen understood this.

"The work style of the Haitians is very intense, and very 'in your face,' so it really took some of the Mexican crew leaders aback," she explained. "Because if you put a Haitian in a row that doesn't have good cutting or picking, or if you cross over into their row, and they consider it theirs, they're going to tell you."

"Related to legal services, we used to say 'right on,'" Maureen continued. "We love them as clients, because they stick to things once they start them. The Mexicans are more about relationships. They would come in and be mad that day, but then maybe this guy's wife was friendly with that guy's cousin, and by the next day they forget about the problems they had. But if Haitians said they were abused in the field, or they didn't get their minimum wage, or if they had bad, uncertified transport or housing, they'd stick to their lawsuit. It's important, you know, because the law is slow."

The other major change that came in the 1990s is the increased percentage of migrating workers who are single men. Some families still travel the circuit together, but not as many as before.

Anne Goodnight and her husband were growers in the 1970s and 1980s and she said that back then, Immokalee was known for families. Single males went to different towns, such as Belle Glade, about an hour northeast of Immokalee. But beginning in the 1990s there was an increase in the number of single males (*solteros*) coming to Immokalee for work. Some were young, like Manuel, just coming to make some money. Others, like Juan, were married, but had left their wives and children at home while they came here to search for a future. Even if the wives and children lived with their husbands in places like Immokalee, only the men went "up the road" in the summer. More and more wives had steady jobs and maintained the permanent households. Some of the women joined their men on weekends if the picking was close enough.

Lesvia Martinez from Guadalupe Family Center sometimes used her weekends or vacation time to work with her husband, Oscar, in the fields in Georgia. When he went for the whole summer season, however, she stayed in Immokalee. She told me once that she had to make a slight change to the items he was packing for his summer trip. He was taking his guitar and his "dress" cowboy boots.

"I understand why you want your guitar," she told him, "so you have something to do at night at the camp, with the other guys. But those boots are for dancing!"

Oscar went north, and the boots stayed in Immokalee.

Transportation for people going up the road is different now, too. From the 1950s through the 1980s, each family had its own truck, and they literally packed up everything they owned and moved from farm to farm, wherever there was work. More recently, workers stay with one company for the whole season, and often the growers provide transportation in vans or small buses. If the workers move around and work for different growers, groups of men will travel together in a truck or van. They save money by sharing the cost of gas and hotel rooms, plus they have the company of friends.

The 1990s also saw some new ethnic groups, including Indians from Mexico's southern states: Oaxaca and Chiapas. They came because in 1993 the Zapatista Army of National Liberation (EZLN) staged an armed uprising, demanding democracy, liberty, and justice for all Mexicans. Southern Mexico became dangerous and there was very little work. These workers usually went to northern Mexico before coming to the United States.

"The Mexican growers went farther down in Mexico and got the Indians as workers," explained one of the Immokalee growers, "but as soon as those Indians learned the business, they all came here because they heard about how much money the U.S. workers make."

"It means a lot more rural people, Indians, who came," explained Brother Jim Harlow, "but because they do not have the extended social networks of the northern and central Mexicans, these new immigrants have to break the ground for the next ones. They have to discover things, like how to get work or where to live."

Ana, the woman who came alone with her three children from Guatemala and was attacked by bandits in the desert, also arrived in Immokalee in the late 1990s. On their first night in Immokalee, she and her children slept in a trailer that the *coyote* helped her find. There were six other people sleeping there, all men. Ana and the children slept in one corner on the floor. One of the men gave them a blanket. The next day the *coyote* came and took her to a job, picking oranges. She owed him money and she had nothing. She could not pay the *coyote* if she was not working.

"We had just walked for four days, and then rode in a packed truck from Tucson," she explained, "and the next day I had to go and work in oranges. Imagine how my feet hurt! That's all I remember was how much my feet hurt. I made twenty dollars that day." The next night the *coyote* said she and the children could stay at his house with him and his wife.

Ana's life has turned out very well, except for the way her family in Guatemala feels about her. During our interview, she talked about the death of her mother, and suddenly began to sob. I could not understand why she was so upset at this moment about her mother's death, until her husband, Manuel, helped me to see that Ana's mother had *just* died, the week before the interview. She had stomach cancer that killed her very quickly. Ana talked to her on the telephone just before she died, and her mother was happy Ana had gone to the United States, because she sent money that paid for morphine. But now Ana's older brothers and sisters were upset because Ana did not come home for the funeral—so upset that they will not speak to her when she calls. Lucy Ortiz said she sees this often among the women she works with.

"Not to be present for family events like births, deaths, weddings, baptisms, etc. is especially emotionally difficult for people who are not at liberty to cross back and forth freely," Lucy explained. "Usually, the families just don't understand. They don't know how hard it is to get home and back."

Ana has decided to accept the fact that her family doesn't understand. She is angry with them too, for acting this way. They do not know what happened to her in the desert.

"I have to stay here because of my children," Ana started to rationalize, but then got to the real reason: the border crossing.

"I know my family doesn't understand, but I suffered coming over here from Mexico. I won't make that crossing again."

I asked Ana what her goals are now. They are simple.

"First, I pray that God keeps us healthy," she said. "Second, that my children grow up to be good men. And third, I want to get a nice, small house for my family."

Ana's Mexican husband, Manuel, wants the same thing. Remember that Manuel was an orphan. He never knew his father, and his mother died when he was only six. He wants to be a father to Ana's children and make the home for them that he never had himself.

"The future of the children is important," he said. "It's important that the children have a place to come home to."

Different types of support organizations developed in the 1990s. Some of the farmworkers, for example, began a formal organization called the "Coalition of Immokalee Workers," an advocate for workers' rights that organizes activities to protest farmworkers' wages. According to the Coalition, the average pay for a thirty-two-pound bucket of tomatoes is forty cents, and this piece-rate has not changed in twenty years.

Originally, the Coalition was a food cooperative for farmworkers, started in 1991 by Guadalupe Social Services, but then it developed into a more activist group, focused on workers' rights. In June of 1993, took the name of Coalition of Immokalee Workers. Pedro Lopez, the first Guatemalan we met, was one of its founders.

Pedro said they got together whenever they had a free day, once a week or whenever there was time, sometimes after work. The Coalition later came under the leadership of Lucas Benitez, who was born in

Guerrero, south of Mexico City. Lucas moved to Immokalee in 1993 and worked for several years picking tomatoes and oranges. He was able to get his legal residency with the help of his extended family. In 1998, the Coalition held a thirty-day hunger strike that drew national attention, including a letter from former President Jimmy Carter. Pedro Lopez was one of the strikers. The Coalition also sponsored a 230-mile organized walk from Fort Myers to Orlando in early 2000, and later a boycott of Taco Bell.

People came to offer new options to the fieldworkers. Harvest for Humanity, for example, started in the late 1990s to provide year-round jobs and houses. Dick and Florence Nogaj (pronounced NO-jay), call the organization they created a "not-for-profit ministry." It consists of Harvest Farm, where crops alternate so workers do not have to migrate, and a housing development called "Jubilation."

Dick was very clear about their philosophy. "We don't believe in handouts, but we do believe in leveraging the resources that were given to us by God." He added, "If all the people in Naples would leverage their resources to help out here, there wouldn't be any poverty in Immokalee."

Harvest Farm is a 110-acre farm that grows red peppers, peaches, beans, citrus, and blueberries. Their goal is a new kind of farm ownership where workers earn a minimum of $8.50 an hour and after three to five years they will be given stock options to buy part of the farm. Jubilation is a housing development that sits on forty acres and has eighty-nine single and multi-family homes designed for limited and moderate income families.

Many of the people who worked full-time in Immokalee during the 1980s left to help people in other places. Sisters Jane Burke and Marie McFadden left at the end of the decade, and Sister Judy Dohner took over Guadalupe Center. Judy brought in many of the staff members that manage Guadalupe Center today. Janie Vidaurri, the organization's director of services, was hired as a secretary in 1993. She is a former fieldworker herself. Her real first name is San Juana, but some Immokalee schoolteachers had trouble pronouncing her name, so they called her Janie. She was born in Reynosa, Mexico, into a migrant worker family. One day her father went to Immokalee to visit his aunt.

"He saw there was a lot of work here," said Janie, "so he decided to come to stay."

Later, he brought his family. Janie's father was here "with papers," because Janie's grandfather came to this country legally long before Janie was born. She is not sure how or why, but I suspect it was similar to the parents of Gloria Contreras, whom we met in Chapter Two. Gloria's grandmother and her brothers and sisters were given citizenship because American men were away in World War II and our country needed labor. Janie's grandfather came the same way. He later petitioned to bring his daughter, Janie's mother, and later she brought her own husband and children. For many years, Janie traveled with her family as they followed the crops to Michigan, North Carolina, and Colorado.

Sister Judy also hired Esther Montero, who today is the Soup Kitchen supervisor. Janie and Esther have known each other since they were children, when Esther's brothers were crew leaders and both girls worked for them in the local fields. At first Esther was a volunteer at the Soup Kitchen, but in May of 1993 she was put on the payroll. Esther has a very special way of dealing with the volunteers who come to serve the poor of Immokalee. Each one is treated as if they were her favorite. She welcomes all the volunteers with hugs and calls them "my love." Two of my Naples friends volunteer twice a month at the Soup Kitchen. When they go, they never say, "We're going out to the Soup Kitchen." Rather they say, "We're going out to see Esther."

Sister Judy looked at Immokalee and saw the gradual progression experienced by families like those of Janie and Esther. People were leaving fieldwork for more stable jobs, but they still needed assistance because, by leaving the fieldwork they lost access to services that were subsidized for farmworkers. One of those services was child care.

These people needed affordable daycare for their children, and many of them still needed help with their own education, so Sister Judy worked on the funding, and in 1996 she opened the Guadalupe Center for Family Education. The parents pay fees for childcare, but on a sliding scale, based on their ability to pay. An after-school program provides tutoring for children in grade school and includes scholarship opportunities for the tutors, most of whom are students at Immokalee High School.

Judy also started the "shoe program" that led me to the Family Center in the first place, when an article about it appeared in the Naples Daily News. About three hundred children get new shoes for the school year through the Guadalupe Center Shoe Program.

The Guadalupe Family Center still serves the non-migrating families of Immokalee with daycare services, and I still teach them music every Wednesday. When I first arrive at the Family Center, sometimes the children see me from the playground. The little two- and three-year-olds come running up, wanting a hug hello, laughing and calling out, "Ms. Carlene! Ms. Carlene!"

The second year I was there, on my birthday Ms. Queenie wrote me a poem. She drew a picture of a guitar in waxed crayon on one side of a 9 X 11 piece of paper and taped the poem on the back. She wrote the poem based on the songs I sang with the children and the stories I told about my father.

> Blow, blow summer wind
> Blow like you will never blow again
> I am looking for my long lost friend
> Listening for that sweet, sweet sound of music,
> Echoing in the distant summer wind.

I can hear the picking of your fingers
Like a gentle whisper in the night,
Blow, blow summer wind.

Sitting on the porch one starry summer night,
Daddy picking those guitar strings
Oh, how those songs to sing
Remembering those days of old
The memories Daddy's guitar holds.

I take Daddy's guitar with me wherever I go
I met a boy named Joe
I teach him to pick that guitar, just like
Daddy taught me.

Girl, you pick that guitar slow
Let the rhythm flow
Daddy, I'll always cherish those guitar memories
I'll pick that guitar high and low
To the end of the rainbow.

A special "note" written on our hearts.
We love you and thank you a lot, Ms. Carlene.
From the Busy Bees

Queenie gave the poem to me while I was singing with the children. They knew about it ahead of time and were very excited to see my reaction. I tried to read it out loud, but only tears came; it was so beautiful. The children stared at me nervously, then looked at each other, then frowned at Ms. Queenie, and then looked back at me. They were confused, because they all expected that I would *like* this present. Of course I explained that I loved it, but later I heard that the children talked about it all day long, telling everyone: "Ms. Queenie made Ms. Carlene cry!"

My favorite thing, now that I've been going to the Family Center for more than five years, is watching the children as they grow. I work with some of them the entire time they attend the Family Center because I work with all the age groups. I see them grow from babies to toddlers to three and four-year-olds. Often I am surprised at how much they have learned. Sometimes I think they are not even listening, but then I find out later that they have heard and learned everything that was taught.

Here's an example. We sing a Kindermusic song called "Hello, Everybody." Its verses are designed to incorporate the children's names as we sing. "If your name is ___, raise your hand!" The children are usually about one-and-a-half years old before they raise their hand only when their own name is called. Up to that point, the teachers raise their hands for them. We make a big deal out of it when they finally get the concept, clapping and telling them what a great job they did. It helps them get in the habit of raising their hands for school, and helps me remember their names.

Two-year-old Priscilla Perez was one of the children I used to think was not paying attention, because she was very quiet. But then I learned that Priscilla would go home and sing the songs I taught to her mother, including "If your name is Mommy, raise your hand!" Her mother is Bruna Perez, the administrative secretary at Guadalupe Center. Before Guadalupe Center, Bruna worked at the Six L's Packinghouse office for four years, doing timekeeping, payroll, and other accounting. "But when they went up the road," Bruna told me, "I wouldn't go up the road. I stayed here in Immokalee."

Bruna also asked me to write down the Haitian Creole words to a song "Hello" that we sing in three languages. When I asked why, Bruna said she was fluent in English and Spanish, so she could sing the first two verses, but two-year-old Priscilla could not understand why her mother wasn't able to sing the Creole verse, too.

Some of the children remember me when they are older. It makes me happy when they do, but it does not bother me when they don't. I know I have given them skills that will help them in their lives: concepts like high notes and low notes, rhythm they learn by strumming my guitar, skills like echoing back what I sing to them, and phonological awareness that will later help them learn to read.

Immokalee Child Care Center (ICCC) expanded in the 1990s, too. In July 1996 it opened an 11,000-square-foot facility where it serves up to one-hundred-fifteen children, ranging in age from four weeks to five years. In April of 2001, Naples artist Flo Huey and her husband Ted added murals of native Florida animals to the walls of the multi-purpose room. The ICCC Mission Statement reads "The mission of ICCC is based on creating a positive, nurturing environment, where relationships are strengthened, children are encouraged, and families are able to begin laying a strong, healthy foundation for their children."

Today the families served by the Immokalee Child Care Center are about sixty percent Latino, thirty percent Black, and the rest White, Haitian, or Native American. ICCC's executive director, Valarie Bostic, described the children of Immokalee in a newsletter:

"When children are young, they aren't aware of the color of their skin, their social status, or how attractive they are. They don't know if they will be cool and poised like the rose, radiant like the sunflower, or bright like the tulip. These things are learned through the different experiences of life which shape who the children become."

There is something very special about being part of the life experiences that shape Immokalee's children.

Additional pre-school and school-support services started up in the 1990s as well. In 1993 Collier County Public Schools created The Learning Center, a pre-kindergarten site that serves children under many government-sponsored programs, including Head Start, Title I Basic, Title I Migrant, and Pre-K Exceptional Education Students.

Many of the children I teach at Guadalupe Family Center move on to The Learning Center when they turn four. I go to this building to sing at Even Start with parents and their children together. We do many songs about body parts, colors, and movements, and the children's songs help the mothers remember English words. The parents enjoy singing in each other's languages; for example, "Hello"—the song Priscilla Perez insisted her mother learn.

> Hello, hello, hello how are you?
> I'm fine, I'm fine, and I hope that you are too.
>
> *Hola, hola, hola ¿como estás?*
> *Muy bien, muy bien, y espero que tu tambien.*
>
> *Bonjou, bonjou, bonjou kijan ou ye?*
> *M' byen, m' byen, m'espere ou menm tou.*

At Even Start, with the children and parents together, we sing Mexican songs like "*Cielito Lindo,*" and the Haitians learn them. Other times we sing Haitian or French songs, like "*Li la Bib-ou*" or "*Frere Jacques,*" and the Latino women learn them. Eduwiges Alvarez, the Mexican woman who was able to give her parents a fiftieth wedding anniversary celebration at a cathedral in Mexico, works at Even Start. She told me the staff and the mothers really like it when we sing in three languages.

She said, "It makes us feel like we are all one."

As important as children, child care, and education were, Immokalee still had unmet needs in the 1990s. One was public transportation. While perhaps not needed in many small towns, it was important in Immokalee because most of the new immigrants did not have cars. They got around by waiting at the side of the road, and people would stop and give them a ride. Sometimes these rides cost between a dollar and five dollars.

I remember noticing this "waiting" before I understood it. At one Good Friday multi-lingual celebration at Our Lady of Guadalupe church, an older man who looked like an Indian from southern Mexico, played the guitar with us. After the services I saw him waiting in the church parking lot. He stood silently, with that look, as if he were already doing what he was supposed to be doing—as if waiting were an activity of its own. At the time, I assumed he was waiting for someone, and I drove away. Now I know he was just waiting for anyone. He was a musician, and we had played our guitars together that night, so after I figured it out I felt badly about not offering him a ride. I decided that next time I would take him, but I never saw him again.

Just before she left Immokalee in 2000, Sister Judy got funding for a bus to make sure there was always a ride. It is only one bus, and it's not a new bus, but it provides transportation within Immokalee. People don't have to walk, carrying their groceries home, and they don't have to sit at the side of the road waiting for a ride, hoping someone will pick them up and won't charge too much money. Volunteers hand-painted the bus, including block lettering that read "THE BUS."

Toward the end of her time in Immokalee, Sister Judy was named the *Naples Daily News* 1999 Citizen of the Year. In June of 2000 she received the Jefferson Award from the American Institute for Public Service, an award founded by Jacqueline Kennedy Onassis and Sen. Robert Taft, Jr., to recognize people whose "progressive leadership and sense of duty to the American people have exemplified the essence of the American spirit."

Umbrella funding organizations also started in the 1990s. Parker Collier founded the Immokalee Foundation, one example, in 1991, dedicated to making it easier for contributors to "provide a brighter future for the children of Immokalee through education, career development, and health care." Don Del Bello, administrative director of the foundation, furnished information about it. More than $1.3 million has been distributed in grants and scholarships since 1992.

Another funding organization started in 2000: the Naples Winter Wine Festival. It started as a conversation among friends who happened to be "avid aficionados" of good food and great wine. The founders secured the interest of more than thirty world-renowned chefs and vintners to help stage an event that would attract some of the nation's most prominent bidders and collectors of fine wine. They wanted to use the funds to make a significant impact on the community.

In 2001, the inaugural year, the Naples Winter Wine Festival raised $2.7 million that it provided to two Collier County organizations. In 2003, $5.1 million was raised and distributed to fourteen organizations, including $750,000 toward the expansion of the Guadalupe Family Center. Soon the "Jelly Beans" (two and a half years old) will have a classroom in a building instead of a trailer, and the long list of people waiting for child care at that center will be accommodated. Every child care organization in Immokalee has a waiting list like Guadalupe's.

There are so many organizations that one might think they would work in competition with each other, but the overall needs are so great that they generally complement one another instead.

"Even though we are all in competition for private funds, I don't see that that has ever stopped any of us from working together," explained Barbara Mainster of RCMA. "It's just a small-town mentality. A lot of us are enamored with Immokalee because the people are super. I am never afraid to be in this town at night. Some wonderful people chose to come here. Those of us who are here are here because we really love it."

Sister Maureen is one of the people who remained in Immokalee after the 1980s, continuing her legal work. She stayed with Florida Rural Legal Services through 1996, but then our government passed what she called "very anti-immigrant legislation." It said that legal service attorneys were not allowed to work with clients unless those clients were legal, permanent residents of the United States. Since many of her clients were seeking political asylum, meaning they were not yet eligible for residency, Maureen was no longer allowed to help them.

Rather than abandon the people she was most devoted to, Maureen got support from her order, and she and three other attorneys who were in the same situation started the Florida Immigrant Advocacy Center (FIAC), with offices now in Immokalee, Miami, and Fort Pierce. In 2001, FIAC received the American Immigration Lawyers Association's Pro Bono Award and Sister Maureen was nominated for the Florida Association for Women Lawyers' Golden Achievement Award.

"I stayed because in immigration law I continue to assist workers and their families get legal residence in the U.S.," she explained. "I have been busy at it for years, and as different laws are enacted, there are new needs and challenges. It is very satisfying work. The people are so hard working. The laws present an intellectual challenge so I can keep growing. I do not envision leaving as long as there is a need here."

Today, Sister Maureen's small office in Immokalee covers ten counties in Southwest Florida that she handles by herself with three paralegals: Ana Rivera, Nadine Pierre, and Sister Kelly Carpenter. Sister Kelly is from Maureen's order, and joined her in 2002 to expand the offices work with abused women and children. She explained that there are three programs: VAWA (Violence Against Women Act); the U Visa; and the Special Immigrant Juvenile program, all created to help victims of domestic violence and other crimes move toward legal residency in the United States. Many of these victims have endured years of violence, beatings and rapes as well as horrific emotional and psychological abuse. They are usually isolated by their abusers and are often unaware there are avenues of escape. Because they do not have papers, their abusers threaten to turn them in if they say anything to anyone. FIAC helps these women and children with legal assistance.

Thus far, Catholic Charities and The Florida Bar Foundation have helped support their work, but the small office continually struggles for funding.

Part of Sister Maureen's work is helping to reunite families by filing petitions for parents to bring their children. In the 1990s there was a great deal of unification of Haitian families, because IRCA, passed in 1986, contained a section specific to Haitians. It allowed them to become legalized if they had arrived in the U.S. before 1982. After they got their papers under IRCA, these new permanent residents could file for immigrant visas for their spouses and children. Maureen helped them with the paperwork, but they waited until the 1990s for the visas to be issued.

I talked with a young woman named Michelle, one of the children from Haiti who was finally permitted to come to join her parents in the 1990s. She was born in 1975, the middle child of seven children. Her English, spoken with a charming French-Haitian accent, is nearly perfect, and she is smart and very gracious.

In Haiti, Michelle's father was in the Haitian army and her mother was an independent businesswoman. Her mother used to go to Santo Domingo and other islands to buy merchandise that she would then sell in Haiti. After Baby Doc left in 1986, she got nervous. Michelle vaguely remembers her father and mother talking in hushed voices about what was happening in the streets. I asked Michelle about her father, wondering about his role in the army.

"They had the *Makout* when he was in the army, but he wasn't part of them," she said. "I don't know all the stories, but I heard some of them…of what the police and the army were doing to people, just killing people. But my father wasn't."

Her father was in the middle of the violence, trying to keep order in a country where there was no order, but when Baby Doc left, Michelle's mother worried that he might not even be able to keep their family safe, so she decided to come to the U.S. for good.

"I don't have a steady job anyway," she reasoned. "So why don't I just stay in the U.S. in case something happens?"

Michelle's father stayed in Haiti and took care of the children, while Michelle's mother got things set up for them all to move to the U.S. It was hard on the children, because they really had no other family.

"We had aunts," Michelle told me, "but you couldn't count on them. They would stay with us for one or two years, and then whenever they started their own families, they would go."

So Michelle became the mother.

"Me and my sisters and brother took care of each other," she explained. "I'm not the oldest, but I was like a manager, like a leader, in trying to watch out for my sisters. You wouldn't believe that on Saturdays I had to do the shopping. You should have seen me, acting like a little lady; I was only about twelve years old. I made sure I had everything on a list, I need to get this and this. Sometimes my dad spent the whole week out and my sisters and brother were looking at me, going, 'All right, where is the food? Because you are the manager.'"

Michelle waited for years to come to the United States.

"I don't know if you know how long it takes to get a visa to come here," she explained. "Like, for me, I didn't expect to come here, because it's been something I've heard since I was a little kid from my mother. She'd always be telling me, 'Oh, I've applied for you to come to the United States.' And then I'm ten, and then I'm fifteen or sixteen, and still nothing. Then you get a paper that says 'Come to the Embassy,' and then you go there, but you have a problem, or they say we can't give you the visa for this or that."

"Because of things like that, I didn't get my hopes up," she continued, "so I figured I better just concentrate on my studies because I don't know if it's going to happen or not. And I think if I can't come to the U.S., I was hoping to go to Paris, because they speak French, and Haitian people go there. I knew people from Haiti who have been waiting forever to go to the U.S. and the family member dies, and everything stops. That means you've been waiting for something for so long and now you can't do anything."

After her long period of waiting, however, Michelle finally got her visa to come to the United States. Today she is happy in her job as outreach coordinator at one of Immokalee's schools, but like most Haitian women I have met, she still has a dream of starting her own business.

Many other immigrants came to Immokalee in the 1990s to begin new lives. Like Michelle, some who came to join their families were educated and conversant in English. They moved immediately into middle-class jobs. Others were alone, uneducated, unfamiliar with English, and grateful just to have a job in the fields. Because of these differences, Immokalee became a small melting pot, not only of people from different cultures, but of people who were on many different levels or steps in their lives. Regardless of what step they're on, they come, and they stay, because there is work in Immokalee.

"It's easy for the Americans to say, 'Just send them back home,'" said Pedro Lopez from Guatemala. "But what would I do if I go home? There is nothing to go back to. We would all be picking coffee for the rest of our lives, and starving. There is no future there."

Pedro said the decision to stay is mostly about his children, but also about the life he wants for himself and his wife. Asking them if they want to go home is much like asking my mother's grandparents if they wanted to go back to Ireland during the famine. Of course they would, but they could not do it. At home there was only bleak poverty with no hope for the future, so they stayed in the U.S. and made a new life. Immokalee's immigrants are doing the same thing.

The immigrants keep in touch with their families and friends, however, and they send money home. A study conducted in 2001 by Bendixen and Associates of Miami showed that immigrants sent eighteen billion dollars from the U.S. to Latin America and the Caribbean. Over nine billion dollars went to Mexico alone.

Sister Maureen had first-hand experience with the results of this money.

"I've walked the hillside of mountains in Queretaro in Mexico, where farmworkers in the U.S. send money," she told me. "Because of that money, the community now has an irrigation holding tank and pipes and hosing so they can provide drip irrigation for orchards of peach trees. It's the best foreign aid we ever heard of, and it goes directly to the families and the villages."

The study showed that the poorest immigrants were usually the most dedicated about sending money home to their families. I remember the people I talked with. Fifteen-year-old Juanita sent one or two hundred dollars a month home to her mother in Mexico. Ana sent money to pay for morphine for her mother. Mexican men like Juan worked here alone for ten years or more, sending money home the whole time.

When help was needed, the immigrants also supported people in their countries whom they didn't even know. Sister Barbara was working at Farm Worker Village when the earthquake hit Mexico City in 1985.

"The people I worked with at Farm Worker Village were very, very poor," she said. "Often there was nothing in the house—maybe a few chairs or a table—but very sparse. Yet when the huge earthquake hit in Mexico, the leaders immediately contacted me and asked for help in sending the money they had raised for the victims."

The new immigrants have come to stay, and many of them have moved out of the fields into better jobs. One path is to get into crew management in the fields, and then into farm management.

Manuel, who married Ana and adopted her three children, is a crew boss with two trucks, but he does not want to leave his new family, so he does not go up the road in the summer. Instead, he works in construction in nearby Naples, but he enjoys managing crews of workers in the fields.

"When there are tomatoes," he said, "I prefer tomatoes."

Oscar Yzaguirre is an example of a field worker who moved up to farm manager. His wife, Cynthia, goes to our church. Patty Swilley, the office manager of Everglades Farms, told me about Oscar.

Oscar was born in Miami in 1963, to Mexican parents. He worked in the fields most of his young life, ending up in Immokalee when he was sixteen years old. He started working in the fields at Sunshine Farms, and then with Johnny Johnson, whom Patty called "Mr. Johnny." Mr. Johnny put Oscar on as assistant foreman, and later, in 1988, Oscar took over all the day-to-day operations of the farm. It wasn't long before Oscar ended up buying out the other owners and took over Everglades Farms.

"Oscar put his whole heart and soul into everything," said Patty. "All the migrant workers would only say good things about him. He was fair, and he treated his guys well. They had the same crew all the time. They all stayed."

Tragically, only a few months after Oscar took over the farm, he was killed in a car accident. His wife, Cynthia, took over the business and was named "Businesswoman of 2002" by the Immokalee Chamber of Commerce. A scholarship has been set up in Oscar's name that provides tuition money for students every year.

Unless the workers move up in farm work, the next step on the social ladder is to move out of fieldwork entirely. Often these next-step jobs are landscaping, construction, golf course maintenance, supermarket jobs, hotel, or restaurant work. Some of these jobs require English.

Learning languages is not easy for most people, and English, in particular, is difficult. The immigrants who work in the fields or the packing houses don't have much opportunity to practice; they work in places where everyone speaks Spanish or Haitian Creole, and their spouses speak Spanish or Haitian. Lastly, perhaps most importantly, there isn't much extra time in the day. Greg Asbed explained how it is for people who work in the fields:

"Generally you wake up around 4:00 a.m. You're standing there trying to get on a bus at 5:00 or earlier. Then you go to the fields, you work all day, and you're home by about 6:00 or 7:00. You're dead tired, you haven't eaten since mid-day, and you have to shower, eat, and spend a little time with your children. Then, the most you can really do is sit around and talk to a few friends before you go to bed and do it all over again."

In the 1990s, more programs were added in Immokalee to teach English. RCMA started a partnership with the schools that provides English literacy classes for adults. Guadalupe Social Services began a "School on Wheels" program, managed by Sister Lorraine Soukup, assisted by Sister Eleanor Frankenberg, both School Sisters of Notre Dame. The program echoes the initial SSND charter of teaching women. Volunteers are first trained in a teaching method that works well for one-on-one lessons. Then, once a week each volunteer goes to the home of an immigrant woman, and for ninety minutes they practice conversational English.

Another example is Sister Margaret Quinlan, IBVM (Institute of the Blessed Virgin Mary), who manages adult education at the Guadalupe Family Center. She provides GED instruction for staff and parents during the day, and parent workshops and "ESL" (English as a second language) classes in the evenings.

Former field workers also get into trades, leaving unskilled manual labor entirely, as Rudy Lopez did when he learned electricity. Usually, the individuals have to take courses to learn their trade. Rudy, as you will remember, had not only encouragement, but also financial help from Chuck Bentley to take courses in electric work.

Nicolas, from Guadalupe Social Services, agreed about the importance of people learning trades, in spite of the fact that I remember him saying that he studied agriculture in Haiti. Today he focuses on education and discourages farm work with the people he sees, especially the young people.

"I always encourage young people not to work in the fields," said Nicolas. "If I were the farmer, I would consider myself a millionaire, because the richness is in the ground, but not to be working in the fields."

He tells them, "Why don't you go to school? As a young person, I want you to learn something. Get a trade. Working in the fields is not a career."

He sighed, and then added, "Some of them listen."

Moving into other types of careers, such as healthcare or childcare, also requires additional education. As we've learned, many of the immigrants only went to school for six years in their home countries, and even the *Tejanos* quit high school as soon as it was legally allowed. In Immokalee and the surrounding areas today, office and service jobs require at least a GED or a high school diploma.

High school degrees were not considered very important in the earlier days of Immokalee. Maria Rodriguez, who manages the Guadalupe Center Clothing Room, came to Immokalee from Texas in 1968, with her parents and thirteen sisters and brothers.

"Back then," she said, "everybody that spoke English and Spanish could get a job at the schools, the clinics, and other places. In the 1980s it was helpful to have Creole and English, too. Now it's more difficult for people to get jobs. They need a GED or high school diploma for everything. For many jobs you also need some college."

When Maria was growing up, the older children in her family had to work in the fields to help support the younger ones. It's different now, though, with the second generation. Maria's four children all graduated from high school and two of them are in college now.

"People my age were first generation," she explained. "People of my parents' generation told us, their kids, 'You're sixteen, you don't want to go to school, OK, you don't have to.' Or they said you had to work because the family needed the money for the younger kids. But when we got older and had our own families, it was different. We wanted our kids to be educated. We said, 'Go to school.' Because farm work is hard, and you don't make that much money."

Assistance for career education is now also available in Immokalee. The Bethune Adult Education Center, for example, added classes in health science (training for medical assistants, nursing assistants, and medical office receptionists) and computer technology (computer applications and maintenance and repair).

A beautiful new building was built next to the Bethune School in the late 1990s, called the "Career and Service Center," owned by the Southwest Florida Workforce Development Board. It is one of five such centers in Southwest Florida; The Immokalee building includes offices for several state and local agencies that provide job search assistance, employment counseling, career and skills assessment, childcare referrals, career preparation workshops, financial aid, and training programs. The center also has a "resource room" to help people get jobs; computers, faxes, and telephones are accessible to everyone.

Many of these people will start new businesses in Immokalee, providing additional job opportunities for others who want to move up and out of fieldwork. They will join the businesses that operate in Immokalee today.

Business is an aspect of Immokalee that people focused on the new immigrants rarely see. In 1999, H.B. "Benny" Starling, Jr. became head of Immokalee's Chamber of Commerce, and in 2003, he filled me in on the community's progress. In four years, Chamber membership increased from fifty to over two hundred. The list in 2003 included many agricultural firms, but gives an idea of the diversity of businesses in Immokalee that many people might never expect. It included many restaurants like Lozano's, Rib City Grill, Kountry Kitchen, Burger Bob's, Vesta's, La Zapateria El Oasis, and Adam-Orieley, Inc. operating McDonald's. Other businesses include The Immokalee Inn, Boone Electric, Bank of America, Winn-Dixie Stores, Walgreen Company, B-Hive Flowers & Gifts, B&L Hardware,

Immokalee Regional Raceway, the Seminole Indian Casino, Mims Welding, Dale's Body Shop, Signs by Linda, Gulfcoast Linen Center, Davis Oil Company, and Buddy's Home Furnishing.

"It is different from other Chambers, because Immokalee is not incorporated," Benny explained. "We have no mayor, no city council, so the Chamber acts as the voice of Immokalee. We can speak as a group to Collier County government on behalf of the businesses here."

The Chamber manages fundraisers, including an auction, and runs the community's Harvest Festival Block Party each March.

"All the ethnic groups get together to celebrate the harvest," said Benny. Twenty-five thousand people attended it in 2002. Six blocks of Main Street were closed off for booths, food, bands, and dancing. The Chamber also runs an annual Awards Banquet in September.

The Chamber includes a division called Immokalee Community Development, Inc. In 2003 this division raised money to support a study that resulted in an award of five-hundred thousand dollars of business incentives for companies to move to Immokalee. Incentives included tax abatement and low or waived impact fees.

Based on my own business background, I would say that one of the main attractions in Immokalee is its labor supply. The new immigrants are often lacking in formal education, but they can easily learn other types of manual labor, such as factory work. Also, of course, they can improve their English and be trained in skilled jobs that lead to successful careers. Today, when farmworkers decide to move up into other jobs, they usually have to travel to Naples, Marco Island, or Fort Myers to get to them. Labor-intensive businesses would do well in Immokalee.

Organizations that have been serving the people of Immokalee for decades continue to grow and change, along with the needs of Immokalee's people. Stan Boynton joined Guadalupe Center as president. Stan has worked in several Latin American countries, most recently in Guatemala, as a small business consultant with the OAS (Organization of American States). Brian Bennett took Brother Jim's place at Guadalupe Social Services. Brian also has a business background, in addition to not-for-profit, working with transitional housing for the homeless, the Columbia Lighthouse for the Blind, and most recently in management with the Ritz-Carlton. The worlds of not-for-profit and business can be quite different, as I learned one year when I was the "Loaned Executive" from SuperValu to the United Way.

"Business will do what is efficient," they told me, "and not-for-profit will do what is equitable." Combining the two should be a very positive thing.

Jim Kean, who volunteers at GSS, has helped on a full-time basis since the mid-1990s. Like the paid caseworkers, Jim identifies needs and then responds appropriately. Because of his years there, he also assists Brian as an unofficial advisor.

RCMA is a major influence in the quality of life of Florida's farmworkers—in Immokalee and elsewhere. RCMA's state headquarters is in Immokalee, but the organization serves over six thousand people in seventeen Florida counties, with a staff of around fourteen hundred people. More than eighty-five percent of the staff are former farmworkers who work together with degreed professionals.

The Immokalee RCMA facility has six separate centers, serving over four hundred children of various ages. Outreach workers spend their days getting parents involved as volunteers and program helpers. They also set up English programs to further help parents prepare their children for public schools. Another program component—school age services—targets older children identified as being at risk of dropping out of school. RCMA provides tutorial, recreational, and home visit services.

In 2000, RCMA opened two Charter Schools in Florida under the direction of Maria Jiminez. One is in Wimauma, Florida, near Tampa, and the other is in Immokalee. The charter school serves one hundred sixty children in kindergarten through fourth grade and will go through sixth grade in the future. RCMA literature calls them "public schools of choice," meaning that they address the special needs of migrant and other low-income rural families. Sister Genevieve Murphy, RSHM, for a time director of Guadalupe Family Center, later moved on to teach at RCMA. (Genevieve came originally from Ireland, and her Irish brogue really stands out against Immokalee's Latino and Haitian accents!) The charter school is important, because, according to RCMA's 2002 Annual Report, children from farmworker families drop out of school at a much higher rate than other children because they come from circumstances that do not prepare them for school in the U.S. RCMA literature outlined the specifics:

Farmworker children start school with limited English, which puts them behind before they even start. Children of families who migrate frequently start school late each year because their parents are still working up North, and they leave school early in the spring when their parents go back "up the road." Parents often cannot help their children with homework, because they lack language skills and education themselves. All these factors can sentence children of farmworkers to lifetimes in the fields. Education is the key to their future, and so is their parents' ability to perceive a bright future for their children. For this reason, RCMA works closely with parents, and involves them in its educational programs. Wendall Rollason, at his 80th birthday party in 1996, explained the importance of this.

"Our most important accomplishment is when we've convinced parents that their children have a genuine opportunity to be what they want to be."

The emphasis on children is well understood by people who work in Immokalee. I complained once to Sister Judy that I felt I should be doing volunteer work that made a greater contribution than just teaching music to preschool children. She explained that there was no greater contribution, because the children are the future of Immokalee.

One of the many advantages of preschool education in Immokalee is that children learn to get along with children from other cultures that speak languages different from their own. I have talked with mothers of Latino children who wish there were more Haitian children in their particular daycare facility so their children could be exposed to different cultures. The children continue multi-cultural friendships throughout school and into their adult lives because different ethnic groups in Immokalee interact in their work, their neighborhoods, and their churches. Albert Lee, who works at Florida Rural Legal Services, said that initially, some of the immigrant groups fought with each other. He gave an example of men from different sides of the conflict in El Salvador. Albert has a wonderful, low voice, and a deep-South black accent, so I remember this comment very clearly.

"That's enough of that fighting," he told the men from El Salvador. "You all live in the United States now, and you boys have got to get along here."

Most of Immokalee's people not only get along, but also treat immigrants of different groups gently, with respect and kindness. Maria Rodriguez from the Guadalupe Center Clothing Room told me a story about this. Maria was born in Texas, but considers herself Mexican because of her heritage. She talked about a Guatemalan woman.

"I knew this Guatemalan family where the man was working up north in the fields," said Maria. "He asked my husband if I would take his wife to the store once a week, so I got to know her."

The woman wanted to thank Maria by giving her a present, but Maria felt bad because this woman was so poor.

"She wanted to give me everything," said Maria, "but she didn't really have anything. So she gave me some beans and Kool-Aid."

Maria did not recognize the type of beans the woman gave her.

"They were big black beans," she told me, "about one inch high. The Guatemalans don't call them beans; they have another name, but they cook them just like beans."

Maria was sensitive to the woman's pride. She knew that it was important to accept presents when they were offered, such as when I first visited Celine in her tiny one-room apartment and she insisted on giving me a bag of vegetables.

"I didn't want to take anything from her," continued Maria, "but I thought it was best to take it, because otherwise it might hurt her feelings. So I took it and she was so happy."

Maria also made good use of the beans.

"I brought the beans over and gave them to a lady from Chiapas," she said. "They are almost the same, you know—people from Guatemala and from Chiapas. That lady from Chiapas was really happy to have them."

The Catholic Church is one place where the groups intermingle and get along very well. On Saturdays and Sundays each ethnic group has its own separate Mass in its own language (Spanish, Haitian Creole, and English). But Holy Days and holidays such as Christmas and Easter are observed in celebrations that combine four cultures, languages, and peoples. Three priests alternate prayers in Spanish, Haitian, and English, and we sing in four languages, including Guatemalan Kanjobal.

Since the 1980s, weekly church bulletins have been written in three languages, and often contain messages for the other cultures. The celebrations specific to each ethnic group, such as the Feast of Saint Michael for the Guatemalans or Our Lady of Perpetual Help for the Haitians, are announced to everyone, and everyone is welcome.

Easter season is my favorite time. For the Immokalee parishioners the Holy Days leading up to Easter are more important than Easter. I asked Lucy Ortiz about this.

"We Mexicans are fixated on pain and suffering," she explained. "That's why we love to join the Good Friday procession and the Saturday night vigil, but do not attend Easter Sunday Mass. We forget that Jesus came down from the cross and that He arose on the third day."

It happens the way she said it, every year. The church is filled on Thursday, Friday, and Saturday nights for tri-lingual celebrations that last for hours, and on Easter Sunday the church is no more crowded than any other day.

Good Friday is my favorite, and one of the best examples of a multi-cultural service. Processions like it are common in Latin America, but there they are celebrated in only one language. In this one, prayers are said in three languages, and the singing is in four.

It usually begins inside the church at 5:00 p.m. Then at 8:00, there is a procession outside. About two hundred people come, a mixture of Mexicans, Haitians, Guatemalans, other Latinos, and a few U.S.-born whites. People who live within about a one-mile radius of the church set up physical representations of stations in front of their homes. They each design their station with whatever materials and creativity they have. Some bring out a dresser and cover it with a purple cloth, on top of which they set a crucifix; others display a picture of Jesus on a chair; others tie balloons on top of a statue of Mary.

Two flatbed trucks lead the procession from the church. On the first there are three life-sized crosses, surrounded by palm plants in containers, with two young people dressed in purple gowns, representing the Virgin Mary and the disciple John. The center cross is draped in purple cloth. On the second flatbed truck are four choirs: Spanish, Haitian, English, and Guatemalan Kanjobal. Guitars back the Spanish, English, and Guatemalan choirs and the Haitians usually sing unaccompanied.

The people follow the priests, who follow the trucks. Each choir sings songs in its own language on the way to its assigned stations. The first station is usually in Spanish, the next in Haitian Creole, then English, and then Guatemalan Kanjobal. When the first station is reached, prayers are said in the language of the singers. Then the procession leaves for the next station, and the next choir sings in its language.

One year my mother came over from her winter home in Stuart, Florida, for Easter, and she came to Immokalee with me for "stations." It happened to be a year where we had to walk behind the crucifix truck because the choir's flatbed truck was in the fields. It is challenging when we don't have a flatbed for the choirs, because we have to put the amplifiers and generator on the crucifix truck, run wires for the guitars and microphones off the back, and then walk behind it with our guitars, holding microphones for each other. Sometimes we have to run, because the truck takes off too fast.

My mother dropped behind as I was playing the guitar, singing, praying, and periodically running. At one point I looked for her, a little nervous that she might be uncomfortable with so many people of different races and colors, but it was not the first time I underestimated my mother. I found her walking in the back of the group, happily talking with a Haitian woman about her age. They might have been old friends.

Institutions like marriage incorporate customs from countries of origin. I was invited to the wedding of Yolanda Contreras and Cesario Aviles at Our Lady of Guadalupe Church. Yolanda ran the after-school program at the Family Center. They both wore white, and marched down the aisle to the music of a *mariachi* band. Part of the ceremony, taken from the Mexican customs of both their families, was the placing of a white lasso loosely around their necks, "to tie the couple together."

I also went to the wedding of "Ms. Delma" Gallegos, who used to teach the Busy Bees at Guadalupe Family Center, when she married Carlos Gonzalez. Delma is Baptist, so the wedding ceremony was a little different from Yolanda's, but also very beautiful. There was a *mariachi* band, and the bridesmaids wore traditional Mexican-style dresses. We would call them "peasant dresses," with long flowing skirts and blouses with billowy sleeves, but they were very dressy—white with gold embroidered stitching. The groomsmen wore white outfits with "peasant shirts" and thin gold ties. Carlos wore a white suit that

Delma says is called a *charro*, and a white sombrero with gold brocade trim.

The schools are one last example of the multi-cultural aspects of Immokalee, as each celebrates the holidays of the dominant ethnic cultures. Long-time schoolteacher Patty Ligas described the holidays celebrated at Village Oaks Elementary School.

"We start in the fall with Colonial and Native American day," she explained. "Seminoles come and make 'fry bread,' show native crafts, bead work, basket weaving, etc. Haitian Independence Day in December and Haitian Flag Day in May are celebrated with music and dance programs. *Cinco De Mayo* is a big celebration, of course, for the Mexicans. The Caribbean Islands are included in this day, too, including Puerto Rico. We also celebrate Black History month with a big celebration in the middle of February."

After one of these celebrations, one of the Haitian tutors asked Patty, "When is the White History Day?"

The children who go to school in Immokalee today have challenges, but they are meeting those challenges and are focused on the future. Many of them go away to school and come back to Immokalee with Bachelors and Masters degrees to work in their community.

I got a good view of their efforts when Cece Brueggen graduated from high school. Cece is the daughter of Joe and Charo Brueggen, and was part of our small church choir. Joe is a resigned priest who now works at the Immokalee Health Department, and Charo is a proud Inca Indian from Peru, who now runs an award-winning daycare business at their home. They met when Joe was doing missionary work in Peru and Charo was the housekeeper at the rectory. They married and have three children who all do very well in school.

The 2002 Immokalee High School graduation was held at the Harborside Convention Center in Fort Myers. So many students were graduating that each family could only have a limited number of guests, so I felt honored to be invited. I also felt honored because Cece wasn't just graduating; she was valedictorian of her class.

I got there a little early and a long line had formed before the doors opened. The Brueggens were not there yet, so I stood in line alone and wondered if I would know anyone. Happily, I ran into several people: Lucy Ortiz, the *Tejana* who married Tali the Puerto Rican baseball player, and who helped me with my research; Maria Rodriguez, who manages the Guadalupe Clothing Room; Lesvia Martinez from the Family Center; and Josie Ayala, a lay minister at our church. Their children or grandchildren were graduating. I was glad to see them, because it made me feel more a part of the community. They were all happy to see me, too. We hugged hello, talked about who we had come to see graduate, and got back to our places on line. I've never felt like part of a community before, at least not like this. It was a wonderful feeling.

I sat with the Brueggens: Joe, Charo, Michelle, and Joey. Patty and Frank Ligas were there too. The students filed in, wearing their caps and gowns, followed by the faculty and the School Board Chair, Anne Goodnight. Yet another person I knew! When the ceremony started, I was moved when I heard this large group of young people and their parents from so many different countries say "The pledge of allegiance to the flag" and sing the "Star Spangled Banner."

As different people gave speeches, I learned that the Immokalee High School class had done some impressive things. This was a class of two-hundred twenty-one students, the largest class Immokalee High had ever had. They were district regional champions and state semi-finalists in football, and boys basketball district champions four years in a row. The track teams won district and regional championships, wrestling and cross-country teams have been to state competitions, and the school has started a golf program. The Immokalee High School BETA Club (Better Education through Achievement) received top honors at the 22nd national convention, and its contribution to the

American Cancer Society was more than double any other schools' in this county.

As the graduates went up to receive their diplomas, I counted them by nationality. (I sometimes wonder if I will ever stop doing research!) Based on their names, over half of them were Latino. About a quarter of the graduates were Haitian, and there were about fifty white and black graduates.

A Mexican girl and a Haitian girl vied for second place, that of salutatorian. The Mexican girl, Elizabet Pacheco Cortes, gave the speech at the graduation, but apparently the decision was not made until graduation day; that's how close the two girls were. Elizabet was headed to Dartmouth College.

Elizabet's speech fit with what I see happening in Immokalee. She based it on a poem called "Stepping Stones."

"Our happiness does not depend on what we have, but what we do with what we have. Our happiness does not depend on what others think of us, but what we think of ourselves. Our happiness is not determined by which of life's stepping stones we are on; it is determined by how prepared we are to take the next step."

The idea of "stepping stones" made me think, because so many of Immokalee's immigrants have been taking steps ever since they got here. Some of them have gone from sleeping under trailers and working in fields to trades or careers, home ownership, and seeing their children go off to college.

Elizabet closed her speech by saying, "I thank God for the opportunities He has given all of us, especially the opportunity to live in the greatest country in the world. God Bless America, and all of us."

When she finished, she repeated the speech in Spanish, because her parents did not speak English.

Cece Brueggen, the valedictorian, gave a speech that was completely practical. That's how she is. The student who introduced Cece did it like this: "If you were to ask anyone in this high school who worked the hardest, took the most demanding classes, and spent the most time doing homework, they would all say Cece Brueggen."

Cece had a 5.0 grade point average, and she took honor's classes most of the time. She is attending the University of Central Florida, majoring in child psychology. She could have gone to any college she wanted, but she didn't want to be too far from home. She hopes to get her Master's degree and come back to Immokalee to open up her own practice. I feel confident about the future of Immokalee because it is in the hands of people like these students.

Immokalee, and other places like it, can offer a window into multi-cultural living with people from many different countries. Part of its appeal is that life is simpler in Immokalee than it is in the coastal communities, and that carries over into the warmth of the people. Tara Norman of Naples, who sings and plays the organ with our small choir at Our Lady of Guadalupe, sent me an email once. It read, "The wonderful thing about being involved in Immokalee is the example that the Mexicans, the Haitians and others have set by accepting me as a minority in their community. These are really fine people."

My favorite times are arriving at and leaving from church. I like saying hello to people from different countries and chatting with them briefly in their own languages; speaking three different languages in the space of an hour is fun. Our little choir usually gets there at 8:30 so we'll be ready to sing at the 9:00 English Mass, and as we're coming in, the Latinos are leaving. I recognize many of them, and say, "*Buenos Dias. ¿Como está?*" They smile and answer me in Spanish, "*Bien, gracias, ¿y usted?*" On our way out, the Haitians are coming in. I know some of them, too, and I smile and say, "*Bonjou. Kijan ou ye?*" They smile and answer me in Haitian Creole, "*Bien meci, e ou menm?*" Celine is always there, and we always talk briefly. I usually ask how her bad leg is feeling, and compliment her on her hat. Celine always wears a hat. She loves hats. She gives me a kiss and wishes me a good day: "*Pase bon joune!*"

Not long ago, I got to church early and listened to the Mexicans play the recessional hymn on their guitars. Then I went up to say hello, and to tell them their music was really good that day. I love the bond among the church musicians; language and culture differences disappear when you all play music. On that particular day, I was surprised to see a Haitian man playing along with the Mexicans.

I smiled and joked with the Haitian man, saying, "Are you Mexican?"

He answered, laughing. "I am everyone!"

All the people I told you about live in Immokalee. They are real people, and I wanted to present them as individuals, rather than just talking about them generally or as groups. One of the things I've learned from the people of Immokalee is that the things we assume about groups of people are not always true. One of the biggest misconceptions I had was that they just get used to fieldwork and it does not bother them. The other was that their emotions are somehow different from ours.

I remember Andy and Gloria's reaction to the first misconception: thinking that the work didn't bother them physically. You may remember that they looked at me like I was crazy. "Are you kidding?" they both exclaimed. "Of course it does! It kills your back! We had aspirins all the time in our lunch pouch."

I also remember Albert Lee, who said his back was killing him within hours, and who told me pointedly, "I say anyone who wants to call farmworkers lazy, they should be made to do that work for at least a week, and I guarantee you they'd learn to respect it."

Rudy Lopez said, "At the end of one day, my hands were full of blisters, and they were swollen. And my back hurt so much!"

And young Juanita, who couldn't even get up after her first day because her back hurt so badly, earning a new nickname: "Ay, ay, ay!"

The other thing I've learned is that people of all cultures suffer just like we do. They feel the same emotions. When I see documentaries of people in the desert at the U.S./Mexico border or see newscasts of Haitians struggling desperately to get their feet on the shores of Miami's beaches, I understand their struggle. I see and feel many things differently from before. Here is an example.

Early one spring there was a story in the *Naples Daily News* about a Mexican man who was killed when he stumbled into the street in front of a car. It happened on Highway 41, not far from two of the biggest vegetable farms in the area. The story said alcohol was involved. I'm sure some people said, "Oh, did you hear? Some drunk Mexican fell in the street and got run over."

The person I used to be would not have thought that, but I probably wouldn't have thought anything. Now that I have met some Mexican people, learned a little about the history of their country, understand how they lived at home and why they come here, my first thought was about his family.

He was probably a husband and a father, just like Juan, who came to the United States to make a little money. He probably called home often and sent money to support his family. He worked hard all week, had too many beers on a Sunday afternoon, stumbled on his way back to the farm, and now he is dead. And somewhere in Mexico a woman is weeping, and children wait for a father who will never come home.

Because they desperately love their families, because they risked everything to get here, and because they work so hard, these farmworkers deserve our compassion and respect. More immigrants came throughout the 1990s, and they continue to come today. They still just want to work. The majority of those who come to Immokalee are still from Mexico, Haiti, and Guatemala, but they also come from Nicaragua, El Salvador, Honduras, Peru, Colombia, and Venezuela.

Many of them have the same needs as those who came in the 1970s and 1980s. They arrive with a few dollars and their clothes in a bag and they speak no English. They live in flophouses or share rundown trailers. They work in the fields all winter, then migrate north for the summer season, taking everything they own with them as they follow the crops. When the weather is good they will not only survive, but will send money home to their families. When the weather is bad they might have no food and no place to live, because they usually do not make enough money to tide them over in the bad times. If field workers get sick or hurt, like Rosalinda, they have no sick pay, no workers' compensation, and no medical insurance.

I think of their lives as "precarious," in that they are uncertain, dependent on chance, and insecure. Farmworkers' lives are still all of those things.

I met two precarious workers from Southern Mexico one Sunday in 2002. They were physically smaller than the Mexicans I knew and very thin, with wrinkled dark brown skin—all signs that they were Indian and had spent their lives in the sun—and they were older, probably in their late fifties. They spoke no English, but came to our English Mass, a sure sign they were new to Immokalee. They followed us after Mass to our monthly congregation breakfast in the building next to the church. They were welcome, because everyone is welcome there, but they sat quietly at a table apart from the rest of us. They kept their eyes down, looking at the table, another sign they were Indian.

These were not the young *solteros* (single men) I had heard about. These were older, hungry, tired men, who looked quietly desperate. I served them breakfast, because it was obvious they were afraid to serve themselves. I was happy and chatty, proud of my new knowledge of immigrants, and my Spanish, that was getting better all the time.

"Are you here so you can send money back to your families in Mexico?" I asked.

They looked up at me, curiously and pitifully—as if I were crazy. Then one of them answered in a quiet, humble voice:

"*Nos faltan dinero.*" ("We have no money.")

Their eyes went back to the table. My chattiness and pride disappeared, and I sat down and talked to them while they ate.

They had just arrived in Immokalee from southern Mexico, from Chiapas, and were looking for work. Like so many of the immigrants, they came to this area because they heard there was work in Immokalee. They just didn't know exactly where to go to find it, so they came to the church. No doubt they had prayed to God to help them.

I never saw them again. That night, if beds were available, they might have slept at Friendship House. Or if they had six dollars, they may have rented a cot in one of the local "flop-houses." More likely, they slept in their clothes under a trailer or in the palmetto bushes. In the morning, someone probably showed them where the buses wait to take workers to the fields. They did not stand the same chance of getting on the bus as the strong young men, but it is likely that someone needed them. Later in the day they probably met someone in the fields—also from Chiapas—and that person helped them find a real place to sleep that night. That's how it works; the ones that have been here for a while help the new ones.

So, despite the number of people who have left fieldwork and gone on to create better futures for themselves and their children, there are still many who labor in the fields. They remain on this first step, either because they don't know how to move on, or don't have the ability. And others will arrive tomorrow, starting out with nothing, like the men I met from Chiapas. By planting and picking the food we eat, they are doing important work—work that most of us would never do.

Now that we've reached the end of this story, I want to ask you just one thing. I wonder if the next time you see farmworkers get off an old school bus at the end of a day, dirty and tired, and watch them go inside a convenience store for a soda, you might look at them with more respect. Think, just for a minute, about where they came from and what they went through to get here. Remember that many of them are just like most of the people I told you about in this book. Be conscious of how hard they work and how little they have to show for it. Maybe you could even give them a little wave, a nod, or a smile.

And one more thing—if you're having a meal and you say grace, how about including words like "Thank you for this food, and for all those who brought it to our table."

Epilogue

Now that this book is done, there are many things I want to do. Of course, I have to get back to my consulting work, and I want to improve my tennis game. I also want to keep on singing with the little children in Immokalee, because it's very rewarding. The children give back so much love, and I love teaching them. I want to keep on singing at Our Lady of Guadalupe Church, too, because I like the connection it gives me to the parish and the things that go on there. I want to learn more Haitian Creole and I want to sit under a tree with some of my Haitian friends and play dominoes. Then I might get back to something a little bigger, something that combines my career with my more recent interest in Immokalee's immigrants.

I'm thinking of an electronic way for the growers to pay the fieldworkers. It's important because many of the immigrants in this and areas all over the United States still don't have bank accounts, especially the farmworkers who migrate. This is a problem for two reasons. First, it is very expensive for the workers to manage their money. It is expensive for them to cash their checks, and it is expensive for them to send money home, using money orders or wire transfer. Second, they carry all their earnings around with them, sometimes even hundreds of dollars in cash. They hold it until they have paid their bills, then they send the rest back home. But farmworkers are often beaten up and robbed because muggers know they carry this cash. It happens not just in Immokalee, but in Naples, too.

I was particularly conscious of this one day when I was buying groceries in our local Publix supermarket. A Latino man, about thirty-five years old, was shopping with his little girl. She was about three years old. I was noticing how gentle this man was with his daughter, and how carefully he was shopping.

They ended up in front of me in the checkout line. When the order was totaled, he pulled out over one hundred dollars in cash—in tens and twenties—from his pocket, but it wasn't enough. He seemed worried that the cashier and I thought he didn't have the money. He was embarrassed, and I felt sorry for him. He asked the cashier would she please wait just a minute, and he took his daughter with him out to the parking lot. He returned a minute later with several hundred dollars in cash that he had left in his truck. That man is the type of person who would benefit from an electronic form of payment.

John Lawson, who is now the Director of Community Outreach with Guadalupe Center, mentioned this to me a while back. He had the idea for an electronic form of paycheck for farmworkers, but didn't know how to make it work. I know how to do it, because I've worked with electronic payment systems before in my career. The payment vehicle would be a form of "stored value cards," like the gift cards used in retail stores now, but they can be payroll cards that can be used in an ATM. They have a secret code (PIN) like a debit card. Instead of a check, the fieldworkers would get their wages updated on a database associated with their card. The program could be designed so that the families back in Mexico or Guatemala or Haiti can take money out of the account shortly after the amount is added to the card here, and at a much lower cost than wire transfers. The card could also be used as a telephone card and to pay for groceries at the supermarket.

Another thing that I would like to see is a souvenir arts and crafts center in Immokalee. It would be a place where the immigrants could sell things they make, like art or objects or clothing—the things that come from their own countries. I have shopped in places like this in Costa Rica and in Mexico. Customers browse among goods that are for sale by various vendors. If one of the vendors doesn't happen to be there, someone else takes care of the sale for them. It is wonderful for shoppers, because all kinds of different things can be found under one roof.

If there were such a place in Immokalee, it could be filled with things from ten different Latin American and Caribbean countries, at least. And it would allow some of the immigrants to stay home with their children and give work to artists and others who could create beautiful things for people to buy. The Guatemalan women could weave skirts, for example. It would be another reason for people from nearby towns to see Immokalee as a destination place, and it would bring money to the town. There are several empty buildings today right on Main Street of Immokalee. Unfortunately, I don't have the skills to make this idea a reality, but I really wish someone else would. It would be a great opportunity for some of the immigrants, and I would like to shop there!

Basically, what I want to leave you with is that a forty-minute drive from Naples, Bonita, Fort Myers or Marco Island, there's a special place that's like being in a different country. Wherever you happen to live, it's very likely there is a similar immigrant town not far from you. I'm not suggesting that you help anybody, or even do anything. Just visit. If you are not sure where to go, start by going to a church. Churches are always welcoming, and people are at their best there.

For those of us who live in Southwest Florida, Immokalee is our "sister town." It's not just some poor place that some people are afraid of and others give money to, it's part of us. It shouldn't be so separate. It shouldn't feel so separate. Many good people live there, and some of them risked everything they had to come to this country. They have enhanced this community as they have enhanced my life. They just want what almost everyone wants: to work, make a better life, and live in peace.

Bibliography

A 2001 Study from the Ohio State University, Department of Economics, Finance & Public Policy on The Impact of Home Ownership on Child Outcomes. Source: Habitat for Humanity of Collier County, Inc., newsletter, Volume 4, Issue 1, Winter 2003.

Austin, Steven L. "Into the Mouth of the Wolf: Guatemalan Refugees Prepare for Repatriation." The American University: Washington, D.C., 1996.

Ashabranner, Brent. *Dark Harvest: Migrant Farmworkers in America.* North Haven, Connecticut: Linnet Books, 1985.

Barron, Roland. "El Heroe Del Pueblo: Rollason 80th Birthday Party." Video.

Becerra, Cesar A. "The Visual Record, 'Giants of the Swamp.'" *South Florida History Magazine* (winter 1994).

Billings, Deborah Lynn. "Identities, Consciousness, and Organizing in Exile: Guatemalan Refugee Women in the Camps of Southern Mexico." University of Michigan, Ph.D. dissertation.

Desmangles, Leslie G. *The Faces of the Gods: Vodou and Roman Catholicism in Haiti.* The University of North Carolina Press, 1992.

Fick, Carolyn E. *The Making of Haiti: The Saint Domingue Revolution from Below.* Knoxville: University of Tennessee Press, 1990.

Gernier, Guillermo J. and Alex Stepick III, eds. *Miami Now! Immigration, Ethnicity, and Social Change.* Gainesville, Florida: University Press of Florida, 1992.

Griffith, David and Ed Kissam. *Working Poor: Farmworkers in the United States.* Philadelphia: Temple University Press, 1995.

Hellman, Judith Adler. *Mexican Lives.* New York: The New Press, 1999.

Jimenez, Francisco. *Breaking Through.* Boston: Houghton Mifflin Company, 2001.

Jimenez, Francisco. *The Circuit: Stories from the Life of a Migrant Child.* Albuquerque: University of New Mexico Press, 1997.

Kobrak, Paul Hans Robert. "Village Troubles: The Civil Patrols in Aguacatan, Guatemala." University of Michigan, 1997. Ph.D. dissertation.

Lewis, Doris Moody. "Immokalee, Formerly 'Gopher Ridge.'" Collier County Public Library: Naples, Florida, 1987.

Martin, Philip L. *Promise Unfulfilled: Unions, Immigration, & the Farm Workers.* Ithaca and London: Cornell University Press, 2003.

Menchu, Rigoberta. *I, Rigoberta Menchu: An Indian Woman in Guatemala.* London and New York: Translation Verso, 1984.

Parkes, Henry Bamford. *A History of Mexico.* Boston: Hoghton Mifflin Company, 1988.

Portes, Alejandro and Alex Stepick. "Haitian Refugees in South Florida, 1983–1986." *Occasional Papers Series*, February, 1987.

Proyect, Louis. "Class and indigenous roots of the Guatemalan revolution." Columbia University. Article 32183, 13 April 1998.

Rey, Terry. *Our Lady of Class Struggle: The Cult of the Virgin Mary in Haiti.* Trenton, NJ: Africa World Press, Inc., 1999.

Riley, Nano and Davida Johns. *Florida's Farmworkers in the Twenty-first Century.* Gainesville, FL: University Press of Florida, 2002.

Rincon, Alejandra. "Those that Fled La Crisis: Guatemalan Migrants to the United States, 1980–1996." Houston, Texas: University of Houston, 1999. Master's Thesis.

Rivera, Tomas. *...And the Earth Did Not Devour Him.* Houston, Texas: Arte Publico Press, 1992.

Rothenberg, Daniel. *With These Hands: The Hidden World of Migrant Farmworkers Today.* Berkeley and Los Angeles: University of California Press, 1998.

Smith, Carol A. *Guatemalan Indians and the State: 1540 to 1988.* Austin, Texas: University of Texas Press, 1990.

Stepick, Alex. *Pride Against Prejudice: Haitians in the United States.* Nancy Foner, Series Editor. "New Immigrants Series." Massachusetts: Allyn & Bacon, 1998.

Stone, Maria. *At The End of the Oxcart Trail.* Naples, Florida: Butterfly Press, 2001.

Stone, Maria. *Ochopee: The Story of the Smallest Post Office.* Naples, Florida: Butterfly Press, Stone Enterprises, Inc., 1989.

Stone, Maria. *We Also Came: Black People of Collier County.* Naples, Florida: Butterfly Press, Stone Enterprises, Inc., 1992.

Stotzky, Irwin P. *Silencing the Guns in Haiti: The Promise of Deliberative Democracy.* Chicago: University of Chicago, 1997.

Tebeau, Charlton W. *Florida's Last Frontier: The History of Collier County*. Miami, Florida: University of Miami Press, 1957.

Thompson, Jr., Charles D. and Melinda F. Wiggins, Editors. *The Human Cost of Food: Farmworkers' Lives, Labor, and Advocacy*. Austin, Texas: University of Texas Press, 2002.

Thompson, Gary David. "International Commodity Trade and Illegal Migration: The U.S. Fresh Winter Vegetable Market and Undocumented Emigration from Mexico." Davis: University of California, March 1987.

U.S. Department of State. "Background Notes: Guatemala."

Wilenz, Amy. *The Rainy Season, Haiti Since Duvalier*. New York: Simon and Schuster, 1989.

Index

0-595-31654-9